CAMBRIDGE TEXTS IN T
HISTORY OF PHILOSOPI

REINHOLD

Letters on the Kantian Philosophy

CAMBRIDGE TEXTS IN THE HISTORY OF PHILOSOPHY

The main objective of Cambridge Texts in the History of Philosophy is to expand the range, variety and quality of texts in the history of philosophy which are available in English. The series includes texts by familiar names (such as Descartes and Kant) and also by less well-known authors. Wherever possible, texts are published in complete and unabridged form, and translations are specially commissioned for the series. Each volume contains a critical introduction together with a guide to further reading and any necessary glossaries and textual apparatus. The volumes are designed for student use at undergraduate and postgraduate level and will be of interest not only to students of philosophy, but also to a wider audience of readers in the history of science, the history of theology and the history of ideas.

For a list of titles published in the series, please see end of book.

KARL LEONHARD REINHOLD

Letters on the Kantian Philosophy

EDITED BY
KARL AMERIKS
University of Notre Dame

TRANSLATED BY
JAMES HEBBELER
University of Notre Dame

CAMBRIDGE
UNIVERSITY PRESS

CAMBRIDGE UNIVERSITY PRESS
Cambridge, New York, Melbourne, Madrid, Cape Town,
Singapore, São Paulo, Delhi, Mexico City

Cambridge University Press
The Edinburgh Building, Cambridge CB2 8RU, UK

Published in the United States of America by Cambridge University Press, New York

www.cambridge.org
Information on this title: www.cambridge.org/9780521537230

First published 2005

A catalogue record for this publication is available from the British Library

ISBN 978-0-521-83023-2 Hardback
ISBN 978-0-521-53723-0 Paperback

Contents

Preface

The editor and the translator of this volume are heavily indebted to many other scholars. Very useful advice on specific points was offered by Alessandro Lazzari, Alexander von Schönborn, Angela Smith, Christian Johnson, Daniel Breazeale, David O'Connor, Doris Jankovits, Eric Watkins, Faustino Fabbianelli, Fred Rush Jr., Gary Gutting, George di Giovanni, Günter Zöller, Lara Ostaric, Manfred Frank, Marcelo Stamm, Martin Bondeli, Megan Halteman Zwart, Noell Birondo, Paul Franks, Sabine Roehr, and Stephen Dumont. The translation benefited especially from the help of Susanne Hebbeler, and some very difficult points in Reinhold's notes were clarified by Andrew Rosato and Patrick Gardner.

In comparing the two versions of the text and working out the best way to display the complex relation between them, the editor was fortunate to have the invaluable advice and assistance of the translator, James Hebbeler. Encouragement and advice from Hilary Gaskin at Cambridge University Press were of enormous help throughout the project.

Introduction

> Analysis and hermeneutics – or rather the 'analytic principle' and the 'hermeneutic principle' – arose in music history (or at least attained historical significance) as opposite ways of unraveling the difficulties posed by the reception of Beethoven.[1]

Reinhold's *Letters on the Kantian Philosophy* is arguably the most influential work ever written concerning Kant. On the basis of the stunning success of the *Letters*, Reinhold was appointed professor of philosophy at Jena, and his engaging lectures quickly drew unprecedented crowds. Overnight, his teaching turned the small university town into the center of the next generation of German thought and the first professional home of the German Idealists: Fichte, Schelling, and Hegel. It also helped to attract to Jena an extraordinary constellation of writers, including Schiller, Hölderlin, Novalis, and Friedrich Schlegel, who all began to focus on Kant and to react to him in terms of the way that the Critical system was initially presented by Reinhold.

Reinhold's success had its preconditions in Kant's difficulties. When the first edition of the *Critique of Pure Reason* appeared in 1781, Mendelssohn and Goethe found it impenetrable in form, and the first reviewers harshly criticized its idealist content. In 1783 Kant issued a shorter account of his Critical philosophy in the *Prolegomena*, but this work is so condensed and so riddled with touchy reactions to criticisms

[1] Carl Dahlhaus, *Nineteenth-Century Music* (Berkeley, University of California Press, 1980), p. 11. Given what happened after Reinhold, Kant may be to subsequent philosophy what Beethoven is to subsequent music.

that it did little to improve the early reputation of the *Critique*. Reinhold dramatically changed this situation by presenting a version of Kant's Critical thought that made it highly accessible and attractive to a readership extending far beyond the ranks of professional philosophy. No wonder that Kant quickly expressed his appreciation to Reinhold:

> I have read the lovely *Letters*, excellent and kind sir, with which you have honored my philosophy. Their combination of thoroughness and charm are matchless and they have not failed to make a great impression in this region. I was therefore all the more eager somehow to express my thanks in writing, most likely in the *Deutscher Merkur*, and at least to indicate briefly that your ideas agree precisely with mine, and that I am grateful for your success in simplifying them.[2]

The *Letters* appeared originally as a series of articles in the leading Weimar journal, *Der Teutsche Merkur*, published in issues from August 1786 to September 1787. The journal was edited by C. M. Wieland, an eminent literary figure who was also Reinhold's father-in-law and energetic ally in defending Enlightenment causes. A book version of the *Letters*, twice as long as the set of original articles, was published in 1790. It made a series of terminological changes, added a few new themes (e.g., aesthetics), and expanded the format from eight to twelve letters.[3] A second volume, dealing with topics such as law, politics, and the will, was added in 1792, and in the twentieth century the two volumes of the 1790s were reissued together in a single volume. Although it is the 1790 version that is now cited most often, because of its greater availability in libraries, it is best to encounter the *Letters* first in the compact format of the original journal version. It is this version, therefore, that constitutes the basic text of the present translation, although an appendix is also provided with all the lengthier additions in the later version.

One look at the titles of the individual letters discloses Reinhold's momentous decision to turn attention away from the abstract epistemological issues at the heart of the *Critique*'s arguments – what Reinhold called its "internal grounds" – and toward its concrete practical and

[2] Kant to Reinhold, December 28, 1787, *Correspondence/Immanuel Kant*, ed. Arnulf Zweig (Cambridge, Cambridge University Press, 1999), p. 271. See also the letters of D. J. Jenisch to Kant, May 14, 1787, L. H. Jakob to Kant, March 26 and July 17, 1786, and Reinhold to Kant (calling him a "second Immanuel"), Oct. 12, 1787.

[3] For details, see below, Note on the texts and translation, and Appendix.

religious "results" (Fourth Letter, p. 117n.). At this time, these results had been discussed by Kant himself only briefly, in remarks in the last sections of the *Critique* (see the Solution of the Third Antinomy, A 546/B 574–A 557/B 585, and the Canon, A 795/B 823–A 830/B 858) and a few short works such as the essay "What Does it Mean to Orient Oneself in Thinking?" (1786).[4] Reinhold's uncanny ability to capture Kant's ultimate positive aims contrasted with other readers at the time, such as Mendelssohn, who had taken the *Critique* to intend an "all-crushing" attack on traditional systems. This was a common and understandable reaction, since Kant claimed to have refuted all theoretical proofs of God and immortality. This situation gave Reinhold a chance to gain fame by effectively bringing out, in contrast, the neglected affirmative goal of the Critical system. It is almost as if Reinhold were clairvoyant in 1786 about the position that Kant was to elaborate only later, in the extensive treatment of the moral argument for God in the *Critique of Practical Reason* (1788) and the *Critique of the Power of Judgment* (1790) – a point that can be totally missed if one reads only the 1790 *Letters*.

There was also a negative side to Reinhold's shift of focus toward later, more popular, and "spiritual" themes, because this shift made the value of the Critical philosophy seem to hinge entirely on Kant's highly controversial moral argument from pure practical reason and the implications of his unusually demanding notion of duty. According to this argument, we all ought to strive for the "highest good," i.e., a situation with an ideal coordination of justice and happiness, and therefore we must "postulate" the conditions that appear necessary to the rational possibility of hoping for this end, namely our own immortality and a God with the requisite power, knowledge, and goodness. The approach of the

[4] In these years, Kant wrote, in addition to the *Prolegomena*, the essays "Idea for a Universal History with a Cosmopolitan Intent" (1784), "An Answer to the Question: What is Enlightenment?" (1784), "On the Conjectural Beginning of the History of Humanity" (1786), and "Remarks on Jakob" (1786). Especially relevant for Reinhold and Kant's work in this decade as a whole is a passage at *Critique of Pure Reason* A 589/B 617: "For granting that there are in the idea of reason obligations which are completely valid, but which in their applications to ourselves would be lacking in all reality – that is, obligations to which there would be no motives – save on the assumption that there exists a supreme being to give effect and confirmation to the practical laws, in such a situation we should be under an obligation to follow those concepts which, though they may not be objectively sufficient, are yet, according to the standard of our reason, preponderant, and in comparison with which we know of nothing that is better or more convincing." Quotations from the *Critique* are from the Norman Kemp Smith translation (London, Macmillan, 1929), with the standard A and/or B references to the first and/or second German editions.

Letters turned attention entirely away from the crucial beginning and middle sections of the *Critique*, which define the core of Kant's system and establish the metaphysical preconditions of the moral argument: the proofs of the synthetic *a priori* structures of space and time, the Transcendental Deduction of the categories, the Analogies argument for the principle of causality, and the restriction of all our determinate theoretical knowledge to a realm of space and time that is transcendentally ideal and not characteristic of things in themselves.

This shift of focus may well be a major factor, still not fully appreciated, in the centuries-long split between two very different schools of approach to Kant and philosophy in general. In Anglophone countries, which did not experience the direct impact of Reinhold's *Letters* (Reinhold's work was not available in English until late in the twentieth century), the "spiritual" side of Kant's thought was more and more neglected in favor of theoretical aspects of the *Critique* that overlap with the broadly naturalist concerns of empiricism and traditional analytic philosophy. In Reinhold's own environment, however, the *Letters*' choice of a much broader range of issues was a first cause, or at least a crucial early sign, of a very different kind of orientation, one that has continued to dominate Continental philosophers. The Jena philosophers and their followers were all mesmerized by the project of trumping Reinhold's work by presenting their own variation of a post-Critical treatment of the "spiritual" interests behind Kant's postulates – an issue that remained incidental, at best, in the analytic tradition.

This is not to say that most writing in the Jena tradition has been explicitly oriented toward spiritual topics. Reinhold himself attempted to make good his relative neglect of Kant's theoretical arguments by beginning to develop, right after the original *Letters*, a system of his own, the so-called Elementary-Philosophy, which was supposed to provide a more adequate general foundation for the Critical philosophy. This was the first of many attempts – by Reinhold as well as his followers – to formulate "internal grounds" better than Kant's own for the sake of most effectively achieving what was taken to be "in spirit" the same admirable "results" that the *Critique* promised.[5] The core materials of the

[5] This strategy is most striking in cases where Kant and Reinhold still allow that God may exist literally as a transcendent person, whereas later writers allow no more than that God may exist "in spirit," i.e., in the fulfilled spirit of human culture. The contrast of letter and spirit was a very common topic of the period.

paradigmatic foundationalist version of this post-Kantian project can be traced in the changes in the 1790 version of the *Letters*, an edition that already gave an indication of Reinhold's fateful intention to move beyond being regarded as a mere catalyst for other philosophers.

The situation of philosophy before the *Letters*

Three main factors – the *Enlightenment*, *Jacobi*, and *Kant* – determined the philosophical context facing Reinhold in the 1780s. To understand the significance of the *Letters*, one needs to appreciate what Reinhold's most deeply entrenched views were before he had even heard of Kant, what the dominant philosophical dispute was at that time in Germany, and what was so remarkable about the specific strategy of resorting to Kant's first Critical writings as a response to this situation.

Reinhold spent his early years in Vienna as a liberal Catholic priest and prolific Enlightenment activist, supporting the far-reaching but controversial reforms initiated during the reign of Emperor Joseph II (1780–90). Feeling it necessary to seek more freedom elsewhere, he left Austria and Catholicism behind forever when he abandoned both his country and the order of the Barnabites on November 18, 1783, three days after his twenty-sixth birthday. The first main influence on Reinhold – and the one with the longest hold on him – was thus the set of progressive practical ideals that he brought along with him when fleeing to Weimar and Protestantism. The second main influence on the *Letters* was the Pantheism Controversy, which erupted in Germany in 1785 upon the publication of F. H. Jacobi's *On the Doctrine of Spinoza in Letters to Mr. Moses Mendelssohn.*[6] Jacobi insisted that Mendelssohn – and thereby in effect all traditional philosophers – had to choose between the alleged fatalistic and Spinozistic position of Lessing and the only alternative Jacobi thought was feasible, a libertarian and anti-rationalist version of Christianity. The third main factor on the scene was the long shadow cast in 1781 by the first edition of Kant's massive *Critique*, a work that befuddled its first readers not only because of its unusual difficulty but also because of its many ambiguous stances. It seemed aimed, for

[6] For a concise review of the Pantheism Controversy, see Allen Wood, "Translator's Introduction," in *Religion and Rational Theology/Immanuel Kant*, tr. and ed. G. di Giovanni and A. Wood (Cambridge, Cambridge University Press, 1996), pp. 3–6. See also below, n. 11.

example, at sharply criticizing, and yet also somehow defending, numerous core claims of commonsense experience, modern science, metaphysical reason, and the Christian tradition.

Reinhold's *Letters* elegantly tied all these themes together by arguing that everyone else had failed to notice the obvious solution, namely that Kant's work had to be read properly and positively from back to front. After this reorientation, it was supposedly easy to see that Kant had succeeded in his *ultimate* aims, which concerned philosophy of religion, and that he had already provided, in a remarkable feat of anticipation, an enlightened solution for the situation of philosophy after Jacobi. Even without presenting anything like a full-length review of the *Critique*, Reinhold presumed that his *Letters* could show how the Kantian philosophy contained the means for meeting Germany's most crying needs – and for bolstering his own hopes of gaining influence as an authoritative spokesman of the age. This was an extraordinary program, and Reinhold came very close to succeeding on all fronts.

The Enlightenment background

Reinhold's optimism was rooted in the most basic philosophical features of his initial concerns. From the time of his earliest writings, the most distinctive feature of Reinhold's commitment to the Enlightenment was his insistence on finding a way to support social reform with a philosophy that met the double demand of being *popular* and *systematic* in the best sense. It is easy to see how this demand arose, even if it ultimately took a rather unusual form. The fundamental practical goal of Enlightenment reforms was to give common people a chance to determine themselves through rationality, and thus to become free from the arbitrariness of natural powers and traditional authorities – in a word, to achieve autonomy. "Enlightened despots" such as Joseph II constantly ran into the paradox, however, of having to "force others to be free," and they often resorted to methods of deception or worse in order to try to wean their subjects away from a deeply engrained attachment to unenlightened beliefs and customs. Initially at least, Reinhold had a very confident "Leibnizian" conviction that there was an alternative, that the Enlightenment did not have to resort to such questionable methods. It could proceed by analysis, a "clearing up" – to use the literal meaning of the verb form of the German term *Aufklärung* – of confused ideas in a way that in principle could be readily acknowledged by anyone with common sense. For Reinhold, this approach required philosophical principles that were more than simply universal in validity and scope (*allgemeingültig*), i.e., applying to and helping all humanity in principle; it also demanded principles that were methodologically universal (*allgemeingeltend*) in the sense of being "universally accepted," or at least such that in fact they could be easily acknowledged. Reinhold was not interested in popularity in a crude sense, but he also did not want to encourage a retreat to authoritarianism by relying on basic principles that could be properly justified only by advanced specialists. Moreover, he was very struck by the fact that recent scientific and legal advances had created a situation in which people were already using principles that were rational not merely "in themselves" but also in a way that everyone could directly appreciate. Reinhold's challenge was to find a means for constructing principles with a similar transparency in the fields of philosophy, morality, and religion, so that all members of modern society could finally lead a thoroughly autonomous life.

All this can help explain why, up to and during the period of the *Letters*, Reinhold was unwilling to promote the Enlightenment by a relatively loose philosophical system or a strategy of division of labor. Even later he continued to insist that a linkage of "popular" and "systematic" credentials in one's principles was not a mere abstract ideal but a deeply felt need of the age, and he went so far as to claim that, "Rights can be recognized by states only when philosophers are clear about them."[7] Moreover, he believed that if principles were to be not only satisfying for philosophers but also capable of holding up as "popular" in the long run, then they had to be organized in a highly systematic way and given an irreversible "scientific" foundation. This insistence on finding a philosophy satisfying the *double demand* of strong conditions of popularity as well as systematicity was a major factor in Reinhold's interest in Kant, since he thought that the *Critique*, and the *Critique* alone, was properly oriented toward meeting this demand. Later, however, as a consequence of ambitious presumptions about the way this demand should be met, Reinhold began to turn away from Kant. By 1790 Reinhold had come to believe that not only Kant's work but even his own

[7] Reinhold, *Über das Fundament des philosophischen Wissens: Über die Möglichkeit der Philosophie als strenge Wissenschaft* (Jena, Mauke, 1791; repr. Hamburg, Meiner, 1978), p. vii. Cf. my *Kant and the Fate of Autonomy* (Cambridge, Cambridge University Press, 2000), p. 123.

initial exposition of the Critical philosophy was inadequate; hence the differences between the two versions of *Letters*. The revolutionary *Critique*, which was to provide by itself a practically sacred new ground for all future philosophy, turned out to need a hasty reformulation in terms of Reinhold's new doctrine of the foundation of philosophy in a single basic faculty of representation (*Vorstellungsvermögen*). This doctrine was grounded in a supposedly transparent and absolutely self-determining "principle of consciousness" (*Satz des Bewusstseins*).[8] Reinhold felt that this principle could do a much better job of meeting the double demand than Kant's system by itself, which now seemed neither absolutely fundamental nor truly universally accessible. Like many readers in our own time, Reinhold worried that Kant appeared to start his system at too "high" a level, one that took ordinary knowledge and notions such as concept, intuition, space, and time as "given" starting points rather than as items derived from a foundation in something absolutely elementary, such as the bare notion of mental representation. In a very short time, Reinhold – like each of his German Idealist successors in turn – changed from playing the role of an after the fact John the Baptist for Kant's "gospel" to setting himself up as the pope of a new infallible system.[9]

The Pantheism Controversy

The initial version of the *Letters* still focused on conveying the value of the end points of the Critical philosophy rather than on seeking an ideal foundational formulation of its starting points. This focus made sense given the role that the Pantheism Controversy played in mediating Reinhold's early interests in the Enlightenment and Kant. The underlying issue here concerned *Jacobi*'s conception of the capacities of philosophy as a theoretical discipline in general. Jacobi's highly negative view of these capacities played a central role in the way that Reinhold and all his so-called Kantian successors began their thinking about the core options in modern philosophy. For Jacobi, not only Spinoza or Lessing but

8 "The representation in consciousness is distinguished by the subject from the subject and the object and related to them both," *Fundament*, p. 78. Cf. George di Giovanni, "The Fact of Consciousness," in *Between Kant and Hegel*, ed. G. di Giovanni (Indianapolis, Hackett, 2000), p. 14.

9 This new period turned out to be brief as well. After objections from others in Jena, Reinhold moved toward a less foundational system in the 1790s, and then often changed his views again to accommodate new positions such as Fichte's philosophy.

traditional theoretical philosophy in general encouraged pantheism because it appeared to be able to do little more than link dependent particulars together with one another as part of a necessarily connected all-inclusive whole. It thus left no room for thinking of oneself as an absolutely free individual, related to other independent individuals and a God who transcends the world-whole. While Jacobi found the most consistent version of deterministic holism in Spinozism, he realized that there was also a skeptical Humean version of it which started from a position that is more epistemological and subjectivist than ontological and rationalist. On this psychologistic version of traditional philosophy, one had to begin simply with certain inner representations, and then, as long as one remained rigorous and consistent, the best that one could end up with was an internal aggregate of necessarily connected (i.e., associated) representations. Here again, ultimate finite individuality and personal freedom were lost, and there was no longer any external nature, any plurality of actual beings, physical or personal, that could be legitimately asserted.

Jacobi was most concerned with the practical implications of this conception of philosophy. It seemed to him that it clearly divested life of any personal meaning, any significant origin or goal, and thus undercut all ordinary belief, morality, and theistic religion.[10] His alternative was to propose that this whole conception had made the mistake of becoming fixated on *demonstration*. We should realize that we do not exist "only to connect," in the sense of merely gathering contingent representations or brute material items together in one whole, however immense. Rather, the fact is that we are always already – when not misled by bad philosophy – open to the direct "revelation" of intrinsically meaningful external matters.[11] There was an obvious consequence of these views for Jacobi's philosophy of religion. Since for him the dominant conception of philosophy could not even justify ordinary claims about any other finite beings, physical or personal, he could contend that believers did not have to be embarrassed

[10] A dramatic reformulation of Jacobi's worries can be found in the transition from part II ("Doubt") to part III ("Faith") of Fichte's 1800 essay, *The Vocation of Man*, ed. P. Preuss (Indianapolis, Hackett, 1987).

[11] See Jacobi's famous statement in *On the Doctrine of Spinoza in Letters to Moses Mendelssohn* (Breslau, Löwe, 1785), p. 31, "in my judgment the greatest service of the scientist [philosophical writer, *Forscher*] is to unveil existence, and to reveal it [*Dasein – zu enthüllen, und zu offenbaren*]." Translation from *Friedrich Heinrich Jacobi, The Main Philosophical Writings and the Novel "Allwill"*, ed. G. di Giovanni (Montreal and Kingston, McGill-Queen's University Press, 1994), p. 194.

by the supernatural beliefs of Christianity, for these were in no worse a position than the everyday claims that this philosophy had put into question. In other words, Jacobi's readers could either accept "traditional" philosophy and a meaningless annihilation of their own selves as ultimate individuals, or they could reject this "nihilistic" position and continue to hold onto their everyday ontology and whatever moral and religious claims also seemed to be "revealed" to them. For Jacobi, the lesson of mainstream theoretical philosophy was that it led at best to a so-called "knowledge" of representations that could never be fulfilling. Jacobi's aim was to bring his readers back to the satisfying non-demonstrative beliefs that they had always held, in such a way that even in a modern context they could continue to lead a life of belief open to others and to faith.

The options that Jacobi insisted on were a huge embarrassment for most Enlightenment philosophers. Jacobi's personal charm, his education and broad contacts (he was a good friend of most of the leading Enlightenment figures, including Goethe), and his reputation and style as a writer made it difficult to dismiss him as a reactionary crackpot. It was therefore all the more disturbing that Jacobi's agenda appeared so opposed to the mainstream of the later German Enlightenment, which assumed precisely that one did *not* have even to think about facing the stark choice of either an unsatisfying "rational" philosophy or a literally supernatural religion. Instead, one could select one of many different, supposedly satisfying forms of rational religion, or "natural theology." The differences between most eighteenth-century successors to Descartes, Leibniz, and Locke were relatively minor in this context. Enlightenment philosophers tended no longer to see any need to insist on the miraculous doctrines of Christian "special revelation," but for a long time they continued to assert that rational philosophy and "natural teleology" point toward at least the likelihood of a God who provides a meaningful existence and final end for human individuals. By the later eighteenth century, however, the corrosive influence of figures such as Hume and Spinoza had led a new generation of philosophers to suspect that none of the old techniques of theoretical philosophy could defend a position encouraging this kind of rational religion, let alone anything like "old-time" supernaturalism.

Kantian practical reason

Reinhold's response to this situation in 1786 was to propose that *Kant* had already provided an ideal way to endorse a version of rational religion after all, one that saved genuine morality, ultimate personal individuality, and the key claims of Christianity. He argued that the discussion between Jacobi and Mendelssohn did not need to be taken to reveal the limits of reason or rational religion as such. It showed only the limits of the traditional "dogmatic" and theoretical metaphysics that was unfamiliar with Kant's Critical vindication of reason and religion on pure practical grounds.

Reinhold's concern with religion was connected to a very serious complication that many readers of the *Critique* chose to ignore or downplay in the 1780s, as many still do to this day, namely that the Critical philosophy by no means excludes transcendent metaphysics and supernatural religion in all senses. As Reinhold astutely recognized, although Kant cleared away *theoretical arguments* for assertions about God, freedom, and immortality, he also promised an elaboration of the rightful claims of pure *practical reason*, and an extended defense of at least some *true* and *substantive non-theoretical beliefs* of a traditional religious nature. For Kant, these beliefs had to be called "pure practical" and "non-theoretical" simply because the only adequate *epistemic ground* for them was a premise set that was not entirely theoretical but included as an essential component some strict moral considerations. It was very important, however, that the *content* of such beliefs – given transcendental idealism and the postulates' conclusions affirming a just God and immortality – still expressed truths specifiable in non-moral terms, for example, the existence of beings with non-spatiotemporal powers.

Reinhold expected his advocacy of Kant's philosophy to have considerable popular impact, and to gain support from the relevant authorities in liberal regimes, because it could provide them with a convenient escape from the threatening extremes that Jacobi had presented. If a rational but non-dogmatic defense of religion was feasible, then the culture wars of *Aberglaube* and *Unglaube* – superstitious faith and crude nonbelief – could be avoided. This strategy would endear Reinhold to the great majority of his readers, who were still relatively traditional. Just as importantly, it would also attract more progressive thinkers who eschewed all supernatural notions but remained very interested in finding some way to secure the secular value inherent in the Critical notion of the highest good, namely the thought of a realm of full human satisfaction and justice. That Kant himself still connected this value to fairly traditional ideas of God, freedom, and immortality was not surprising, given the fact that this complex of ideas had a very well-known anticipation and democratic pedigree in favorite texts of the time, such as the threefold creed of Rousseau's "Savoyard Vicar" (1762).[12] In progressive Jena, "results" at least *somewhat like* Kant's postulates thus became a common goal, even while practically everyone, including Reinhold himself soon, also thought it necessary to come up with better "premises" than Kant's own.[13] This was true even of figures such as the young Schelling, who as a student was extremely disturbed by the attempts of theologians in Tübingen to modify the general argument form of Kant's postulates for their own orthodox ends. The "Earliest System Program of German Idealism" (1796 or 1797) was perhaps the most famous expression of this desire of the leaders of the new generation to succeed Reinhold by reaching the *underlying* "spiritual" goal of Kant's postulates in a more radical way of their own.

Historicity, systematicity, and common sense

Even if it is understandable why Kant's general ideal of the highest good proved highly attractive at the time, it should also be clear on reflection that the philosophical energy behind these appropriations of Kant had to be grounded in something other than the practical arguments of the *Critique* itself. These arguments were woefully condensed, and they did not even seem to be very good representations of Kant's own best thinking at the time. They appeared to insist, quite dogmatically, that we have a "pure" moral "need" to obtain deserved rewards for our moral striving, and yet the very "purity" of this intention seemed in tension with the admission that we have a psychological weakness requiring the thought of God, or of a God-like punishing and rewarding force, to "spur" us on. No wonder that Kant had to work very hard, in his 1786 "Orientation" essay, to try to distinguish his concept of a *necessary need* of pure practical reason as such from anything like the contingent sensible drives or random desires for the supernatural that he took to be the starting point for the unacceptable position of figures such as Jacobi and his ally Wizenmann.

12 Jean-Jacques Rousseau, *Emile*, tr. B. Foxley (London, J. M. Dent, 1911), pp. 228–78.

13 See Schelling's letter to Hegel, Jan. 5, 1795, which claims that Kant's philosophy has only given the "conclusions," for which the "premises" are still needed, and that "all imaginable dogmas have been stamped as postulates of pure reason," in *Briefe von und an Hegel*, ed. J. Hoffmeister (Hamburg, Meiner, 1981), vol. 1, p. 13. Reinhold's work was discussed intensively in the Stift in Tübingen and was the focus of Schelling's earliest writing.

Instead of providing expository details and *direct support* for the moral argument at the center of its own interpretation of the Critical philosophy,[14] the *Letters* introduced three quite different ways of indirectly building a case for Kant: historical, systematic, and commonsensical. First, Reinhold repeatedly illustrated the remarkable way in which Kant sensed and responded to the most basic *needs of the age*, needs that had themselves to be understood in the context of the *whole history* of human culture. This point reflected Reinhold's deep methodological conviction that philosophies and religions in general had to be assessed in terms of their historical responsiveness to the needs of reason in a particular era – a theme that the German Idealists, especially Hegel, followed up on in great detail.

Second, Reinhold repeatedly hinted that Kant had a deep and convincing general analysis of the *subjective structure of our faculties*, and that this structure provided the hidden "internal grounds" and technical authority needed for the Critical philosophy's "scientific" standing. Reinhold assumed that only the absolutely firm grounds of a scientific philosophy could provide an effective program for achieving the kind of reliable practical "results" needed to complete the Enlightenment and to resolve the Pantheism Controversy. He therefore devoted half of the *Letters* to the seemingly out of place topic of philosophy of mind in order to contend that Kant's theory of subjectivity could do much more than answer the specific problem of immortality: the theory could also explain the whole history of the mind–body problem and resolve the main issues of epistemology. By the time of the 1790 edition, however, reflection on these issues led Reinhold beyond Kant's own account and to an emphasis on the notion of a basic faculty of representation. This notion became the foundation of Reinhold's new Elementary-Philosophy, and the previous neglect of the notion provided him with a convenient explanation for the *Critique*'s inability to gain full acceptance after all, even after the extraordinary impact of the initial version of the *Letters*.[15]

[14] For sympathetic treatments of the moral argument, see Allen Wood, *Kant's Moral Religion* (Ithaca, Cornell University Press, 1970), and Robert M. Adams, "Moral Arguments for Theistic Belief," in *Rationality and Religious Belief*, ed. C. F. Delaney (Notre Dame, University of Notre Dame Press, 1979), pp. 116–40. Hume and Kant notwithstanding, traditional non-moral arguments for God have also received significant defenses in recent analytic philosophy, notably in the work of Richard Swinburne and Alvin Plantinga.

[15] Similar considerations were soon used by Fichte to claim that nothing like Reinhold's program could succeed until its theory of subjectivity was fundamentally improved. This tactic continues to be repeated by successors of Reinhold and Fichte.

Both of these points connect with the third general theme that concerned Reinhold, namely the philosophical importance of the Enlightenment notion of *common sense*. Explicit respect for *sound* common sense was central to Reinhold's historical characterization of our own enlightened era, and for him it also provided a systematic standard for adequate theories of subjectivity. Hence he sought a philosophy with premises that were immediately evident and that used as simple notions as possible, such as representation. Even apart from specific issues concerning history and mind, however, common sense had a general methodological value for Reinhold as an irreplaceable touchstone for any philosophy aiming to be both morally responsible and properly popular and systematic.

In sum, while the broadly metaphysical project of a defense of core Christian doctrines (a transcendent God and an immortal soul) on the basis of a foundationalist version of a "Kantian" science of subjectivity dominated the relatively familiar surface of the *Letters*, the articulation of this project was determined throughout by Reinhold's much less well-known, and highly original, appreciation for the philosophical significance of historicity and common sense. Most post-Cartesian philosophers had insisted that one must emphasize either historicity, like Herder and his followers (who modeled philosophy on art and interpretation), or systematicity, like Leibniz and his followers (who modeled philosophy on mathematics and logic) – but *not both* at once. Although Reinhold had special respect for Herder and Leibniz, the *Letters* exhibited a new and immediately influential style of writing that aimed at leading modern philosophy beyond the forced choice of either relativistic historicism or systematic ahistoricity. What made Reinhold's approach even more remarkable was the way that it was combined with a very strong respect for common sense, a respect that could easily seem incompatible with taking very seriously *either* history or traditional systematic philosophy, especially after the impact of modern science. Kant was an influence here too, for, as Reinhold saw, the Critical philosophy was distinctive in aiming to do justice to common sense and philosophical systematicity together – even though Kant severely criticized Herder and never incorporated history into his *methodology* to the degree that Reinhold did.[16] Ironically, it was

[16] See my "Reinhold on Systematicity, Popularity and 'The Historical Turn,'" in *System and Context: Early Romantic and Early Idealistic Constellations/System und Kontext. Frühromantische und Frühidealistische Konstellationen*, ed. R. Ahlers, *The New Athenaeum* 7 (2004), 109–38.

precisely the difficulties in the reception of Kant's own writing that forced Reinhold eventually to insist all the more on an "historical turn" in philosophy, and to stress that a special hermeneutical perspective was needed in order for us properly to appropriate the underlying rationality of our philosophical development and its ultimate compatibility with common sense. His aim was to display the complex "fate" that innovative philosophies repeatedly underwent, as they struggled to be understood and to survive throughout the non-transparent dialectic of history, where progress regularly occurred, as Hegel was to insist, "behind the back of consciousness."[17]

All this explains why the titles and contents of the individual Letters are very unlike what would be expected simply by considering the *Critique*'s table of contents and the reactions of its other readers. In place of transcendental arguments about space, time, categories, and idealism, Reinhold's readers were treated to new visions of philosophy as essentially historical, "scientific," and practical (in a moral sense) – visions that all turned out to be extremely influential, even if they at first appeared to contradict one another.[18]

The situation of philosophy within the *Letters*

Reinhold's prior encounter with the Enlightenment, Jacobi, and Kant came to be expressed in the *Letters* as an historically framed defense of common sense, rational Christianity, and Critical subjectivity. Reinhold's Enlightenment orientation is most evident in the First and Fourth Letters, which claim that the core doctrines of both the founder of Christianity and the *Critique*'s "gospel of pure reason" were nothing other than the most appropriate responses of reason to the deepest "needs" of common sense (First Letter, p. 121) in the historical situations in which these doctrines were introduced. The Second and Third

[17] G. W. F. Hegel, "Introduction," in *Phenomenology of Spirit*, tr. A. V. Miller (Oxford, Oxford University Press, 1977), p. 56.

[18] Despite their high-flown metaphysical language, the Idealists largely followed Reinhold's pragmatic example in their methodology, although Schelling and Hegel had a very different reaction to Jacobi. Rather than rushing away from the thought of the all-determining world-whole and insisting on free individuality, like Reinhold (and then Fichte), they explored the new option of giving this whole a human face, of showing that it has an *internal teleological* form, so that something like the highest good can be achieved *necessarily within* nature by a "cunning of reason" that need not be regarded as "purely" practical.

Letters contend, more specifically, that the current era desperately needs an enlightened version of Christianity that secures God's existence as a postulate of moral reason and thus avoids the extremes of Jacobi's anti-rationalism and Mendelssohn's dogmatism. The postulate of a future life, a topic that Kant himself never treats at length, determines the Fifth through Eighth Letters, the whole second half of the work. The practical goal of satisfying the "unified interests of morality and religion" turns out to depend on letting "Critical grounds of cognition" supplant more traditional "metaphysical" theories of the soul. Only a balanced Critical account of the functional interconnection of our spontaneous and receptive powers of subjectivity can provide a basic philosophical "science" of our faculties that delivers us from the twin evils of "spiritualism and materialism."

Reason's "need"

All these concerns surface explicitly in the title of the First Letter, "The Need for a Critique of Reason," a need that is spelled out further in the 1790 title in the typical Reinholdian phrases "spirit of the age," "present state of the sciences," and "universal reformation." The words "need," "critique," and "reason" point directly to Kant's claim that the Critical demonstration of restrictions on what is determinable by pure theoretical reason is the prerequisite to conceiving a possible satisfaction of practical reason's fundamental "need" to achieve the highest good.[19] Although the commonsense notion of just rewards (which is central to the ideal of the highest good) is not intrinsically historical, Reinhold's claim is that, at crucial turning points in our culture, our concern with this notion needed to be vividly stimulated by the moral visions of revolutionary religious figures (Jesus and his followers) and then metaphysically secured by a philosophy (Kant and his followers) that properly defines the bounds of reason. The "spirit of the age" in Germany in 1786 is defined by confusion about these points. Hence, the "present state" of its philosophical "science" requires a "universal reformation" in order to overcome a fundamental misunderstanding about reason itself that is

[19] The crucial consideration here, which Reinhold does not explain, is that according to Kant the exact laws of nature, which necessarily structure our experience, are still compatible with our absolute freedom and immateriality, given the metaphysical ideality of space and time.

creating despair about the possible satisfaction of humanity's most basic interests.

The First Letter introduces this problem through a summary of worries that incline Reinhold's imaginary correspondent toward pessimism about the Enlightenment in Germany. Sharply conflicting results in metaphysics, especially about the existence of God, have led to "indifference" about reason itself, despite the danger of increasing authoritarianism in politics and nonreasonable attitudes of superstition and nonbelief in religion (pp. 99–105). Reinhold's optimistic reply is that conflicting metaphysical arguments do not by themselves nullify the possibility that reason has a proper and constant concern here, one that can be satisfied once it is reoriented toward grounds that clearly have a chance of universal acceptance (pp. 105–9). As long as there is the possibility of a "rational metaphysics" on such grounds, there may be an escape from the stale options of traditional metaphysics, which deals dogmatically with concepts alone, and "hyper-physics," which makes claims about supernatural powers but lacks a proper basis in intuition to back its claims (pp. 110–16). These extreme options can have a crucial historical role, however, as part of a teleology of reason, wherein reason's own "expectations" disclose the shortcomings of past metaphysical attempts in a systematic way that indirectly points to the new kind of practical metaphysics that is needed now (pp. 117–22). Not surprisingly, precisely this kind of metaphysics is found in Kant's *Critique*, which Reinhold claims, contrary to other interpretations, is neither simply negative and "all-crushing" nor dogmatic and "neologistic"; it has positive "results" that can be "simply" explained and lead to philosophical and religious peace (pp. 123–6). In closing remarks, Reinhold acknowledges the "metacritical" worry that there are continuing disputes about the *Critique* itself and the source of its own authority (how can it non-question-beggingly use reason to evaluate reason?), but he invokes a comparison with Newton to suggest that it is not surprising if a revolutionary approach meets initial resistance because it makes use of new ideas (pp. 126–7).

God's existence as a "result"

The Second Letter focuses on Kant's positive "result" concerning the existence of God. Reinhold begins by claiming that a significant sign of the power of reason may be found in the "fact" that all cultures have affirmed God's existence. The present age, nevertheless, takes a very dim view of reason because traditional demonstrations of God now appear to be very weak, and so we seem to be heading toward two bleak options: "that reason must remove faith" or "faith must be without reason" (pp. 129–31). Here again, the *Critique* points to a saving possibility, a "rational faith" that escapes these options and meets the "need of the age" for a stable system, while showing not only the weaknesses of traditional theoretical arguments for a personal God but also the "impossibility" of any disproofs (including pantheism) of such a God's existence (pp. 132–3). By establishing the limits of theoretical reason and then making use of "practical reason," Kant's position is like faith, for it invokes a non-theoretical ground (namely moral demands) and affirms God, and it is also like reason in general, for it appeals to considerations that are necessary, universal, non-sensory, and systematic (pp. 134–5). Moreover, his approach reveals how reason, as practical, can satisfy the most common person, and not only philosophical experts, because morality is addressed to all (normal, mature) human beings as such and can be appreciated even by those who lack special intelligence or skills. Reason even shows a way to heal class divisions, since the deepest ground of the Critical philosophy lies in an awareness that everyone can have of their own rational self, which is supposedly the same as the proper ground for the proof of God and as old and as universally accessible as common sense (pp. 136–7).[20] Instead of elaborating on exactly how the *Critique* argues from this ground, Reinhold turns at this point to Kant's 1786 "Orientation" essay. It is here that Kant directly responds to the Pantheism Controversy by indicating that his moral argument for God provides an alternative to both Jacobi's supernatural anti-rationalism and Mendelssohn's theoretical rationalism. What Reinhold adds is a typical historical claim that these erroneous extremes were also very valuable, since their development helped to disclose the limits of what philosophy can accomplish within the old dogmatic orientations. Those who say that Jacobi is like Kant are right only in that both philosophers acknowledge some limits to theoretical demonstration. Much more important is the fact that Kant still relies on reason of a universal kind (moral), whereas Jacobi seems to go beyond rationality altogether through immediate and

[20] The most striking passage in this regard is in the Third Letter, where Reinhold calls the moral argument for God "as intuitive and illuminating as the self-consciousness that a human being has of its rational nature" (pp. 30–1).

particular claims about the supernatural.[21] On the whole, Kant is more like Mendelssohn, who wisely insisted on relying on rational grounds but had too much confidence in theoretical as opposed to practical reason (pp. 138–41).

The unity of morality and religion

The Third Letter attends to the worry, motivated no doubt by Mendelssohn's concerns, that Kant's energetic efforts at "toppling" old proofs of God can give the impression of a basically negative program. Reinhold's reply is that the *Critique* not only affirms God but also achieves a general positive objective in showing how reason provides a "ground of cognition" that secures the "necessary relation of morality to religion" (pp. 3–5). Kant unifies morality and religion "by the head," using an argument for God from pure practical reason to save an era endangered by "morality without religion," whereas Jesus unified morality and religion "by the heart," using an appeal to moral feeling and images of God as a loving and universal father to save an era endangered by "religion without morality" (pp. 6–9).[22] The common democratic orientation of Jesus and Kant, which promises salvation to all as "world citizens," is contrasted with the tyranny of the intervening "orthodox" period, which is found not only in the elitism of the Roman church but also in strands of the Reformation tradition that stress theological claims at the expense of basic moral claims. Reinhold proposes an analogy: Kant's "religion of pure morality" relates to genuine Christianity as, more generally, the true theory of morality relates to proper moral practice (pp. 10–14). This practical orientation is secured by the *Critique*'s proof of the restricted nature of our faculties, which (if sound) undermines the claims of those who assume that we have a speculative faculty for determining – or disproving – the existence of anything beyond the sensible world, either by mere concepts or alleged revelation

[21] This contrast is complicated by the fact that Jacobi, like Kant, contrasted the mere rationality of the understanding with the orientation toward the "unconditioned" that is definitive of reason. They also both affirmed the distinctive need and power of reason to assert something "unconditioned," but Kant, unlike Jacobi, insisted that this power can be properly exercised only through the means of universal practical reason. Cf. my "The Critique of Metaphysics: The Structure and Fate of Kant's Dialectic," in *The Cambridge Companion to Kant and Modern Philosophy*, ed. P. Guyer (Cambridge, Cambridge University Press, forthcoming).

[22] Cf. Hegel, *Early Theological Writings*, tr. T. M. Knox (Chicago, University of Chicago Press, 1948).

(pp. 15–21). Here again Reinhold does not pause to explain Kant's main grounds for this crucial "restriction thesis," namely the *Critique*'s controversial arguments for transcendental idealism.[23] Instead, he quotes a long passage from the "Orientation" essay, which argues that our rational moral conception of God is a "first" condition that would have to be met by any purported intuition of the divine (pp. 22–6).[24] After dismissing any purely theoretical cognition of the divine, Reinhold touts the systematic advantages of the Kantian moral cognition of God. It builds on the conceptual richness of traditional metaphysical approaches while being able – unlike such metaphysics – to affirm concrete individual existence, a result that hyperphysical appeals to intuition can reach only illegitimately (pp. 27–32). The last part of the letter places the moral argument for God in the context of a three-stage universal history of religion: first there was crude historical faith, then there was a crude theology of reason, involving hyperphysical or dogmatic claims, and now, in a third era, higher forms of faith and reason are properly combined in Kant's pure moral religion (pp. 34–9). The main point of this story goes beyond religion. It exemplifies Reinhold's more general view that philosophical advances usually incorporate both historical and systematic approaches, and that this occurs through a process of dialectical development within the whole history of culture, which culminates in reason's reconstructive narrative of its own fulfillment.

The history of religion

This narrative approach is made explicit in the title of Reinhold's Fourth Letter, which concerns the "previous course" of conviction in the postulates of God and immortality. Its first pages provide some of Reinhold's

[23] These arguments depend on very specific and complex claims about how we are limited in *all our determinate theoretical* knowledge by pure forms of space and time, forms that have to be understood as merely "transcendentally ideal" and not applying at all to "things in themselves" beyond sensible appearances. It is no accident that later Reinhold, and then his successors, relied on "shorter" and supposedly better arguments for "idealism" that bypass Kant's specific considerations about space and time. This procedure led to considerable confusion about the meaning and structure of the main arguments and conclusions of the *Critique*. See my *Kant and the Fate of Autonomy*, chs. 2–3, and *Interpreting Kant's Critiques* (Oxford, Clarendon Press, 2003), chs. 3 and 5.

[24] This may sound as if it is being allowed that we might have such an intuition, but Reinhold goes on to insist that our intuition is sensible and finite, and so we cannot have any intuition, and hence any theoretical cognition, that could demonstrate the existence of an infinite being. This still is not to go so far as the claim that caused scandal in both the Pantheism Controversy and Fichte's later Atheism Controversy (1798–9), namely that the very existence of an infinite personal being is impossible.

clearest statements about how these two "articles of faith" show the harmony of Kant's "systematic philosophy of religion" with both common sense and historical tradition, since Jesus also "rested content with the deliverances of common sense" in favor of these articles (pp. 117–21). Historical development is important nonetheless because in the infancy of Christianity a "pure" reliance on moral considerations would have "undermined conviction." In the pre-Kantian world, intuitions and concepts were inadequately thematized. Sensible intuitions were at first overly emphasized by common people just as, later, bare concepts were overly emphasized by philosophers (pp. 122–30). Reinhold's account of this process introduces what is perhaps one of the earliest explicit formulations of the alienation version of the "projection" theory of religion (p. 132).[25] The account explains belief in miracles and incomprehensible divine powers as a hypostatization of powers desired by our own weak reason, a reason that misunderstands its own systematic capacities by picturing them in external, authoritarian terms (pp. 131–4). Building on Jacobi's analysis, Reinhold describes this development in terms of another analogy: "Rome" (dogmatic Catholicism) completes the alienated systematic development of hyperphysical thought just as Spinoza "completes" the alienated systematic development of theoretical metaphysics (pp. 134–7). Reinhold regards Spinoza as the best of the traditional metaphysicians because he appreciates that a theoretical assertion of the existence of a divine person should involve, like all existence claims, intuition and not mere concepts. Reinhold sums up the perplexities of modern philosophy of religion in terms of its inevitable difficulties in trying to bring together the notions of (a) a necessary being and (b) the "noncomprehensibility" of divine existence without yet appreciating (c) the command of practical reason. The advantages of relying on practical reason are that it does not try to prove God from concepts alone – and *in this sense* it allows that God's existence is not "comprehensible" – and yet it alone can show

[25] Cf. J. G. Fichte, *Versuch einer Critik aller Offenbarung* (Königsberg, 1792), §2, "The idea of God [the Giver of Law through the moral law in us] is based on an externalization [*Entäusserung*] of our moral law of something subjective in us into a being outside us; and this projection [*Übertragung*] is the specific principle of a religion instrumental in the determination of the will." Cited by George di Giovanni, "The First Twenty Years of Critique: The Spinoza Connection," in *The Cambridge Companion to Kant*, ed. P. Guyer (Cambridge, Cambridge University Press, 1992), p. 433. Reinhold's version of the theory already anticipates the dialectical twist of German Idealism, according to which extreme alienation is a fortunate and ultimately rational process that enables a later and deeper recovery of oneself through another.

that God exists and the concept of a necessary being is instantiated (pp. 138–42).[26]

Immortality as a "result"

The second basic "article of faith," immortality, dominates the rest of the *Letters*, although only in the Fifth Letter is it discussed directly in relation to Kant's moral argument. Even there, Reinhold focuses on the context and results of Kant's postulate rather than the unusually unpersuasive argument for it, which is simply that pure practical reason requires us to believe that we have the opportunity to work toward the highest good in a way that is not limited by the mere natural course of human existence.[27] Once again Reinhold's main aim is to show how a basic idea of the *Critique* fits all at once the fundamentally historical, systematic, and commonsensical character of reason. He stresses that even though the idea of some kind of an afterlife naturally occurs to common sense, history reveals that the "pure" conception of an immortal soul is a relatively late development, one that requires considerable time for the underlying notion of a mind–body distinction to be adequately developed beforehand (pp. 167–72). The first step in this process is simply the commonsense religious interest – manifested initially without any concern for proof – in a good or bad fate after death as a consequence of actions in this life. Once again, the second step is a dialectical development of extreme positions: bare historical and then bare metaphysical grounds for immortality assist in raising popular interest in the issue and in the tools of mere reason, but their inadequacy leads to the formulation of the moral argument (pp. 173–8). In a final clarification, Reinhold explains that the moral argument does not appeal in an improper way to the feelings of hope and fear, since it insists that first we must please God morally, and not in any manner that involves a hypocritical enslavement to our own passions or an external authority. The key idea is not,

[26] Unfortunately, Reinhold expresses this point simply by concluding, "practical reason requires them to believe what they cannot comprehend" (p. 139) – as if it is a great virtue that the Critical view can be put this way. This is one of several awkward formulations that may have led Reinhold's readers away from Kant rather than toward him.

[27] See Kant, *Critique of Pure Reason*, A 827/B 855f.; *Lectures on Metaphysics/Immanuel Kant*, ed. and tr. K. Ameriks and S. Naragon (Cambridge, Cambridge University Press, 1997), and the review of Kant's concern with immortality throughout his career in my *Kant's Theory of Mind* (Oxford, Oxford University Press, 2nd ed., 2000), ch. 5.

"be good simply because there will be a reward later" (a motive that is futile because it would destroy one's goodness from the start), but "because, and only because, you genuinely are striving to be good, you can hope for a proper reward later" (pp. 179–84).

Critique of "metaphysical grounds"

The Sixth Letter attacks "metaphysical grounds of cognition" for the doctrine of immortality. Although Reinhold's own view of this doctrine is in a sense also highly metaphysical in its presuppositions and implications, the main point that he intends to make is clear enough, namely that traditional *strictly theoretical* arguments for immortality are highly problematic, especially after the *Critique*. Instead of displaying the full "internal grounds" for this Kantian position, however, Reinhold once again calls attention to the benefits of its results: sound arguments from "metaphysical" grounds alone would supposedly hurt, rather than promote, the unity of religion and morality because they would make interest in morality unnecessary (pp. 68–70). The most complicated philosophical issues arise when Reinhold tries to specify exactly what can be theoretically said about the soul nevertheless, once we get beyond all the fallacies of (traditional) metaphysics.[28] He allows that there is nothing "wrong" about a theoretical use of the notion of the soul *if* it is simply meant to designate appearances that are not like those of "outer sense" (pp. 70–2). This may seem to be a mere phenomenological point, but Reinhold goes on to give it a very strong meaning by suggesting that the fact the mind does not appear extended to us implies that it need not be subject to the processes of corruption to which bodies are vulnerable. It is unclear whether he takes this claim as *evidence* that our mind *cannot* in any way go out of existence, or rather as merely a "defensive" way of saying that we do not *have* to say that it must be corruptible simply because bodies are. Unlike Kant himself, Reinhold here does not invoke the doctrine of the transcendental ideality of bodies, and this also leaves it unclear exactly why he thinks that we must ultimately (theoretically, and not merely qua appearance) regard ourselves as beings that are not bodies.

[28] This is a difficult undertaking because of the complexity of the Paralogisms section of the *Critique*, which Kant went on to revise extensively in his second edition. See the Preface to the second edition of my *Kant's Theory of Mind*.

I have shifted here from the question of what we should say about the "soul" to what we should say about the ultimate nature of the "self" precisely in order to raise the issue of the difference between these two notions. Much of the strength of Kant's own position depends on keeping this distinction in mind, and on recognizing that even if the term "soul" can be used to designate a certain kind of temporal appearance that need not, or perhaps cannot, correspond exactly to a soul-substance of this distinctive mental kind "in itself" (because nothing in itself is temporal), this still does not settle the question of our own ultimate nature. There were metaphysicians at the time – Kant and Reinhold call them "spiritualists" – who thought that our ultimate nature would have to be something like an indestructible simple mental being, a monad that is defined as a "spirit" because it has higher rational powers and is invulnerable to destruction in a way that is *theoretically* demonstrable. Reinhold reminds his readers of a famous passage in the *Critique* which, among other things, challenges this spiritualist view by saying that our best evidence allows us to speak only about an "I or he or it (the thing) which thinks ... = *X*" (A 346/B 404). That is, even if there is a self, subject, or "*X*" that can be said to exist in some way as more than "mere appearance," this is *not* to say that there is any evidence yet that it is *specifically* a soul-substance or spirit. Reinhold obscures this point somewhat in saying that we "can call" the soul "spirit," or "simple," or "substance" (pp. 72–4) as long as we do not claim *thereby* to be able either to determine an object of outer sense within experience or to claim immortality beyond experience. This may be true, but it is an unfortunate way of putting things because it does not state a categorical denial of spiritualism, which is, after all, one of the two main substantive points of the Critical theory of mind. Nor are matters helped when Reinhold adds that any mere metaphysical representation of the self is "unimportant" and that, in any case, we "know nothing" about this self (pp. 75–80). This way of putting things could lead one to forget that Kant implies that we *do know* (theoretically) at least the very important truth that some kind of self exists and it *cannot* be *known* as spirit – and yet it also *cannot* be spatial or material in itself. This is the second main substantive point of the Critical theory of mind, one which Reinhold also endorses, namely that "materialism" or "naturalism" must also be excluded.[29] But once again, rather than elaborating on this highly

[29] See Kant, *Critique of Pure Reason* A 379, A 383, B 420; *Prolegomena* §§46 and 57; and cf. my *Kant's Theory of Mind*, p. 36.

controversial claim and Kant's crucial underlying arguments for it concerning the transcendental ideality of space and time, Reinhold concludes by reiterating the practical advantages of Kant's moral argument, the fact that it can respond in a rational way to concerns about the self that other philosophers, such as Jacobi, react to in ways that may encourage wild fantasies.

The history of rational psychology

The Seventh and Eighth Letters turn to the history of the concept of a simple thinking substance, and, in particular, the ways in which the ancient schools each emphasize one of the features of mind in a one-sided manner, thereby encouraging either materialism or spiritualism. The Critical philosophy, in contrast, avoids the extremes of a reduction of mind to body, or of body to mind, and its balanced theory of faculties of sensibility and understanding shows how the distinctive complexity and unity of the mind can be described without the introduction of a confusing plurality of souls, as in some ancient theories. Reinhold's account here might at first seem like an anachronistic dead-end, but recent scholarship has indicated that in its time it was embraced by leading Plato scholars, and its general strategy clearly had an effect on very similar accounts of mind by the German Idealists. For today's readers, the main challenge of this section lies in determining exactly what Reinhold is saying about the finer points of Kant's theory of mind.

Reinhold begins with the observation that the *Critique*'s aim is to get beyond traditional debates on mind–body dualism by sharply distinguishing proper affirmations about different types of representations (inner–outer), and their apparent rules, from improper metaphysical claims about differences in "things in themselves" (pp. 142–6). Note that this is a general methodological distinction that many philosophers might make without appealing to any of Kant's specific arguments for transcendental idealism. Reinhold follows Kant closely, however, in stressing that traditional metaphysical concepts such as simplicity and substance are not very informative with respect to the mind, whereas it is useful to think of it in functional terms, in terms of the "power of thinking" and the faculties of sensibility and understanding (pp. 147–54). He also follows Kant in rejecting the materialist reduction of the epistemological features of receptivity to mere actions of the body (which could never account for pure forms of intuition), and in rejecting the spiritualist elevation of the active intellect to a demonstrably independent soul (pp. 155–65). Reinhold's final remarks put to rest two hypothetical objections to his historical account of ancient theories: that it underplays the role of the notion of the "world-soul" and the possibility that ancient talk about a separate soul was merely figurative (pp. 247–55; 274–8).

Reinhold's main concern is to show specific ways in which the Kantian theory systematically improves on the four main ancient schools. The Epicurean, or "psychological," theory has a model that is too passive and cannot explain laws generated by the spontaneity of the understanding. The Stoic, or "moral," theory has a model that is too elevated and attributes causal powers to the intellect (e.g., to generate desires) that are really due to the senses. The Aristotelian, or "logical," theory introduces an active intellect that remains mysteriously independent of the sensible realm. The Platonic, or "metaphysical," theory improperly claims insight into the nature of the soul in itself (pp. 256–66). More generally, these theories make inner sense too much like understanding, as if mere passive awareness, even of one's self, could guarantee knowledge; or, they make outer sense too much unlike understanding, as if perception were a physical process not already informed by the intellect.

It is right here, almost hidden away at the end of the *Letters*' historical remarks, that one can find its most perceptive theoretical observations on the Critical philosophy. Reinhold's final argument nicely anticipates aspects of Kant's famous second edition Refutation of Idealism (B274–9). Reinhold criticizes Greek philosophers who were reluctant to give the body an essential role in our fundamental epistemic processes because they assumed that our immortality could be secured only if it is attached to a soul that is always purely rational. They feared that an epistemological dependence on outer sense could make us metaphysically dependent on the physical domain. Kant's breakthrough is to work out a theory of knowledge that allows outer sense a central epistemic role without committing itself to materialism or falling back into a "myth of the given." His theory thus does justice to what is best in materialism's motives (its denial of "bald" Platonic epistemology),[30] while not identifying epistemic issues with the metaphysical issue of an existence possibly independent of bodies – and hence it can do justice to what is best in spiritualism's

[30] Cf. John McDowell, *Mind and World* (Cambridge, MA, Harvard University Press, 1994).

motives (its anti-"naturalism") as well (pp. 267–73). Here again, Reinhold seems clairvoyant, since Kant himself did not explain this line of argument very clearly prior to 1787. In this instance, Reinhold may have been a catalyst for not only Kant's reputation but also some substantive advances within the Critical philosophy itself.

A final note: the complex nature of Kant's systematic approach to traditional metaphysics can also explain why, even before the arguments of the *Critique* were known, he was treated with a kind of respect that made his work open to an appropriation like Reinhold's. Kant was unusually well situated for taking on a central role in German philosophy because he was someone who could be regarded as being able to make a very informed criticism of metaphysics *from within*. His criticism had to be taken very seriously by traditionalists because it came from a position unlike that of the assorted skeptics, radical empiricists, and avowedly anti-systematic thinkers who were the typical enemies of the discipline. At the same time, precisely because Kant was such a talented Enlightenment "insider," his Critical views could also become an attractive instrument for generations of revolutionaries, many of whom, by no accident, still call themselves "Critical" thinkers in a general sense. After Reinhold, the *Critique* became a common starting point for writers who, impatient with thoroughly rethinking metaphysics on its own "internal grounds," were most concerned with the "result" of completing the Enlightenment immediately and undermining "the establishment" altogether. For these reasons, the final legacy of the *Letters* may rest not so much in its metaphysical discussions and optimistic attitude but in the way that it unwittingly stimulated a new genre of highly popular narratives of the self-destruction of all earlier philosophy, now including Kant's and Reinhold's systems as well. The effect of the *Letters* can be found not only in the structure of the ambitious positive programs of the German Idealists but also in the mocking retrospectives on "German ideology" offered by Heine, Marx, Nietzsche, and their followers.

Chronology

1757 October 26, Karl Leonhard Reinhold born in Vienna

1772 Studies with Jesuits at St. Anna's in Vienna

1773 Order of the Jesuits suppressed by Pope Clement XIV

1774 Studies with Order of the Barnabites

1780 Ordained as priest

1781 First edition of Kant's *Critique of Pure Reason* (Riga)

1782 Joins Masonic lodge "To True Harmony" in Vienna and befriends the writers Aloys Blumauer, J. B. Alxinger, J. F. Ratschky, and the lodge master, Ignaz von Born; numerous reviews on Enlightenment themes

1783 Abandons priesthood, flees to Leipzig, develops interest in the radical Illuminati movement led by Adam Weishaupt

1784 Moves to Weimar, befriends C. M. Wieland, editor of *Der Teutsche Merkur*; "Thoughts on Enlightenment" and supportive review of Herder's *Ideas on a Philosophy of History of Humanity* in *Merkur*; Kant writes "An Answer to the Question: What is Enlightenment?"

1785 Becomes co-editor of *Merkur*, marries Wieland's daughter Sophie, with Herder officiating; essays on "despotic principles" in Austrian politics; *Pantheismustreit* begins

1786 Becomes converted to Critical Philosophy upon studying *Critique of Pure Reason*; first of a series of eight "Letters on the Kantian Philosophy" in *Merkur*, "On the Mysteries of the Ancient Hebrews," review of J. Gurlitt, *Outlines of a History of Philosophy*

1787 Awarded *Magister Philosophiae* and named *Professor Extraordinarius* of philosophy in Jena, lectures on Kant; critical review of Herder's *God: Some Conversations*

1788 Praised by Kant in "On the Use of Teleological Principles" in *Merkur*; lectures and essays on aesthetics, review of critical work on Kant by the orthodox Tübingen professor J. F. Flatt, a teacher of Hegel, Hölderlin, and Schelling

1789 *On the Previous Fate of the Kantian Philosophy* (Jena), *Essay on a New Theory of the Human Faculty of Representation* (Jena)

1790 *Letters on the Kantian Philosophy*, revised and expanded to twelve letters, appears in its first authorized book form (Leipzig), *Contributions to the Correction of Previous Misunderstandings of the Philosophers*, vol. I, *Concerning the Foundation of Elementary-Philosophy* (Jena)

1791 *On the Foundation of Philosophical Knowledge, Accompanied by Elucidations of the Theory of the Faculty of Representation* (Jena), "On the Concept of the History of Philosophy: An Academic Lecture," review of third edition of Kant's *Critique of Pure Reason*

1792 Reinhold's Elementary-Philosophy begins to receive intense criticism from works such as G. E. Schulze's *Aenesidemus* (Helmstädt); *Letters on the Kantian Philosophy*, vol. II (Leipzig), review of German edition of Hume's philosophical works

1793 "Philosophical Correspondence with Salomon Maimon" (published by Maimon without Reinhold's authorization), review of Kant's *Critique of the Power of Judgment*

1794 Accepts call to Professor in Kiel (Denmark); *Contributions to the Correction of Previous Misunderstandings of Philosophers*, vol. II, *Concerning the Foundations of Philosophical Knowledge, of Metaphysics, Morality, Moral Religion, and the Doctrine of Taste* (Jena), review of Kant's *Religion within the Boundaries of Mere Reason*

1796 Prize Essay on the Question "What Progress Has Metaphysics Made in Germany since the Time of Leibniz and Wolff?," *Selection of Assorted Essays*, part I (Jena)

1797 Moves toward the position of Fichte's *Wissenschaftslehre*; *Selection of Assorted Essays*, part II (Jena)

1798 *The Fundamental Concepts and Principles of Ethics: Deliberations of Sound Common Sense, for the Purpose of Evaluating Moral, Rightful, Political and Religious Matters* (Lübeck and Leipzig), review of several works by Fichte

1799 Moves toward the position of Jacobi; *Public Letter to J. C. Lavater and J. G. Fichte Concerning Belief in God* (Hamburg)

1800 Moves toward the position of C. G. Bardili; review of Schelling's *System of Transcendental Idealism*

1801 *Contributions toward a More Convenient Survey of the State of Philosophy at the Beginning of the Nineteenth Century* (Hamburg, three of eventually six volumes)

1803 *On the Relation of Sound Understanding and of Philosophical Reason to Common Sense and Speculative Reason* (Hamburg)

1804 *C. G. Bardilis and C. L. Reinhold's Correspondence Concerning the Essence [Wesen] of Philosophy and the Absurdity [Unwesen] of Speculation*, edited by Reinhold (Munich)

1805 *Prolegomena to Analysis in Philosophy* (Berlin)

1806 *Essay on a Critique of Logic from the Viewpoint of Language* (Kiel)

1808 Moves away from Bardili's "logical realism"; "On a New Answer to the Old Question: What is Truth?"

1812 *Foundation of a Synonomics for the General Use of Language in the Philosophical Sciences* (Kiel)

1823 12 April, dies in Kiel

Further reading

An excellent brief overview of Reinhold's early career is given in René Wellek, "Between Kant and Fichte: Karl Leonhard Reinhold," *Journal of the History of Ideas* 45 (1984), 323–7. Very helpful information on the background of Reinhold's thought can be found in general studies on the period such as Manfred Kuehn, *Scottish Common Sense in Germany, 1768–1800* (Kingston and Montreal, McGill-Queen's University Press, 1987), Theodore Ziolkowski, *German Romanticism and its Institutions* (Princeton, Princeton University Press, 1990), Terry Pinkard, *German Philosophy 1760–1869: The Legacy of Idealism* (Cambridge, Cambridge University Press, 2002), Dieter Henrich, *Between Kant and Hegel: Lectures on German Idealism* (Cambridge, MA, Harvard University Press, 2003), and Manfred Frank, *The Philosophical Foundations of Early German Romanticism* (Albany, SUNY Press, 2004). Especially useful are Sabine Roehr, *A Primer on the German Enlightenment: with a Translation of Karl Leonhard Reinhold's "Fundamental Concepts and Principles of Ethics"* (Columbia, University of Missouri Press, 1995) and *What is Enlightenment? Eighteenth Century Answers and Twentieth Century Questions*, ed. James Schmidt (Berkeley, University of California Press, 1996). Prior to the *Letters*, the translated essay in Roehr's book was the longest work by Reinhold available in English. Schmidt's volume contains Reinhold's "Thoughts on Enlightenment," a good starting point for appreciating Reinhold's broader concerns. To learn about Reinhold's own systematic position, an ideal text to begin with is the excerpt "The Foundation of Knowledge," in *Between Kant and Hegel: Texts in the Development of Post-Kantian Idealism*, ed. George di Giovanni (Indianapolis, Hackett, rev. ed., 2000), pp. 52–106.

The best preparation for understanding Reinhold's philosophy is to study Kant's main works, all of which are now available in other volumes in this series, with new introductions by contemporary philosophers. Also highly relevant are Reinhold's other immediate predecessors, especially Lessing, Herder, and Jacobi. Since Fichte, Hegel, Schelling, Schiller, Hölderlin, Novalis, and Friedrich Schlegel all developed their thought in reaction to Reinhold's reading of Kant, the study of these figures is also essential to fully appreciating Reinhold's significance. A harsh critique of Reinhold can be found in G. W. F. Hegel, *Difference Between the Systems of Fichte and Schelling*, ed. W. Cerf and H. S. Harris (Albany, SUNY Press, 1977). In many ways, this work appropriates the "historical turn" of Reinhold's philosophical methodology, but it is indicative of Hegel's influence that the rest of the full title of this work is rarely even cited: *in Connection with the First Fascicle of Reinhold's "Contributions to a more Convenient Survey of the State of Philosophy at the Beginning of the Nineteenth Century.*"

The main critical studies in English of Reinhold's philosophy are Rolf-Peter Horstmann, "Maimon's Criticism of Reinhold's 'Satz des Bewusstseins,'" in *Proceedings of the Third International Kant Congress*, ed. L. W. Beck (Dordrecht, Reidel, 1972), pp. 330–8; Daniel Breazeale, "Between Kant and Fichte: K. L. Reinhold's 'Elementary Philosophy,'" *Review of Metaphysics* 35 (1981/2), 785–821; Frederick Beiser, *The Fate of Reason: German Philosophy from Kant to Fichte* (Cambridge, MA, Harvard University Press, 1988), ch. 8; Karl Ameriks, *Kant and the Fate of Autonomy: Problems in the Appropriation of the Critical Philosophy* (Cambridge, Cambridge University Press, 2000), ch. 2; and Paul Franks, "All or Nothing: Systematicity and Nihilism in Jacobi, Reinhold, and Maimon," in *The Cambridge Companion to German Idealism*, ed. K. Ameriks (Cambridge, Cambridge University Press, 2000), ch. 5.

Recent German editions of Reinhold's work are *Schriften zur Religionskritik und Aufklärung 1782–1784*, ed. Z. Batscha (Bremen and Wolffenbüttel, Jacobi, 1977); *Über das Fundament des philosophischen Wissens: Über die Möglichkeit der Philosophie als strenge Wissenschaft*, ed. W. Schrader (Hamburg, Meiner, 1978); *Korrespondenz 1773–1788*, ed. R. Lauth, E. Heller, and K. Hiller (Stuttgart, Frommann-Holzboog, 1983); *Die hebräischen Mysterien oder die älteste religiöse Freimauerei*, ed. J. Assmann (Neckergemünd, 2001); *Beiträge zur Berichtigung bisheriger*

Missverständnisse der Philosophen. Erster Band, das Fundament der Elementarphilosophie betreffend, ed. F. Fabbianelli (Hamburg, Meiner, 2003); and *Beiträge zur Berichtigung bisheriger Missverständnisse der Philosophen. Zweiter Band, die Fundamente des philosophischen Wissens, der Metaphysik, Moral, moralischen Religion und Geschmackslehre betreffend*, ed. F. Fabbianelli (Hamburg, Meiner, 2004). Reinhold's main systematic work, *Versuch einer neuen Theorie des menschlichen Vorstellungsvermögens*, has been reprinted (Darmstadt, Wissenschaftliche Buchgesellschaft, 1963), as has his contribution to *Preisschriften über die Frage: Welche Fortschritte hat die Metaphysik seit Leibnitzens und Wolffs Zeiten in Deutschland gemacht?* (Königl. Preuss. Akademie der Wissenschaften, Darmstadt, 1971); excerpts from his influential discussions of freedom of the will are reprinted in *Materialen zu Kants "Kritik der praktischen Vernunft"*, ed. Rüdiger Bittner and Konrad Cramer (Frankfurt, Suhrkamp, 1975), pp. 252–74 and 310–24. The 1790 version of the *Letters* is scheduled to appear soon in a new German edition edited by Martin Bondeli. Essential to all research in this area is *Karl Leonhard Reinhold: eine annotierte Bibliographie*, ed. A. von Schönborn (Stuttgart, Frommann-Holzboog, 1991).

A renaissance in Reinhold studies began with *Philosophie aus einem Prinzip: Karl Leonhard Reinhold*, ed. R. Lauth (Bonn, Bouvier, 1974). Since then, the importance of philosophical reactions to Reinhold in the "constellations" of his successors in Jena has become a main theme in modern European philosophy. See especially the extensive studies by Dieter Henrich, *Konstellationen: Probleme und Debatten am Ursprung der idealistischen Philosophie (1789–1795)* (Stuttgart, Klett-Cotta, 1991) and *Grundlegung aus dem Ich: Untersuchungen zur Vorgeschichte des Idealismus Tübingen–Jena (1790–1794)*, 2 vols. (Suhrkamp, Frankfurt, 2004); and Manfred Frank, "*Unendliche Annäherung.*" *Die Anfänge der philosophischen Frühromantik* (Frankfurt, Suhrkamp, 1997). See also Marcelo Stamm, "Das Programm des methodologischen Monismus. Subjekttheoretische und methodologische Aspekte der Elementarphilosophie K. L. Reinholds," *Neue Hefte für Philosophie* 35 (1995), 18–31. Two important studies for specialists are Martin Bondeli, *Der Anfangsproblem bei Karl Leonhard Reinhold* (Frankfurt, Klostermann, 1995), and Alessandro Lazzari, "*Das Eine, was der Menschheit Noth ist*" (Stuttgart-Bad Cannstatt, Frommann-Holzboog, 2004). Bondeli and Lazzari are among the editors of a continuing series of volumes of essays from recent Reinhold congresses. Fundamental concepts of Reinhold's practical philosophy are discussed in Gerold Prauss,

Kant über Freiheit als Autonomie (Frankfurt, Klostermann, 1983) and Henry E. Allison, *Kant's Theory of Freedom* (Cambridge, Cambridge University Press, 1990). The historical intrigues of Reinhold's career are the focus of Gerhard W. Fuchs, *Karl Leonhard Reinhold – Illuminat und Philosoph* (Frankfurt, Peter Lang, 1994). A helpful overview of Reinhold's early career and its relation to the *Letters* in particular is given in Yun Ku Kim, *Religion, Moral und Aufklärung: Reinholds philosophischer Werdegang* (Frankfurt, Peter Lang, 1996).

Note on the texts and translation

Details about the relation between the main text, i.e., the letters as they originally appeared in the *Merkur*, and the materials in the Appendix taken from the expanded 1790 edition are given in the table at the end of this note and the list at the beginning of the Appendix. For the 1790 edition, the translation is based on the text as it appears in *Briefe über die Kantische Philosophie*, edited and introduced by Raymund Schmidt (Leipzig, Reclam, 1923). For the *Merkur* version, the translation is based on copies of volumes in the special collection of the library of the University of Chicago. Reinhold's own footnotes to the text, which are not very numerous (and are often incomplete), are indicated by alphabetical letter symbols, with editor's interpolations in square brackets. There is also a sequence of editor's footnotes, which are indicated by arabic numbers and concern minor textual matters or, on a few occasions, provide clarifications of key historical and philosophical complexities. Page numbers in brackets in the text give the *Merkur* page numbers or, in the Appendix, page numbers of the 1923 Reclam (photomechanical) reprint of the 1790 edition. All page numbers referenced in the editor's footnotes are to the *Merkur* or Reclam pagination.

No German volume contains both the *Merkur* and 1790 versions, and the Reclam reprint does not document the very numerous additions and small changes that Reinhold made in the later edition. The Appendix constructed for this translation includes all the longer sections (i.e., roughly anything longer than a block of a couple sentences) that were added or heavily revised for the 1790 edition. It would have been extravagant to try to list all the changes here, but an effort was made to note any changes that clearly appeared to have significant philosophical implications. There are many minor changes that Reinhold made that were merely incidental stylistic corrections or adjustments. By far the most common changes reflect Reinhold's desire to introduce terminology concerning the faculty of representation, which by 1790 had become the central and distinctive theme of his own first system (he called it the "Elementary-Philosophy" because it aimed at explaining all knowledge and action in terms of the elements of this one basic faculty). He also needed to bring his expressions in line with Kant's terminology in works published after the *Merkur* letters appeared. Some typical changes of this kind are flagged near the beginning of the text. In the Appendix, the italics in the translation correspond exactly to the 1790 edition. This policy is not followed for the *Merkur* edition, except for Reinhold's notes, where he was clearly going out of his way to emphasize particular points. The use of italics in the *Merkur* is quite excessive by current standards, is not always easy to discern with certainty, and varies from letter to letter without any clear principle. To keep the translation of this text uncluttered, italics are used only for foreign terms and book titles.

This is not the place to discuss in detail the philosophical differences between the two versions of the *Letters*, but the notes and Appendix have been designed with the aim of giving readers a chance to trace these differences. After the *Letters* first appeared, influential commentators began speaking of a "Kantian-Reinholdian" philosophy, as if there were no significant difference between Kant's system and Reinhold's. There were, in fact, considerable differences between Kant and Reinhold, and they became apparent by 1790 when Reinhold began to develop, for the first time, a system of his own – although he was even then trying to present himself as still true to Kant.

Because the *Merkur* was a journal with a very wide audience, the style of Reinhold's writing, especially at the very beginning of the *Letters*, is more literary than is typical of his philosophical works. Readers should not be put off by the unusually dense first few pages and the dialogue that the author constructs between himself and an imaginary philosophical partner. The text becomes much easier to read as it goes on, and although the 1790 additions are relatively abstract, they usually are even clearer than the original letters, which were extremely popular in their time. There are a few key terms, however, that can be easily misunderstood and deserve explanation beforehand.

Geist is a term that Reinhold helped make central in post-Kantian philosophy. It is tempting to translate it as "mind" rather than "spirit," given the mystical connotation of the latter term in English. Nonetheless, there are several reasons why "spirit" is used here. Its very awkwardness is a reminder that German does not have a single word for "mind," and that the main term that it has used (*Geist*) always carries with it a heavy load of metaphysical and theological meanings. *Geist* is also the term that, by no accident, is central to Hegel's *Phenomenology of Spirit* (1807), and in that work the social, religious, and historical layers of the term's meaning (as when one speaks of the "spirit of the age") are a reminder that it is highly inappropriate to think of the term simply in the individual and psychological sense that dominates the English meaning of the word "mind" (and corresponds more closely to *Gemüt*). The limitation of resources in German here, especially at this time, also comes out in the fact that in this work when Reinhold speaks about what is translated as "minds" he usually uses the term *Köpfe*, which literally means "heads." Clarity about *Geist* is crucial to understanding central aspects of Kant's and Reinhold's philosophies. The *Critique* does not use *Geist* positively but employs instead the term "I," or even "soul" (*Seele*), which indicates a subject or mind considered in a merely philosophical or psychological way. Kant's main opponent in his criticism of rational psychology is precisely "spiritualism," and a central – and often misunderstood – point of Kant's discussion is that a vigorous denial of "spirit" in the sense of the spiritualist notion of a *theoretically demonstrable*, *fully independent*, and *purely mental* substance is still compatible with allowing that some kind of mind or thinker exists (even if it may need to be referred to merely as an "I or he *or* it that thinks"). Reinhold attempts to take a somewhat similar in-between position by criticizing the extreme positions of Cartesian spiritualism and atheist materialism, but at times he falls back into affirmations of our *Geistigkeit*, or spirituality, and thus betrays a terminological confusion that contrasts with Kant's more careful mode of expression (see below, nn. 154–7).

One of the most common phrases in the text is "Critique of Reason." This is because Reinhold adopts the unusual procedure of using, without italics, the short phrase *Kritik der Vernunft* rather than giving the slightly longer full title of Kant's *Critique of Pure Reason*, which is *Kritik der reinen Vernunft*. The translation renders Reinhold's words literally as "Critique of Reason" but capitalizes the nouns, so that the phrase is not overlooked (elsewhere, capitalized English terms like this are used only to refer to a subsection of a book, e.g., Transcendental Dialectic). It is difficult in any case to find an appropriate practice here that would count as reproducing the German "exactly"; titles usually are not italicized by Reinhold, and in German capitals are used for all nouns, not only for principal words in titles. Reinhold must have given his own "unusual procedure" some thought, because he employs it repeatedly in the *Letters*. He may have been trying to suggest that Kant's book perfectly exhibits the procedure of reason itself, and so the full matter under discussion is not simply Kant's specific account of a critique of pure reason but is the general idea, and ideal process, of a critique of reason by reason itself. It should also be kept in mind that at this time Reinhold did not know that there would be other *Critiques* by Kant: the *Critique of Practical Reason* (1788) and the *Critique of the Power of Judgment* (1790). Moreover, what Reinhold is discussing in the *Letters* is often not limited to the *Critique of Pure Reason* but includes philosophical points made in Kant's essays in the mid 1780s. Nonetheless, Reinhold's procedure is very unusual because in almost all instances he is certainly referring to Kant's book, and so readers should certainly keep that book and its full title in mind wherever the capitalized phrase "Critique of Reason" occurs in the translation. Reinhold's procedure has some philosophical costs. In leaving out the word "pure," Reinhold obscures the fact that Kant did *not* intend to critique (in the sense of "challenge" or "restrict" and not merely "examine") reason *in general* (including logic and pure practical reason) but simply to challenge theoretical uses of reason that proceed *too* "purely," that is, without recognition of the need to refer to sensory, spatiotemporal contexts in order to make warranted determinate claims.

Another important and easily misunderstood phrase is "common sense." The phrases *gesunder Menschenverstand*, which literally signifies "healthy (or sound) human understanding," and *gemeiner Menschenverstand*, which literally signifies "common human understanding," are often treated as equivalent and as meaning "common sense," and they are translated that way here, whereas the closely related phrase *gemeiner Verstand* is translated as "common understanding." Any phrase including the term "common" (*gemein*) is especially significant for Reinhold because he is so concerned with taking a mediating approach, with finding terms common to various principles, and, above all, with utilizing principles that can bridge the gap between common people and specialists. In translating philosophers such as Reinhold, one cannot avoid using the phrase "common sense," but it is misleading in so far as it obscures the fact that the corresponding German phrase includes a term which, on its own, means "understanding" (*Verstand*) rather than "sense"; this reflects the broadly rationalist tendency of German thought. Reinhold's interest in the issue is closely related to, but not limited by, his concern with Kant. In the *Prolegomena to Any Future Metaphysics that Will Be Able to Come Forward as Science* (4: 259), Kant makes use of a distinction between *gemeiner* and *gesunder Verstand*, emphasizing the normative connotation of the latter and indicating that ultimately (contrary to some interpretations) he is not against common sense as such. Similarly, near the very end of the *Critique*, Kant asks, "Do you really require that a mode of knowledge which concerns all humanity should transcend common understanding and be revealed to you only by philosophers?" (A831/B859). This kind of explicit reference to the understanding drops out, however, in the *Critique of the Power of Judgment* in contexts where Kant uses the terms *Gemeinsinn* and its Latin equivalent, *sensus communis*. These terms designate a specific aesthetic capacity that has to do primarily with sensibility (and hence they do not mean the same thing as *gesunder/gemeiner Menschenverstand*), and so, even if it is understandable, it is an unfortunate complication that these terms have also been translated (elsewhere) as "common sense." It is no wonder that the meaning of "common sense" was frequently debated by German writers in this era; see, e.g., Reinhold, "Ueber Populäritat und gesunden Menschenverstand. Fragment eines Briefwechsels," *Der neue Teutsche Merkur* 3 (1791), 419–29. (The ascription to Reinhold of this anonymously published essay is discussed in Alessandro Lazzari, "*Das Eine, was der Menschheit Noth ist*": *Einheit und Freiheit in der Philosophie Karl Leonhard Reinholds (1789–1792)* (Stuttgart-Bad Cannstatt, Frommann-Holzboog, 2004), p. 241; see also K. Ameriks, "A Commonsense Kant?"*Proceedings and Addresses of the American Philosophical Association* 79 (2005).)

Except for the A and B editions of the *Critique of Pure Reason*, all page references to Kant's work give the volume number, followed by a colon and page number, of the standard German Academy edition, *Kant's Gesammelte Schriften* (Berlin, 1900–). Passages cited from the *Critique* are from the Norman Kemp Smith translation (London, Macmillan, 1929).

The following pages offer a table that displays the relation between the two versions of Reinhold's *Letters*. See also the detailed list of contents at the beginning of the Appendix.

<table>
<tr><th>1786–7 edition, Weimar, pagination in Der Teutsche Merkur</th><th>1790 edition, Leipzig, pagination in 1923 Reclam reprint</th></tr>
<tr><td></td><td>Preface (9–13)</td></tr>
<tr><td>First Letter (August 1786, vol. III, 99–127)
"The need for a Critique of Reason"</td><td>First Letter (17–44)
"The spirit of our age and the present state of the sciences heralds a universal reformation of philosophy"

Second Letter (44–74)
"Continuation of the preceding letter: The need for a highest rule of taste, for guiding principles for positive theology and jurisprudence, and, above all, for a first basic principle of natural right and morality"

Third Letter (74–97)
"The shaking in the domain of the philosophy of religion heralds a reformation of this philosophy: my judgment regarding the Kantian philosophy in general"</td></tr>
<tr><td colspan="2">99–105 (Merkur) ≈ 17–22 (Reclam)
105–23 (Merkur) ≈ 74–91 (Reclam)</td></tr>
<tr><td>Second Letter (August 1786, vol. III, 127–41)
"The result of the Kantian philosophy on the question of God's existence"</td><td>Fourth Letter (97–123)
"The result of the Kantian philosophy on the question of God's existence, compared with the general as well as particular results of previous philosophy"</td></tr>
<tr><td colspan="2">127–32 (Merkur) ≈ 97–101 (Reclam)
132–41 (Merkur) ≈ 116–23 (Reclam)</td></tr>
<tr><td>Third Letter (January 1787, vol. I, 3–39)
"The result of the Critique of Reason concerning the necessary connection between morality and religion"</td><td>Fifth Letter (123–37)
"The result of the Critique of Reason concerning the necessary connection between morality and religion"</td></tr>
</table>

<table>
<tr><td></td><td>Sixth Letter (138–52)
"Kantian rational faith compared to the metaphysical and hyperphysical grounds of conviction"</td></tr>
<tr><td colspan="2">3–39 (Merkur) ≈ 123–52 (Reclam)</td></tr>
<tr><td>Fourth Letter (February 1787, vol. I, 117–42)
"On the elements and the previous course of conviction in the basic truths of religion"</td><td>Seventh Letter (152–72)
"On the elements and the previous course of conviction in the basic truths of religion"</td></tr>
<tr><td colspan="2">117–42 (Merkur) ≈ 152–72 (Reclam)</td></tr>
<tr><td>Fifth Letter (May 1787, vol. II, 167–85)
"The result of the Critique of Reason concerning the future life"</td><td>Eighth Letter (172–89)
"The result of the Critique of Reason concerning the future life"</td></tr>
<tr><td colspan="2">167–85 (Merkur) ≈ 172–89 (Reclam)</td></tr>
<tr><td>Sixth Letter (July 1787, vol. III, 67–88)
"Continuation of the preceding letter: The united interests of religion and morality in the clearing away of the metaphysical ground for cognition of a future life"</td><td>Ninth Letter (189–210)
"Elucidation of the metaphysical ground for cognition of the immortality of the soul with regard to its origin as well as its consequences"</td></tr>
<tr><td colspan="2">67–73 (Merkur) ≈ 189–94 (Reclam)
77–88 (Merkur) ≈ 199–210 (Reclam)</td></tr>
<tr><td>Seventh Letter (August 1787, vol. III, 142–65)
"A sketch of a history of reason's psychological concept of a simple thinking substance"</td><td>Tenth Letter (210–30)
"The basic outlines for a history of the idea of spirit"</td></tr>
<tr><td colspan="2">142–65 (Merkur) ≈ 210–30 (Reclam)</td></tr>
<tr><td>Eighth Letter (September 1787, vol. III, 247–78)
"Continuation of the preceding letter: The master key to the rational psychology of the Greeks"</td><td>Eleventh Letter (230–63)
"The key to the rational psychology of the Greeks"</td></tr>
<tr><td colspan="2">247–64 (Merkur) ≈ 230–45 (Reclam)
266–78 (Merkur) ≈ 251–63 (Reclam)</td></tr>
</table>

	Twelfth Letter (263–92) "Suggestions regarding the influence of the undeveloped and misunderstood basic truths of religion on civic and moral culture"

[99] First Letter: The need for a Critique of Reason

So you continue to insist on the opinion, dear friend, that the enlightenment of our German fatherland has been waning in Protestant domains ever since it began rising in Catholic domains? Given the comparison you drew, I wonder whether you have, on the one hand, taken into account a truly greater swiftness that has diminished since its initial zeal and, on the other, an apparent slowness that is based on an optical illusion. Has not this slowness become more prominent the further the enlightenment, much like the sun, advances in relation to its horizon?[1] – But, according to your own assurance, you have compared the course of Protestantism only to itself and have found that it is not, for instance, merely moving forward more slowly [100] but rather that it is actually at the point of retreating. Given the perspective in which you were able to arrange them in your letter, the many facts on which you base this claim certainly offer no comforting view of the future; and I confess to you that I have not found one among them I could deny or even call into doubt.[2] By deriving the plausibility of your claim more from the combined effect of your reasons

[1] The comparison between the Enlightenment and the sun is one of Reinhold's most frequently used images. It is a commonplace of the period, found often in the work of other Masonic figures such as Mozart. See the discussion of Reinhold and his associates in Vienna, in Nicholas Till, ch. 10, "Freemasonry and the Catholic Enlightenment," in *Mozart and the Enlightenment: Truth, Virtue and Beauty in Mozart's Operas* (New York and London, W. W. Norton, 1992).

[2] The 1790 ed. (pp. 17–18) replaces the following two sentences with: "But I am also refraining from any objections that I could bring against the questionableness of some of these facts because you want to have the plausibility of your opinion judged more by the combined effect of *all* the reasons cited than by the force of *any one* taken individually. In order to show you that I have wholly understood you, I want to take your most essential remarks out of the sequence of facts and inferences that accompany them in your letter and to repeat them here in my own words."

than from the force of any one taken individually, you anticipate the objections I could make against many of the inferences you have drawn. I think, therefore, that those reasons will lose nothing when I take them out of the sequence of facts and remarks that accompany them in your letter and place them here one after another for my own purposes. – You write:[3]

> Ever since the free use of reason in religious matters began to lose for its old defenders the charm of a forbidden fruit, the former zeal for the rights of reason has been displaced by indifference,[4] which on occasion has already broken out into hate and contempt and threatens to pass over into a universal mistrust. Those who are not already convinced that reason has gone too far in our day do at least fear that it will go too far and are seeking either to restore its old arbitrary [101] limits or to invent new ones. – The exclusive right of reason to decide on the meaning of the Bible – that right with whose recognition the whole of Protestantism either stands or falls – is being attacked even by Protestant theologians with a zeal that has contributed in no small way to the reawakening of the old hopes and institutions of the Roman reunifiers. – The appeals of reason to sensation, to common sense,[5] to intuitive sense, to a feeling for the divine, etc. are becoming ever louder and more frequent, and from every one of these petty tribunals verdicts are being obtained against the perfectly legitimate claims of reason. – The science from which all the other sciences borrow their principles, the science that from time immemorial constituted the most distinctive and important employment of reason, and through whose development Leibniz, Wolff, and Baumgarten[6] have rendered such a great service to the true priorities of our age – in a word, metaphysics – is being neglected in a way that contrasts oddly with the claims of our century to the honorary title of "the philosophical." Like an insignificant and ramshackle fortification, metaphysics is being surrendered to its enemies, against whom it had only recently been serving reason so well. Out of the ruins of this science, hot-headed enthusiasts and cold-hearted sophists are at

[3] This is one of several passages that Reinhold puts in quotation marks, sometimes as part of the internal dialogue with the correspondent that he invents for the letters, and sometimes simply to express positions under consideration that were common at the time.

[4] Cf. Immanuel Kant (1724–1804), Preface to *Critique of Pure Reason* (Riga, 1781), A x: "the prevailing mood is that of weariness and complete *indifferentism*."

[5] *Gesunder Menschenverstand*. See above, Note on the texts and translation.

[6] Gottfried Wilhelm Leibniz (1646–1716), Christian Wolff (1679–1754), Alexander Gottlieb Baumgarten (1714–62).

present busier than ever [102] propping up anew the old systems of superstition and nonbelief.[7] Far from offsetting[8] one another, these systems are instead gaining new strength as a result of their mutual struggle, draining the energy of the human spirit with pointless quarreling in the scholarly world, and perpetuating opposition between the understanding and the heart in the moral world. The hopes of the well-meaning who wish to see this unholy feud settled through the mediation of reason are disappearing at the same rate that reason itself is passing the most unprecedented tests of its efficacy and strength in so many other fields of human knowledge. Reason, which has never before been called in as judge so universally and for the most insignificant details, is being accused ever more loudly as a disturber of the peace in the most important affairs of humankind. And while its ostensible triumph over old prejudices is announced with shouts of victory by beardless youths, men take the stand before men and accuse reason of high treason against humanity.[9] They argue that it demonstrates the opposite of what God reveals, and, without themselves knowing it or wanting to, they sharpen the dulled weapons of superstition and nonbelief alike.[a] – [103] Compare, dear friend, our academies of the arts and sciences to the public and private societies that work under all sorts of names and pretexts for the continuation of our immaturity,[10] and whose diversity has the

[7] *Aberglaube, Unglaube.* Reinhold uses this combination of terms frequently because they have a common root, *Glaube*, but unfortunately this fact is lost in English translation. Moreover, there is no sensible alternative to translating *Glaube* sometimes as "belief" and sometimes as "faith" (and *Unglaube* as "nonbelief" but *unglaubig* as "faithless"). Friedrich Heinrich Jacobi (1743–1819) exploited this ambiguity by making use of David Hume's (1711–76) nontheist statements that we must rely on "belief" to encourage the view that we must rely on theist faith. See his *David Hume on Faith, or Idealism and Realism, a Dialogue* (Breslau, 1787), translated in *Friedrich Heinrich Jacobi, The Main Philosophical Writings and the Novel "Allwill"*, ed. G. di Giovanni (Montreal and Kingston, McGill-Queen's University Press, 1994), pp. 253–338.

[8] *Aufheben.* Reinhold uses this term in many key passages in a way that seems to foreshadow (and may have influenced) the frequent dialectical use of the term by G. W. F. Hegel (1770–1831). The term is often translated in different ways in different contexts, e.g., as "suspend" or "nullify." See below, n. 40 and n. 119.

[9] Cf. 1790 ed., p. 12 (Appendix, section A), where Reinhold cites a related passage from Horace.

[a] See *Results of Jacobi's and Mendelssohn's Philosophy Critically Assessed, etc.* [This work was written by Thomas Wizenmann [1759–87], a young supporter of Friedrich Jacobi. Its full title is: *Die Resultate der Jacobischen und Mendelssohnschen Philosophie; kritisch untersucht von einem Freywilligen* (*Results of the Jacobian and Mendelssohnian Philosophy Critically Assessed by an Impartial Observer*) (Leipzig, 1786). On Wizenmann, see Frederick Beiser, *The Fate of Reason* (Cambridge, MA, Harvard University Press, 1986), ch. 4. This footnote is omitted in the 1790 edition.]

[10] Cf. Kant, "An Answer to the Question, What is Enlightenment?" (Berlin, 1784), which begins, "Enlightenment is humanity's emergence from its self-incurred immaturity" (8: 85).

> systematic appearance of driving reason into a corner from several sides simultaneously. Which of these two very opposed kinds of associations is at present more flourishing and active? Which of the two has a larger number of members, more enthusiasm in its endeavors, and a more numerous and receptive public to show for itself? – Finally, granted that priestcraft and despotism have perhaps never before had so many causes for complaint against reason, reason, precisely because of this fact, has also never before had so much cause to fear the worst from both of them. As long as it did nothing more than clear away, as a result of the Reformation, the prejudices in the hierarchical system that opposed the freedom of priestcraft and the absolute power of despotism, reason had nothing but the misunderstood interest of both against itself. But once reason proceeds further and asserts principles that are incompatible with the continuing existence of priestcraft and despotism, then nothing is more certain than that both of them will summon all the strength that their old holdings procure for them in order to suppress the voice of their enemy. Soon they will [104] need no other pretext for this end than the abuses that our writing mobs are committing with their publications and freedom of the press – abuses which are becoming ever more rampant and which might ultimately bring even the better thinking servants of religion and the state to the point of regarding as the lesser evil those well-known remedies which eliminate freedom together with licentiousness.

You have urgently called upon me to write you my opinion concerning the likely outcome of all these phenomena taken collectively. When I now confess to you that my opinion is exactly the opposite of yours, I know that I am claiming something quite paradoxical to you. Yet I also know that for the time being I already have your heart on my side, and thus I hope to come to agreement with your mind all the sooner.

Your letter has portrayed aptly enough the disarray in which the concerns of reason in matters of religion now find themselves among us. And however much the individual features of your portrait must lose some of their determinateness in the sketch that I have drawn up of them, I still believe that every more attentive observer of our age will rediscover even in this sketch the most pertinent recent events, together with their heroes, as well as some of his own observations regarding them. [105] Each individual phenomenon that appears in this sketch would, when taken by itself, make me more or less alarmed; each deserves the attention of every friend of humanity, and most of them have already attracted this attention. But when I view them as a whole in their connection with one another and with the causes and occasions that gave rise to them, I become very inclined to regard them as reliable harbingers of one of the most far-reaching and beneficent revolutions that has ever occurred at one and the same time in the scholarly and moral world.[11]

If the phenomena that you, my friend, have arranged together in your portrait actually share a common ground,[12] then this ground is none other than the old and still persistent misunderstanding, which today is more lively – or rather, more visible – than ever before, regarding the right and power of reason in matters of religion. It is especially characteristic of our age that the disputing factions are latching directly onto reason itself, which they elevate or degrade depending on whether or not they believe that they have cause to be satisfied with its decisions. Those who are dissatisfied press against reason and storm it for better answers, or [106] they give up all hope and either take up sides with the faction against reason or become indifferent spectators of the conflict. This is roughly the contour shaping the history of the current state of our higher enlightenment regarding speculative religion, which has a much larger influence on the rest of the affairs in our moral world than the indifferent spectators usually care to admit.

The age-old and never-ending dispute over many all-important questions is itself the most convincing proof that the answers reason has so far given to these questions – or rather, the answers that have been given in the name of reason – lack evidence and universal validity. The most striking example of such a question is that which concerns the existence of God. Let us stay with this example.

We shall suppose once and for all that it was reason which, from the first stages of its development, unceasingly raised this question. I know that believers and nonbelievers reject this supposition. Believers claim that reason could never arrive at this question on its own, and nonbelievers claim that reason declares this question to be superfluous. But I know that you, my friend, are neither a believer nor a nonbeliever of this sort, and that

[11] See Appendix, sections B and C for the additions that Reinhold inserted at this point in the text in the 1790 edition. After these additions, which include the introduction of a separate letter, the 1790 edition adds further revisions of the *Merkur* text that begin here. See Appendix, section D.

[12] *Gemeinschaftlichen Grund.* See above, n. 5. The search for a common ground can be regarded as what Reinhold always took to be his most fundamental task.

you are in agreement with me that reason [107] not only can raise this question but also must raise it. – Now given this supposition, it had to become impossible for reason to pass by systems or aggregates of its most distinctive concepts or the science of its notions, principles, and basic principles[13] – in a word, [the science of] metaphysics, which subsequently was so denounced. It turned out that the whole subject matter of the question could be thought in no other way than with concepts that became more metaphysical the more they were purified from the foreign admixtures of fantasy and the sediment of common prejudices, and the more firmly one's eyes were fixed upon them in continual examination. The relation of all other proofs for God's existence to the metaphysical concept of an unconditioned necessary existence became more and more visible. And men appeared who asserted more or less clearly that while natural as well as even supernatural revelation could indeed confirm reason's concepts of the deity, it could not replace them. Even our faith-theologians[14] did not find it superfluous to add the ontological argument to their proofs derived from supernatural sources. And although in their typical compendiums they usually placed this argument last, they still always found themselves compelled to privilege it and to recognize, even against their wills, its first-rank status whenever dealing with nonbelievers [108]. Our modern enemies and despisers of metaphysics ultimately have no other way out (as experience teaches) than to observe a strict silence on the whole question or to roam about in a labyrinth of indeterminate feelings. If one forces the silent to start talking or those in the labyrinth to give an intelligible account of their philosophy of the heart, they will both speak metaphysics just like the nobleman who spoke prose without knowing it or wanting to.[15]

But however unavoidable it might have always been, and may now still be, to consult metaphysics about God's existence, all the answers obtained by such questioning to date have been, and still are, ill-suited for universal conviction. This holds not only, for instance, with respect to those classes for whom no scientific proof exists but also among men who have spent the greater part of their lives dealing with the sciences – and indeed, even with metaphysical investigations. Writers whose

[13] *Notionen, Principien und Grundsätze.*

[14] *Glaubenstheologen*, theologians such as the Pietists, who proceed by relying on faith as opposed to reason or tradition.

[15] An allusion to Molière's M. Jourdain, who spoke prose before comprehending the meaning of the term "prose."

philosophical spirit one cannot possibly deny without wholly abandoning the philosophical spirit oneself have declared all metaphysical proofs for God's existence to be inadequate. They have either come over to the opinion that reason can decide absolutely nothing in regard to this question, or they have gone so far as to believe that they have established a negative answer already with the premises [109] of those proofs. In truth, the manifold use that skeptics as well as pantheists, etc. have made of their claims about metaphysics has contributed in no small way to the confirmation of the old opinion regarding the hereditary perversion of reason. It has also helped preserve the reputation of those proofs for God's existence which were believed to have been found outside the domain of reason and nature, for had the domain of reason been more soundly expanded, such proofs would have suffered a proportionate loss of reputation. "Hence, despite all previous efforts, we still do not have a metaphysics that can answer this immense and often-raised question with universally illuminating certainty." This is a fact that cannot be denied by any of our present-day philosophical factions no matter how lofty the opinion may otherwise be that each faction entertains regarding the answer it has already found.

But from the fact that we have no such metaphysics, it in no way follows that we cannot have one. Those who claim this impossibility for the benefit of faith – a faith to which they have every right to help themselves in the absence of knowledge – must concede the other equally undeniable fact "that so far they have been just as incapable of procuring universal validity for the very principles of their faith [110]." For it is precisely among the most skilled and astute thinkers that these principles generally find the least acceptance. In the meantime, as long as the possibility has not yet been demonstrated of a metaphysics that could give a universally valid answer to the question of God's existence, the faith-theologians, who declare all heretofore fruitless endeavors of reason to be an argument against that possibility, cannot be dismissed. But these theologians are no more capable of refuting those who cite as an argument for that possibility the persistence of these efforts, the significant interest that humanity must take in a decisive answer, and the ever-growing inadequacy of every answer offered to date.

The doubt that arises from this argument and counterargument is one of the chief conditions under which that new metaphysics, if it indeed should be possible, could become actual and find acceptance. By resisting dogmatic claims about both the actual possession of such a science and its impossibility, this doubt removes the insurmountable obstacles, inevitably posed by our naturalists and supernaturalists alike, to the seeking out, development, and propagation of the new science. Both types of [111] dogmatists can no longer repress this doubt once it has taken hold, for it robs them of their weapons the very moment it appears. And this doubt has the significant advantage that its two opponents can never make common cause against it but rather will wear one another out amongst themselves the more they lash out against it. The more keenly they insist on their claims, the more the weaknesses of the arguments on both sides come to light and the more it becomes apparent to the impartial spectator how ill-suited for universal conviction their solutions to the immense problem are – solutions that are endlessly repeated by the one side in the name of metaphysical reason and by the other in the name of hyperphysical revelation.[b]

That this is presently the case among us seems to me to be indicated by just those signs of our time that appear to you, my friend, to be so alarming. They are the evident effects and distinguishing marks of a universal shaking of all our previous doctrinal structures – a shaking that is assaulting everything with a zeal and strength the likes of which we have never before seen. The incompatibility of these doctrinal structures has become so obvious that their supporters, who in the meantime had learned how to get along better [112], are attempting all for naught to keep themselves from polemics in their presentations. They contradict each other, even against their own wills, as soon as they make arguments, and it turns out in the end that each has merely refuted the other's opinion without having proven his own. In an actual struggle the aggressor always carries the day, provided he is not a blockhead. The deist drives pantheism out from all fortifications, while the pantheist tears down the bastions of deism.[16] The supernaturalists among the

[b] *Hyperphysics* is the author's term for every supernatural theory of the supernatural. [This footnote is omitted in the 1790 edition.]

[16] The 1790 ed. (p. 81) replaces this sentence with: "The *theist* believes that he has driven *atheism* out from all fortifications [*Verschanzungen*], while the atheist triumphs over the wrecked bastions [*Bollwerke*] of theism." The 1790 ed. often replaces "deism" with "theism" and "pantheism" with "atheism." Cf. also Kant, *Critique of Pure Reason*, A 849/B 877: "although metaphysics cannot be the foundation [*Grundveste*] of religion, it must always continue to be a bulwark [*Bollwerk*] of it." *Verschanzungen* (which can also be translated as "entrenchments") and *Bollwerke*, like *Grundfeste*

Protestants have no infallible church and consequently no territory of their own impervious to reason, no territory upon whose ground their doctrinal structures would be safe from attack. As a result they see no other means for themselves than to use the dissension among the philosophers to their advantage and to carry out their construction, wherever possible, atop the ruins of the systems of reason that their opponents have destroyed by themselves. And so they press with all their might to demonstrate from the contradictions of those systems the inadequacy of reason and the indispensability of a supernatural surrogate for it. But as soon as that struggle commences which is supposed to expose the weaknesses of their opponents, it turns out to be impossible for them to remain indifferent thereby. In order to keep the pantheists at bay they must side with the deists; yet in doing so they have to give up the very claims they had made earlier. [113] Hence, the frequent contradictions among the supporters of the supernaturalist faction: while some claim the impossibility for proving God's existence from reason, others claim its indispensability; while some presuppose God's existence in their proof of revelation, others prove it from revelation; while some think that they know in advance what they subsequently believe on the basis of the word,[17] others believe even before they know whom they are supposed to believe.

Depending on the standpoint you want to take, dear friend, you will look upon this general wavering of our accepted systems either as a danger to reason for the philosophers or as a danger to faith for the theologians. While those factions which have been driven into a corner revert to extreme measures, exaggerate their claims in the heat of battle, and leave their defenses wide open – defenses which even their opponents' attack had not exposed – the peaceful spectator sees, not without concern, the defenders of reason fighting for the cause of nonbelief and the guardians of faith fighting for the cause of superstition. And this accounts for the riddle concerning how these two opposing sicknesses progress so violently at the same rate.

In the meantime, dear friend, let us not stop at all the disorder that seems to be seizing our attention because of its noise and sensation [114].

and *Schutzwehr*, are terms from military science that Reinhold and Kant frequently use in explaining epistemological points, especially in religious contexts. *Grundfeste* signifies a constructed foundation and is often used to suggest an offensive intention of launching attacks or building a new foundational philosophical system, whereas *Schutzwehr* literally signifies a defensive instrument for warding off attacks. See also below, n. 147 and n. 148.

[17] I.e., presumably from scripture on a literalist interpretation.

While this fight continues to be waged by a few hotheads, the conviction is spreading ever further among the more rational supporters of each system[18] that there is no hope for gaining universal acceptance of their system. This conviction, which we perhaps have more to thank for today's tolerance and freedom of thought than we imagine, undeniably has no small part in the indifference[19] that is so clearly taking the upper hand against both metaphysics and its supernatural surrogate – an indifference that appears quite strange next to the blustering impetuousness with which one defends metaphysical and hyperphysical results. Most of the modern philosophical and theological writers who feel the energy and the calling to think for themselves have become weary of investigations from which so little approval and so much opposition stand to be expected. The success of many excellent works in which philosophers have studied human beings and physical nature, and theologians the Bible and morality, lies open for the world to see. But just as, on the one hand, the indifference of sound minds to metaphysics and hyperphysics is increasing with this very success, and, on the other, the impossibility of proving previous systems is becoming ever more obvious from the continued struggle between factions, [115] it is likewise bound to become impossible even for philosophers and theologians of this kind to presuppose as found the answer to the question of God's existence. And because they still can neither avoid this question nor leave it unanswered, they too will feel themselves compelled to listen to the aforementioned doubt concerning the possibility of a universally satisfying answer.

This doubt has very little in common with ordinary skepticism, which rests satisfied with mere ignorance, for the more its meaning is grasped, the more it carries with itself a pressing need for its resolution. The all-important and ever-active interest that humanity takes in a conviction regarding God's existence, and that even the unholy followers of superstition and nonbelief so loudly proclaim, makes all indifference impossible here and transforms that doubt into the following specific question: Is a universally satisfying answer to the question of God's existence

[18] The 1790 ed. (p. 82) replaces "While this fight continues to be waged by a few hotheads, the conviction is spreading ever further among the more rational supporters of each system" with "While this fight continues to be waged by fanaticism on both sides, the conviction is becoming ever more rampant among a certain class of cold-blooded naturalists and supernaturalists."

[19] See above, First Letter, p. 100.

possible? Or rather (since this possibility cannot be demonstrated by an already-existing answer, but first must be investigated): How is such an answer possible?

This problem lies, as it were, at the point where the two paths of metaphysics and hyperphysics come to an end, where both paths trail off backwards into the infinite and [116] lead further and further away from the goal – the point from which the only remaining path is the one that moves forward. Once we find ourselves at this point, we have left both stray paths behind. And since we cannot remain at a standstill, we must take up the path before us – which is to say, we must solve the problem. Seeking the conditions of this solution outside the domain of reason or confusing this domain with our previous metaphysics would be tantamount to moving backwards and losing our way again on one of the previous paths. Thus, there is nothing left to do than to become acquainted, above all, with that still unknown domain of reason in which these conditions must lie. And the newly entered path leads to a new and second problem: What is possible through reason proper?

I think, dear friend, I see you shaking your head over this problem. Not, for example, because you remain unconvinced that its solution is the only possible path that could at all lead to our goal. "But (I hear you saying) this problem still remains a problem after everything that has been accomplished in speculative philosophy to date by the whole lot of men, great and small, and precisely this little fact provides a strong presumption that it will also [117] remain a problem forever." – Admittedly, in the foregoing I was able to indicate only very perfunctorily the course that the human spirit had to take in order to arrive at this problem; nonetheless, it seems to me that your objection can be answered from what has already been said. Every fate that our philosophy has experienced until now had to be undergone before one could think in earnest of posing this problem, let alone solving it. Doing either was absolutely impossible on the dogmatist's path – that is, on the path most often taken. And yet this path to the solution of our problem was not only unavoidable in itself but even necessary as a preparation for that solution. Without the efforts of the dogmatists, which were sustained by flattering illusion, we never would have obtained those magnificent preliminary exercises to which reason owes that degree of development which it requires for such an exceedingly difficult undertaking. As long as this degree of development was not present, skepticism was not capable of much beyond prodding the dogmatists. The dogmatists thus proceeded unhindered on their paths and had to proceed far enough for them or their spectators to see that these paths were leading them farther away from their goal the further they advanced along them. Before this point in time it would have been neither advisable nor possible [118] to hold them up in their advances. Nothing is more understandable than why this moment did not come sooner. The history of peoples and epochs that have achieved something noteworthy in the sciences shows us clearly enough the causes by which the course of philosophy was so often interrupted. After the revival of the sciences among us, the dogmatists needed a fairly long time before they could appear in two main sects, the orthodox and heterodox, that would more or less keep one another in balance. While the latter were allowed to take care of their natural necessities in a sufficiently free and open manner, the former felt themselves forced to call on reason for help. But in the struggle between their systems, both sects have brought matters to the point where their dispute is considered rather insignificant – however important the motivation behind it may have been – and even professional philosophers and theologians want no part in it.

You would be doing our age a severe injustice, my friend, if you were to take the aversion of our better minds to metaphysical and theological squabbling to be an aversion to all profound investigations in general and to an investigation into the importance of our problem in particular. Everything depends on whether extraordinary circumstances will impress this importance upon the heart of our thinkers, and this, I believe, we may [119] expect from just those phenomena of our day which seem to my friend to be harbingers of so much evil.[20] As metaphysical as the question, What is possible through pure reason?, may sound, it still rings out loudly at present in the voice of our unmetaphysical age. We have almost no theological battles any more except for those which are being carried out explicitly for and against reason. "Only through reason is true cognition of God possible" and "Through reason true cognition of God is impossible" are the slogans of the disputing factions, and the actual and alleged proofs for these two claims are the most common weapons with which one takes the field against the other. In this way, one endeavors to find out what reason is or is not capable of

[20] See above, First Letter, pp. 99–103.

achieving; that is, one seeks proofs for one's old opinions in the faculty of reason itself. The lack of such proofs, which have still not been found – or rather, the lack of universally valid premises for these previous proofs – is thus the difficulty that both factions run into, and the genuine point of the old misunderstanding that we are finally more nearly approaching. An indeterminate but vivid feeling of this difficulty expresses itself in the despair that has become very visible in recent times concerning the possibility of establishing opinions through proofs of reason or resolving doubts through grounds of reason. [120] This despair has contributed in no small way to the present indifference toward metaphysics. It is undeniably what is prompting some to support their tottering metaphysics with mysticism and the Kabbalah, and tempting others to heed the invitations of secret societies that promise satisfaction from their wealth of traditions and revelations. Moreover, it is compelling some to appeal with their reason to feeling, to human understanding,[21] to intuitive sense, to history, etc. Finally, it is this despair that lies at the basis of that phenomenon which you, my friend, observed so accurately and which is so characteristic of our age: an express hatred of reason. Certainly it is possible that the base self-interest of the wretched, who in their occupations have so much to fear from reason, plays a part in this sad occurrence. But let us be fair! The universally recognized probity of many a writer who has declared himself loudly and openly against reason in matters of religion vouchsafes for us by itself that the sole cause of such strange conduct in an affair in which precisely the best heart takes the strongest interest was the betrayed expectation of a satisfying answer for the mind. But these writers themselves specify this cause clearly enough, for they blame reason for the lack of universally valid principles that [121] would allow the question of God's existence to be answered. In so far as the proofs by which they sought to confirm this accusation are taken from previous metaphysics and directed against previous metaphysics, it becomes evident that these writers are confusing reason with metaphysics and charging the former with what can actually be rendered only to the account of the latter. As a result of this accusation, their opponents are forced to seek out for the

[21] *Menschenverstand.* This could refer, for example, to John Locke (1632–1702), *An Essay on Human Understanding* (London, 1690), or David Hume, *An Enquiry Concerning Human Understanding* (London, 1748). See also above, n. 5.

first time those universally valid principles which they believed they had found long ago, and finally to admit as well that they had previously thanked reason for a possession that they had actually owed to none but metaphysics.

It inevitably turned out, then, that reason was misconstrued by both of our factions. How much comes together in bringing this important truth to light for our contemporaries! Never before has one so manifestly expected too much and too little from reason than in the present day. The idolatry that is being practiced with reason on the one hand and the disgust that is shown to it on the other are approaching the absurd. Meanwhile both the exaggerated panegyrics and defamations that one is becoming accustomed to encountering with regard to reason have at no other time been so universally attacked and so deftly refuted. Ultimately even the most rational and moderate supporters of each [122] faction are bound to arrive at the thought of seeking the ground for the exaggerations that they note in their own comrades in the principles shared by the whole faction. For even they are being unanimously accused of making exaggerated claims for and against reason – and precisely by the most rational and moderate supporters of the opposing faction. One side is just as universally and thoroughly convinced that too much is being expected of reason as the other side is convinced that too little is being expected of it – or what amounts to the same thing, each side is blaming the other for misconstruing reason. Since each side must now justify before its opponent its cognition of reason, each feels compelled to find new grounds beyond those which previously had satisfied only itself – grounds that would also be illuminating for its opponent. Each side must therefore go beyond its previous cognition and seek out principles it has not yet discovered. In a word, each must ground its previous cognition of reason anew. Hence, neither side can be any more content with its own cognition of reason than it is with its opponents' cognition of reason, and the need for a new investigation into the faculty of reason must ultimately become universally accepted by thinking minds, just as they are already now convinced that reason has been misconstrued.

[123] The problem regarding what is possible through reason is thus prepared, set as a task, and necessitated by the prevailing circumstances of our day. It would indeed be no small merit of our century to have drawn out the old and unholy misunderstanding from the obscurity of confused concepts and to have brought it down to the simplest terms.

It has cost the world the bloody and unbloody wars between orthodoxy and heterodoxy, made inevitable nonbelief and superstition, squandered the energies of the human spirit with useless speculations, and seemed to all appearances as if it would have to continue forever. It would indeed be no small merit to have made more accessible a problem whose solution promises for our descendants nothing less than the end of all philosophical and theological heresies and, in the realm of speculation, an everlasting peace of which not even Saint-Pierre[22] had dreamed. But even the solution itself has been reserved for our century, and surely a more shining crown could not be placed on its merits.

I know, dear friend, that[23] you have not read Kant's *Critique of Pure Reason* yourself, and that because of your circumstances it will likely be a while before you can read it. But I do not know whether you have become acquainted with this masterpiece of the philosophical spirit through news that has reached your ears [124] apart from the point of view from which, in this extensive letter, I have presented the subject matter it treats. Surely you have heard those speaking with awe about the all-crushing Kant and his profound work.[24] But perhaps you have also read assessments of this work in which one marvels at the astuteness of the man yet claims with astonishment to have discovered in the work itself God knows what neological[25] attempts at making idealism into a system, resuscitating old scholastic hairsplitting, introducing into philosophy unnecessary new forms of speech, and even undermining conviction in indispensable truths, etc.[26] Perhaps one has even named for you famous philosophers who have passed similar judgments on this book, or who have at least declared it to be absolutely incomprehensible. In that case,

[22] Charles Irénée Castel (Abbé) de Saint-Pierre (1658–1743), author of *Projet pour rendre la paix perpétuelle en Europe* (*Project for Obtaining Perpetual Peace in Europe*), 3 vols. (Utrecht, 1713/1717).

[23] See Appendix, section D for the heavily revised and expanded version of the text included in the 1790 edition (pp. 92ff.) that begins here and ends where the First Letter comes to a conclusion in the *Merkur*, p. 127.

[24] See below, n. 42 and n. 81.

[25] The Neologians were eighteenth-century Protestant German theologians (e.g., Johann Salomo Semler [1725–91]) who attempted to reconcile rationalist and Christian traditions. See Dieter Henrich, *Between Kant and Hegel: Lectures on German Idealism* (Cambridge, MA, Harvard University Press, 2003), p. 107, n. 10.

[26] See the 1782 "Garve-Feder" review of the *Critique*, translated in the Appendix to Kant, *Prolegomena to Any Future Metaphysics that Will Be Able to Come Forward as Science* (Königsberg, 1783), ed. Gary Hatfield (Cambridge, Cambridge University Press, 2nd ed., 2004), pp. 201–7.

you will be able to thank me all the more for making you familiar in a preliminary way with a work that, according to my innermost conviction, is just what the most pressing philosophical needs of our time call for – a work that secures in so many ways a better future for our descendants. But in any case, if I want to convince you fully of the coming of [125] that fortunate revolution which appears to me heralded by those phenomena of our day which you find so terrible, I am obliged to show you that the immense problem of whose importance and indispensability I have been speaking until now has actually been solved.

Do not worry that I shall presume to lead you into the depths of speculation from which Kant has unearthed so many previously undiscovered treasures of the human spirit. Your future leisure time will allow you to find your surest guide in the book itself. I can and shall content myself with extracting the principal results of the Critique of Reason[27] and showing you in those same results the solution of just as many important disputes, disputes that have been carried on until now as a result of the universal misunderstanding of reason. In this way, you will come to know the tree by its fruits.

Before I proceed in my next letter to the matter at hand, I believe that there is still one small doubt to ward off, one that the previous fate of Kant's work could occasion in you. The solution to the immense problem, if it is to meet our needs – or rather, if it is to deserve this name at all – must be apodictically certain through and through, and consequently it must be suited to the most universal conviction. It is a well-known fact, however, that the Critique of Reason has in no way effected such a conviction in all of those who have read it. [126] Without going into a detailed explanation of the many causes of this fact – causes which for the most part lie outside the Critique of Reason – I want only to remind you of Newton's works,[28] which experienced the very same fate for a long period of time despite their mathematical evidence. For Newton could still count on at least the best minds and the most adept mathematicians to understand him most readily – a hope that Kant cannot maintain so generally with respect to the most skilled and famous philosophers of his time. The deeper those philosophers have entrenched themselves in their dogmatic or skeptical manners of representation, and

[27] *Kritik der Vernunft*. See above, Note on the texts and translation.
[28] Isaac Newton (1642–1727).

the more abundant the laurels they have gathered along their own paths, the more difficult it must become for them to adopt a wholly new manner of representation and to take up a wholly new path on which only a single one of their contemporaries is proceeding. Kant has overthrown the previous dogmatism and skepticism just as surely as Copernicus and Newton have overthrown the Ptolemaic and Tychonian systems.[29] But for similar reasons, dogmatists and skeptics will carry on in their business[30] for a while longer just as the defenders of those two world systems carried on in their own after the better world system had been discovered and demonstrated. Nonetheless, the acceptance that Kant has already found among his contemporaries [127] is as notable as his reception has been honorable, and he will find an even better reception and acceptance the more our opponents and defenders of reason become inclined, as a result of the ever-growing perplexity of their dealings, to accept the mediation offered to them.

[29] Nicolaus Copernicus (1473–1543), Ptolemy (Claudius Ptolemaeus) (second century BC), Tycho Brahe (1546–1601).
[30] *Wesen.*

[127] Second Letter: The result of the Kantian philosophy on the question of God's existence

What I claimed in my last letter concerning the lack of a universally satisfying answer to the question of God's existence actually applies more to the grounds and proofs for this answer than to the answer itself. An affirmative answer to this question is given by all eras and peoples with a majority vote, which on close inspection is nothing less than unanimous. This judgment, which is pronounced by such universal agreement and confirmed by the equally universal interest of humanity, is therefore a judgment of common sense and must rest on irrefutable and universally evident grounds.[31] These grounds, taken together as a whole, must have been ever present and continuously operative and, consequently, are capable of being discovered and developed but not invented or altered. Nevertheless, the actual role that [128] reason – when viewed as a separate faculty – had in these grounds[32] could have remained forever unrecognized, undetermined, and unproven without this role having therefore been less real or the arguments themselves less persuasive. The seven elementary colors have always radiated the color white as a result of their uniform mixture – even before Newton discovered the existence of these seven elementary colors in every ray of light and the effect of their uniform

[31] The 1790 ed. (p. 97) inserts "and on irresistible motivations."

[32] The 1790 ed. (p. 98) inserts a footnote: "For the development of its faculty, *reason* requires the antecedent functions of *sensibility* and *understanding*; and to this extent, of course, the conviction in God's existence depends on sensibility and understanding as well. But the *matter* for the representation of an actual *body* is *given* to sensibility by means of an impression from outside, whereas, as the Critical philosophy shows, the *matter* for the representation of the *deity* can be, and actually is, determined solely in the *form* of reason."

mixture. A Newtonian who would deny sensation of the color white in all those who either do not know or do not wish to concede the theory of the seven colors would be acting just as foolishly as a metaphysician who would accept no conviction in God's existence that is not built explicitly on grounds of reason. Conversely, an ignorant person who appeals to how things look in order to deny the seven different colors in the color white would perhaps be making a more tolerable judgment than the typical defenders of faith who appeal to common sense[33] in order to deny reason any role in their conviction in God's existence.

This role was able to surface only gradually and only to the extent that, as society achieved higher degrees of culture, the need for more definite and explicit direction from [129] reason became more pressing. Superstition and nonbelief had already inflicted their devastation very extensively before theologians saw it as necessary to devote greater attention to the questions of whether faith may conflict with reason and whether reason can ground faith. Yet at the same time, one can accept it as a fact confirmed by the experience of all eras that in all cultivated nations reason has always come to the aid of universal conviction in God's existence to the same degree that this conviction has run into danger in its foundations. Perhaps never before have these foundations been as universally and emphatically shaken as they have been in our day. On this account alone, one could hope that, for the sake of this universal conviction, reason would undertake something that it had never done before. Never before has reason's role in this conviction become such a lively and open topic of discussion; never before has reason been so urgently called upon to specify that role in a definite and universally satisfying way. This role has become the true bone of contention between our two main factions, which accuse one another of nothing more often and more emphatically than charging to reason's account either too much or too little with regard to the grounds of conviction in God's existence. For both of them it is becoming less and less possible to dismiss, by means of these systems alone, the accusations made against their [130] systems. One faction appeals in vain to demonstrations[34] that exceed the capacities

[33] *Gemeiner Menschenverstand*; see above, n. 5. At the end of the next paragraph, *gemeinster Menschenverstand* is translated as "most elementary common sense."

[34] The 1790 ed. (p. 99) replaces "demonstrations" with "objective grounds of reason" here and throughout – presumably to leave room for the notion of legitimate "subjective" arguments from pure practical reason. Cf. above, n. 27, and below, n. 72 and n. n.

of common sense, and that encounter strong opposition among the most skilled of thinkers. The other appeals in vain to facts whose intrinsic unlikelihood is in our day beginning to strike the most elementary common sense, while the historical indemonstrability of these facts is becoming more and more obvious as a result of investigations by our philologists and historians. If members of the one faction want to save an apodictic certainty that would make all faith superfluous, then there is nothing left for them to do but to show the exact role, disputed by their opponents, that reason has in that certainty. If members of the other faction want to justify a faith that would make all grounds of reason superfluous, then they must refute, from the essence of reason itself, the role of reason that their opponents claim for it in the universal belief in God's existence.

The question, What role does reason have in our conviction in God's existence?, thus divides into two other questions that are provoked by the needs of our age, namely: Does reason contain apodictic proofs for God's existence – proofs that make all faith dispensable? and, Can there be a faith in God's existence [131] that requires no grounds of reason? The *Critique of Pure Reason* answers both questions negatively. Just as it demonstrates from the essence of speculative reason the impossibility of all apodictic proofs, it demonstrates from the essence of practical reason the necessity of a moral faith in God's existence. Consequently it compels naturalists to abandon, in favor of a rational faith, their ungrounded claims to knowledge, and supernaturalists to accept their faith from reason. To be sure, these answers must come very unexpectedly for both factions. But once the entire domain of pure reason becomes visible to them, they must give themselves over to what appears before them – that which leads the one faction to feel the absence in this domain of something it long believed that domain to possess, and that which forces the other to become aware of something present in it that it had never suspected. Both will be compensated amply enough for their disappointed expectations by a discovery that surpasses even the boldest of their previous claims. Until now, they no doubt believed that they had adequately refuted the alleged arguments against God's existence. But probably neither of them had ever thought that the impossibility of such proofs can be discovered in the essence of reason itself and apodictically demonstrated. The supposed universal validity of their refuting counter-arguments was refuted by an experience of the [132] contrary, and however skillfully they presumed to have avoided the weapons of their opponents in every attack, the simple fact that these opponents kept returning with the same weapons must have removed all hope of ever bringing the dispute to an end. Kant shattered these weapons and thereby made that very dispute impossible for the future. He displayed as a chimera the atheism that today more than ever haunts the moral world in the forms of fatalism, materialism, and pantheism,[35] and he did so with a vivacity that our modern theologians cannot claim in their unmasking of the devil. So if there should still be fatalists, etc. in the present or future, they will be people who have either not read or not understood the *Critique of Pure Reason*.[36]

I know, dear friend, how much these claims of mine imply. But, on the supposition that Kant irrefutably demonstrated the impossibility of apodictic proofs for or against God's existence and found the true ground of conviction in a faith commanded by reason, you cannot possibly find my claims to be exaggerated. For the time being, of course, you must accept this supposition on my word. But with every result that I present to you in my future letters [133], I hope to lead you closer to your own insight and conviction. My present letter is intended to make you acquainted only in a preliminary way with the answer that the *Critique of Pure Reason* has supplied to the question of God's existence. To be sure, in order to find this answer along with its proofs, Kant first had to solve the immense and exceedingly difficult problem of what is possible through pure reason. But for now, in order to be able to judge with the highest probability the soundness of this answer as well as its grounds, we need nothing more than to consider the answer itself, together with the circumstances that make a new answer necessary at all, and the conditions that these circumstances dictate.

The new answer, which is supposed to meet the needs of our age, cannot so much as contain new arguments for God's existence, but rather it must test, sort out, and confirm what is universally valid in previous ones. It must completely overthrow the [old] wavering systems for the sole purpose of erecting a new system from their usable ruins, one that

[35] The 1790 ed. (p. 101) replaces "pantheism" with "*Spinozism*" here and elsewhere.

[36] *Kritik d. r. V.* This abbreviation (for Kant's *Kritik der reinen Vernunft*) is used occasionally elsewhere, but henceforth the full title is given in the translation, without a note. See Appendix, section E for the material included in the 1790 edition that Reinhold inserts at this point in the text and that concludes with a heavily revised version of the following two paragraphs.

will not only not lose anything but rather will gain more and more internal stability as well as external usefulness with every future advance of the human spirit. It must satisfy the rational demands of previous factions, strike down forever their illegitimate [134] claims, indicate the ground of their misunderstanding as well as the point of agreement between their opinions, and thus forever put an end to all of their previous disputes. Finally, this answer must be illuminating to the most astute thinkers in its grounds and to the most elementary common sense in its result.

The Kantian answer fulfills all of these conditions. The grounds that it derives from reason for conviction in God's existence, and which lead to faith, are as old as this conviction itself. The question of God's existence was always the occupation of reason's highest concern and the most general subject of faith. Yet never before has reason's occupation with such important questions been so rigorously examined, never before have the roles that both reason[37] and faith must have in the answer been sorted out so precisely, and never before have the legitimate claims of both to universal conviction been so clearly exhibited and so completely confirmed, as with this new answer. In so far as it is founded on a faith commanded by practical reason, this answer topples the doctrinal structures of both apodictic proofs and blind faith and establishes a new system through a most successful union of the clarified principal arguments of both doctrinal structures. In the new system, reason [135] ceases to be presumptuous and faith ceases to be blind, and instead of opposing one another as before, they mutually support one another in perpetual harmony. The deist[38] who wants to have his [faculty of] reason accepted as providing conviction in God's existence, and the believer[39] who wants to have his faith accepted as providing this conviction both find their rational demands validated, just as, conversely, they find their inadmissible claims dismissed – whether the claim of the deist not to admit any faith alongside his reason, or the claim of the believer not to admit any reason beyond his faith. Both now meet on the line that has become visible marking the limits beyond which knowledge may not proceed and the boundaries from within which faith may not remove itself. The deist

[37] The 1790 ed. (p. 118) replaces "reason" with "*knowledge*" here and throughout – presumably to leave room for the notion of pure practical reason.
[38] The 1790 ed. (p. 118) replaces "deist" with "*theist*" here and throughout.
[39] The 1790 ed. (p. 118) replaces "believer" with "*supernaturalist*" here and throughout.

accepts faith on the command of his reason, the believer embraces reason for the sake of his faith, and their discord is settled forever. – The unholy distinction between an esoteric and an exoteric religion is thereby at last overcome.[40] Faith of the usual kind, which excluded arguments from reason, was made just as little for thinking minds as the usual proofs from reason, which displaced faith, were made for the common man. Yet, for this very reason the religions of these two classes of humanity stood in conflict with one another – not because of a mere superficial difference in manners of representation but because of a difference in fundamental concepts themselves. The Kantian answer [136] unites both in so far as it satisfies the most astute thinker with its arguments and the most elementary understanding with its result. Its arguments, which lead to faith, are forever secured against all objections of skilled reason, the sources of these objections are cut off, and all dogmatic proofs for and against God's existence – by which faith was made either superfluous or impossible – are annihilated. The most skilled metaphysician – or what in the future will be one and the same, the philosopher who knows the essence and limits of reason most precisely – will thus also be the most inclined to listen to the voice of practical reason, which commands faith. This is the voice that rings out loudly enough for the most elementary understanding as well. Whereas the oracles of speculative reason prove to be ambiguous for philosophers – and are as good as not even there for the great masses – practical reason, in its legislation of morality, gives rulings by itself that are both intelligible and illuminating in their essential content for all classes of humanity. And just as the sage feels it necessary to presuppose a highest being as the principle of the moral and physical laws of nature, a principle that is wise and powerful enough to determine and bring about the happiness of rational beings as a necessary consequence of moral laws, so too [137] the most common man feels compelled to accept a future rewarder and punisher of the actions that his conscience approves and condemns (even against his own will). In the Kantian answer it is thus one and the same ground of reason that offers faith to the most enlightened as well as to the most elementary understanding – that is, a faith that stands up to the most rigorous examination by the former and is illuminating for the most ordinary capacities of the latter. What a recommendation for the *Critique of Pure Reason* that

[40] *Aufgehoben.*

through an investigation which, in a certain sense, exhausted all the depths of speculative philosophy, it discovered and confirmed precisely that ground for cognition of God's existence which the history of all eras and peoples shows to be the oldest, most universal, and most effective! And, finally, what a recommendation that it rigorously proved, and did not merely make probable, the wise arrangement of providence, which, in a matter equally important to all human beings, can provide no more advantage to an understanding cultivated by chance circumstances than it can to a less cultivated understanding!

It emerges clearly enough from what has already been said that the well-known dispute between Jacobi and Mendelssohn – a dispute which you, dear friend, because of an overly worked up anxiousness, have found so alarming – had already been decided [138] several years ago by the time[41] it actually erupted. In the Preface to his excellent *Morning Hours*, Mendelssohn himself confesses that he "knew the work of the all-crushing Kant only from the insufficient reports of his friends or from scholarly notices that are seldom much more instructive."[42] And Jacobi, in his polemical writings on behalf of faith, cites the *Critique of Pure Reason* in a way that[43] makes the fact that he has not thoroughly grasped it at least as obvious as the fact that he has read it. Still, if Mendelssohn had not been prevented by the state of his health from studying the Critique of Reason, we would probably have been deprived of a work[44] that with rare clarity expounds ontological pseudo-arguments on the basis of their fundamental concepts, presents these arguments in their strongest possible forms, and seeks to supplement them with new ones. In short, we would have been deprived of a work that presents the whole matter of dogmatic deism with a resplendent order, thoroughness, and precision that must greatly ease the office of the Critique of Reason and hasten the end of the dispute that is carrying on before its court of law. And if Jacobi had grasped the entirety of Kant's view, we would not have received his outstanding new presentation and sharpening of the

[41] Translating *wenn* as "by the time," to avoid ambiguity and to make clear Reinhold's idea that Kant's writings had a solution (in 1781) for the Pantheism Controversy even before it erupted (in 1785). See above, Editor's Introduction.

[42] Moses Mendelssohn (1729–86), *Morning Hours, or Lectures on the Existence of God* (*Morgenstunden oder Vorlesungen über das Dasein Gottes*), part I (Berlin, 1785), in *Moses Mendelssohns gesammelte Schriften*, ed. G. B. Mendelssohn (Leipzig, 1843), 2: 235. Cf. above, n. 24, and below, n. 81.

[43] The 1790 ed. (p. 121) inserts "provided I have understood him correctly."

[44] Mendelssohn's *Morning Hours*.

proofs of atheism, which likewise seems to be just what the Critique of Reason now calls for.[45] Moreover, we would have one less striking example to offer of how much the [139] efforts of even the most profound and astute men must fall short whenever they want to pass over reason entirely in their accounts of their conviction in God's existence.

Just try for a moment, my friend, to see what you are able to understand by a faith "that is at once the element of all human activity and cognition;[c] [a faith] by which we know that we have a body; [a faith] that is supposed to be perceptual evidence and intuitive cognition – or rather, a conviction of perceptual evidence that is itself called revelation;[d] [a faith that is] a new source of immediate evidence in human beings themselves, which does not presuppose the truth of a religion but carries immediately with it a conviction in God and divine things; [a faith that is] an immediate certainty of our relationship to the deity; [a faith that is] a certainty in God's existence as a fact for us through appearances, events, revelation, testimony; and finally [a faith that is] even historical knowledge of God." If, as the author of the well-known *Results* (who, according to Jacobi's own assurance,[e] grasped his opinion [140] entirely and from the ground up) assures us, it was unfamiliarity with the spirit of Jacobi that prompted Mendelssohn to consider Jacobi's faith to be theological and orthodox, then it seems to have been no less an unfamiliarity with the spirit of Kant that prompted Mr. Jacobi to confuse his historical faith with the philosophical faith that the *Critique of Pure Reason* demonstrates, and to suppose that for the last

[45] The 1790 ed. (p. 121) omits the following sentence as well as the first sentence of the next paragraph.

[c] [Jacobi,] *Concerning the Doctrine of Spinoza* [in *Letters to Herr Moses Mendelssohn* (Breslau, 1785)], pp. 122, 162. [Translated in *Friedrich Heinrich Jacobi*, pp. 173–251.]

[d] [Wizenmann,] *Results of Jacobi's and Mendelssohn's Philosophy Critically Assessed by an Impartial Observer*, pp. 18, 24, 154, 158, 184, 253. [Cf. above, First Letter, p. 102, n. a.]

[e] [Jacobi,] "Preliminary Report," in *Answer to Mendelssohn's Accusations* [*Concerning Letters on the Doctrine of Spinoza*]. ["Vorbericht," in *Wider Mendelssohns Beschuldigungen betreffend die Briefe über die Lehre des Spinoza* (Leipzig, 1786). This is Jacobi's reply to Mendelssohn's *To Lessing's Friends: An Appendix to Mr. Jacobi's Correspondence Concerning the Doctrine of Spinoza* (*An die Freunde Lessings. Ein Anhang zu Herrn Jacobis Briefwechsel über die Lehre des Spinoza*) (Berlin, 1786), which appeared a few days after Mendelssohn's death on January 6, 1786. Jacobi had not only to defend his interpretation of Lessing but also to ward off accusations by Mendelssohn's friends. Some of them suspected that Mendelssohn died because of stress resulting from the controversy over the publication by Jacobi of discussions revealing the allegedly Spinozist views of Mendelssohn's longtime friend Gotthold Ephraim Lessing (1729–81). On Lessing's own position, see Barry Nisbet, "Introduction," *Lessing: Writings on Philosophy and Religion*, ed. H. B. Nisbet (Cambridge, Cambridge University Press, 2005).]

six years Kant has been teaching the same thing as his own view.[46] Given the way in which Mr. Jacobi explained his faith, it was very excusable that Mendelssohn arrived at the idea of regarding this faith to be something not too unlike common orthodoxy. In contrast to Jacobi, Mendelssohn very likely could have combined the faith that Kant derived from the moral law – and which is nothing more than a supposition proven to be necessary from mere grounds of reason – with his own principle "whose aim is to make acceptable no other conviction in doctrines of eternal truths than conviction through grounds of reason."[47] – Be that as it may, the dispute between Jacobi and Mendelssohn still has the merit of exposing the dialectical ambiguity of our metaphysics and bringing it to more widespread attention. [141] Mendelssohn protected and defended a demonstrative form of deism, and, since the new source of conviction[48] was as good as closed off to him, he considered it to be the only provable system among all others. Jacobi, in contrast, "having compared one philosophy against another, protects and defends atheism, and as long as no new source of evidence is opened, he accepts it as the most coherent of all systems."[f] Both men found the grounds for their very opposed opinions in one and the same science – in our previous metaphysics – and they presented them in a way that attests most appropriately to their universally recognized astuteness and their long-term familiarity with this science. How much, therefore, must this remarkable and striking fact – namely that our previous metaphysics must necessarily favor contradictory results – prove useful for the

[46] The 1790 ed. (p. 122) adds in a footnote here: "See p. 101 of the same *Answer*." This refers to Jacobi's *Answer to Mendelssohn's Accusations*. See above, n. e.

[47] Reinhold does not give a source for this quotation, but it comes almost verbatim from Mendelssohn's posthumously published reply, *To Lessing's Friends*. See *The Spinoza Conversations between Lessing and Jacobi: Texts with Excerpts from the Ensuing Controversy*, tr. G. Vallée, J. B. Lawson, and C. G. Chapple (Lanham, MD, University Press of America, 1988), p. 137. For the full context, see Alexander Altmann, *Moses Mendelssohn: A Biographical Study* (London and Portland, The Littman Library of Jewish Civilization, 1998), ch. 8.

[48] See Kant's moral argument for God as a postulate of pure practical reason, which is presented briefly in the *Critique of Pure Reason* (A 633/B 661f.; A 809/B 837f.) and "What Does it Mean to Orient Oneself in Thinking?" (*Berlinische Monatschrift*, 1786; 8: 137–41), and is elaborated at length in later works such as the *Critique of Practical Reason* (Halle, 1788) and the *Critique of the Power of Judgment* (Berlin and Libau, 1790). For a translation of the 1786 essay and related materials, see Kant, *Religion within the Boundaries of Mere Reason and Other Writings*, ed. A. Wood and G. di Giovanni, with an Introduction by Robert M. Adams (Cambridge, Cambridge University Press, 1998).

[f] [Wizenmann,] *Results*, p. 154.

profound proofs with which the Critique of Reason has overcome this metaphysics![49] How much must it also demand that the thinking minds among our contemporaries give a hearing to the proposals for a better metaphysics that this very Critique of Reason offers for the taking!

[49] See Kant's discussion, in the *Critique of Pure Reason*'s Transcendental Dialectic, of the "antinomies" that lead traditional rational cosmology into inevitable contradictions, e.g., concerning the spatiotemporal magnitude of the world.

[3] Third Letter: The result of the Critique of Reason concerning the necessary connection between morality and religion

Confirmation of the rumor that the public presentation of the Critique of Reason is forbidden at a certain German university would not be nearly as unexpected for me as denial of that rumor would have been for you, my friend, who have so little hope in the enlightenment of our age. Is there anything that does not worry you about that faction of religious zealots which is busier than ever and whose members are used to deriving their conviction from any source but reason? I, in contrast, credit the opposing and better faction (the term "faction" taken here in its positive sense[50]) [4] with an ever-increasing upper hand; I do expect, particularly from this side, the fiercest and most effective resistance against the new philosophy[51] without, however, fearing it, even in its strongest outbursts. Just as, through its establishment of rational faith, the Critique of Reason has fallen out of favor with the enthusiasts on both sides – those who in no way accept their faith from reason, and those who, bent on knowledge, do not even want to have faith in reason – so too, through its annihilation of all demonstrative proofs for the existence of God, it will also have to

[50] *Partei.* This term is sometimes translated as "party" (see below, Appendix, n. 10), and in English this implies the kind of positive advocacy in mind here, but in the passage above, as in most of Reinhold's philosophical discussions, "faction" is the more appropriate translation.

[51] The 1790 ed. (p. 124) inserts a footnote: "This expectation, ever since the time when I first expressed it, has been fulfilled by most of our professional philosophers, partly in their own books and dissertations and partly in collections and series, in most of our scholarly newspapers, bulletins, and critical journals, and from most of our philosophical podiums."

take hold with the enlightened defenders of religion. Along with the late Mendelssohn, these defenders of religion regard demonstrative proofs as the fundamental truths of all religion, or at least they agree with the opinion that "no worshiper of the deity should dismiss the least ground of proof that carries with it even some power of persuasion."[g] You, my friend, who confess to belonging to this class yourself, offer me no small proof of your confidence and impartial love of the truth by calling on me to speak for the Critique of Reason on this topic.

In your last letter you ask: "What can religion gain by toppling the proofs [5] to which such a considerable number of greater and lesser thinkers concede nothing less than the force of conviction? What can it gain by toppling the proofs to which religion owes so many of its victories over the skepticism of nonbelievers and reason its reputation – a reputation that believers are granting to reason more and more in matters of religion?" – I believe that I can respond to this question with confidence: "By the clearing away of these proofs in the manner accomplished by the Critique of Reason, religion gains nothing less than a single, unshakeable, and universally valid ground of cognition, one which completes by means of reason the unification of religion and morality that was introduced through Christianity by means of the heart." I hope to explain this answer to your satisfaction.

Established at a time when the division between religion and morality appeared to have reached its highest point, this unification is a merit of Christianity that even its enemies cannot deny, and yet one that its friends do not know how to prize adequately when they demand still something greater in order to bestow on its exalted founder that title of honor, "savior of humanity." Among the general masses of his contemporaries, Christ had found religion without morality, and among a few philosophical sects, morality without religion. In accordance with the [6] way of thinking of him who had sent him, his attention had to be directed toward the larger group without neglecting the smaller. And religion, for which the general disposition and preparation were already in place, had to become the foundation for a new moral edifice that would suit the needs of both the common man and the enlightened thinker. Christ's teaching thus established a mediating concept for human beings by

[g] [Mendelssohn,] *On Evidence in Metaphysical Sciences (Abhandlung über die Evidenz in metaphysischen Wissenschaften)*, the new edition (Berlin, 1786), p. 102. [Translated differently in *Moses Mendelssohn: Philosophical Writings*, ed. D. Dahlstrom (Cambridge, Cambridge University Press, 1997), p. 292.]

which the most subtle speculation and the most sensory manner of representation could be connected with equal ease. And wherever, according to this teaching,[52] the highest being was thought of as a father whose family was the human race, morality became illuminating for even the most elementary understanding, and religion became moving for the most cold-blooded philosopher. Morality and religion were now not only reconciled with one another but also united by an internal relation according to which morality depended upon religion, at least in so far as it was indebted to religion for its dissemination and effectiveness. Religious sanction secured for the more refined and lofty rules of morality a general acceptance that otherwise would not have been found in the crude and uncultivated understanding of the common man. Moreover, religious sanction gave these rules that higher degree of interest without which they commonly have little effect on the colder heart of the thinker. The common man now forgave his enemies "for the sake of the heavenly [7] father, who lets his sun rise over those who are good and those who are evil," and thus fulfilled a duty whose existence many moral philosophers were not able to dream of until recently. The cold thinker, in contrast, who actually had been led to the conviction of this duty by his philosophy, now discovered in his religion – which teaches him to see in his enemy "the son of the universal father of humanity" – the motivation with which he was able to counter the stubbornness of his heart. – In this way Christianity formed world citizens in the truest sense, and with this grand undertaking it had an advantage over philosophy in so far as it in no way let itself be limited, as philosophy was, to those classes of humanity that blind chance destined to be part of higher culture. Thus, its actual purpose was, and will be for all time,[53] partly to make the moral claims of reason tangible for the understanding of the common man, partly to gain them a place in the thinker's heart, and consequently to be the benefactor of reason in the moral cultivation of humanity. Far from advancing claims that would silence philosophy, or, even less, that would make philosophy superfluous or annihilate it from the face of the earth, Christianity was assigned the task of turning the results of the profound observations of

[52] The 1790 ed. (p. 125) replaces "this teaching" with "the teaching *of Jesus*." Very similar themes are expressed in "The Life of Jesus," an early fragment by Hegel, in *Three Essays, 1793–1795*, tr. J. Dobbins and P. Fuss (Notre Dame, University of Notre Dame Press, 1984), pp. 104–65.

[53] A quotation mark has been taken out here (there is no closing quotation mark).

the wise into the common possession of all social classes. [8] It was to transform into warm love and active use the cold approval that these results had found in a small number of thinking minds until then, and – as Socrates[54] had attempted in vain – to pull philosophy down out of the fruitless regions of speculation and introduce it into the actual world. – I need not worry, dear friend, that you will fail to recognize Christianity in these main points, no matter how idealistic they may appear to many others. At least this is how it seems in so far as it presents itself through the teaching and examples of its founder to the healthy eyes of an impartial researcher: it laid the foundation for the fortunate unification of religion and morality and never entirely lost its beneficent influence on the education of humanity, even in the midst of all the ill-treatment that it had to suffer from superstition and nonbelief.

Why must I speak here of the monstrosity that misused the name of Christianity so long ago and very nearly suffocated its spirit? And why can I give it no other name than that under which it wreaked so much havoc – namely "orthodoxy"? During the time when the free and scientific cultivation of reason collapsed with the Roman Empire and was buried under its rubble by despots and barbarians, this offspring of ignorance and pride[55] achieved domination [9] over the human spirit. In a short period of time it became just as easy for it to impress upon thinking minds the prejudices of the vulgar as to urge upon the common man the unintelligible propositions of a corrupt scholastic wisdom – and indeed as divine pronouncements. Moreover, it became easy to substitute these same pronouncements for the simple and commonly useful teachings of the Gospel and to make blind faith in their authority accepted not only as the first of all moral duties but also as adequate compensation for neglecting all the rest. The more this monstrosity of ignorance and pride succeeded in suppressing the use of that faculty which elevates humanity to a moral existence, the more it destroyed the fruits of that beautiful union which Christ[56] had established between religion and morality. In place of the great and moving portrait that Christ had put forward of the heavenly father it foisted an image in which everything was incomprehensible. No wonder that image became thoroughly immoral, whereas the adventurous manners of representation that

[54] Socrates (470–399 BC). [55] The 1790 ed. (p. 128) inserts here "of the *Neoplatonists*."
[56] The 1790 ed. (p. 128) replaces "Christ" with "Christianity."

paganism entertained of its gods boasted a number of moving and uplifting features of humanity. Humanity was much worse off at that point than it had been with the previous division between religion and morality. Religion became a sanction of immorality, and under the pretext of religion whole nations, advanced schools, and tribunals now issued decisions and carried [10] out atrocities the likes of which one will scarcely find in the history of fanaticism prior to the introduction of Christianity. – Reason began to recover with the revival of the sciences, and then even its friends seemed to unite with its enemies in driving the division between religion and morality to an extreme. While reason's enemies denied, in the name of God, all merit to any action that arose merely from rational motives,[h] its friends once again sought and found their morality in the writings of the ancients and in their own reason. In so doing, they became all the more inclined to find religion dispensable in general, for in many instances they had worked in vain for years to separate the true and beneficial features of religion from the many crude errors that they had absorbed in the religious instruction of their youth.

As a result of the Reformation, reason has regained the free use of its powers – at least in one half of the Christian world – and especially in recent times has recovered quite markedly from the natural consequences of its earlier captivity. Yet however much reason may have accomplished since the Reformation in terms of restoring the unity between religion and morality, [11] the success of its efforts until now has indisputably been more of a preparation for this grand undertaking than a completion of it. Who does not know that the factions of the orthodox, which are indifferent to the morality of reason, and the factions of the moralists, which are indifferent to religion,[57] are at present most zealously at work distorting the concepts of their contemporaries through their unfortunate misunderstanding? The orthodox will admit morality at most as a chapter of their theology, and the moralists will not admit theology even as a chapter of their morality. The moralists strive to make all religion

[h] That is, from what is comprehensible, natural. Even the virtues of a Socrates were declared to be glaring vices. [For a review of discussions of Socrates at this time, see Dominique Bourel, "Nachwort zur Entstehung des *Phädon*," in Moses Mendelssohn, *Phädon oder über die Unsterblichkeit der Seele (Phaedo, or Concerning the Immortality of the Soul)* (Berlin and Stettin, 1767), ed. D. Bourel (Hamburg, Meiner, 1979), pp. 164–6.]

[57] The 1790 ed. (p. 129) replaces "factions of the moralists, which are indifferent to religion" with "factions of the *naturalists*, which are indifferent to the *morality of religion*."

dispensable to their reason, and the orthodox strive to secure their religion against all reason. Their common misunderstanding thus lies in the fact that they fail to recognize the religion of pure reason,[58] which relates to Christianity – or to what is equivalent, the religion of the pure heart – as the theoretical doctrine of morals[59] relates to the practical.

In our era the reunification of religion and morality, or the restoration of Christianity, depends mostly on the establishment and dissemination of this cognition of God, which is grounded in pure reason[60] – just as at the introduction of Christianity the unification of religion and morality depended mostly on the establishing and disseminating of pure morality. Pure religion is [12] the need of the present age in precisely the same sense that pure morality was the need of the age eighteen centuries ago. And because we have, on the whole, far more to show for ourselves with regard to morality than with regard to religion, a restorer of Christianity ought to use the more universal disposition toward morality in precisely the same way that the founder of Christianity used the more universal disposition toward religion in his time: he must start from morality as Christ started from religion. In a word, just as at an earlier time religion, as one of the most common and effective motivations of the human heart, had to be set in motion in order to provide access to a morality that was little known and very much opposed to ruling customs, so in our time this very morality, which belongs among the most certain, cultivated, and popular of cognitions, must become the foundation for all those who want to do their share in putting pure Christianity back in possession of that which has been usurped by superstition and nonbelief.

58 The 1790 ed. (p. 130) inserts a footnote here: "This expression as such should in no way denote *natural* religion but rather religion *to the extent that* it is necessarily thought according to the principles of the Critical philosophy and is fully misconstrued by its *naturalist* as well as *supernaturalist* followers."

59 *Sittenlehre*. The term "morals" is used in translating this term, and in contexts where Reinhold speaks of "corruption of morals." Otherwise, in this volume the terms *Sittlichkeit*, *Moral*, and *Moralität* are all translated as "morality" because Reinhold constantly moves back and forth between them as if they are interchangeable. For example, in the 1790 ed., p. 32 (Appendix, section B), Reinhold uses *Moral* and then *Moralität* in the phrase "truths of religion and morality." "Morality" is the more common term in contemporary Anglophone philosophy, but the term "morals" can still be found in many places, e.g., in discussions referring back to Kant's main texts in the field, the titles of which are usually given as *Groundwork* [or *Foundations*] *of the Metaphysics of Morals* (Riga, 1785), and *The Metaphysics of Morals* (Königsberg, 1797). See also below, n. 158, and 1790 ed., pp. 65–6 (Appendix, section C).

60 The 1790 ed. (p. 130) replaces "of this cognition of God, which is grounded in pure reason" with "of a ground for cognition of the basic truths of religion that is equally illuminating for philosophizing reason and common sense."

Philosophy has remained, even to this day, a debtor to that religion which established and disseminated the most sublime and important results of practical reason in the actual world. The point in time when philosophy can and must repay this great service has presently arrived. Reason [13] is being urgently pressed to secure cognition and worship of the deity[61] against unphilosophical errors, to justify it against philosophical doubts, and to bolster it against enthusiasm and indifference, which are increasing at the same rate. If philosophy, in its own way, is to do to religion what Christianity in its way did to morality, then as Christians led from religion to morality by means of the heart, so philosophy must lead from morality back to religion by means of reason. That is to say, for a religion that has been misunderstood and questioned, philosophy must derive a ground of proof from universally recognized principles of morality – just as Christianity drew from religion the motivations with which it disseminated and invigorated morality.

One might ask whether before now our philosophy could well pride itself on having clarified the necessary connection between the fundamental concepts of morality and religion or on having supplied the formula that expresses this connection in an illuminating and determinate manner. – To be sure, it derived the moral law from the nature of practical reason (or of the rational will) with an evidence whose triumphant power shines already from the mere fact that, in our day, only seldom – and never without first renouncing the title of philosopher [14] – does an orthodox thinker appear who would free atheists of the binding force of the moral law. Reason thus made the ground for cognition of morality independent of religion in so far as it made it possible to avoid the usual circle[62] in the derivation of religion from morality, and of course it gained much as a result. But it also gave rise to the prejudice that declares religion dispensable with respect to morality. Hence, in order to secure the necessary connection between morality and religion, philosophy needed to derive religion from morality. Until now, however, the two main factions that constitute nearly the entire Christian world have stood opposed to this. One faction builds its religion on hyperphysical events and the other on metaphysical speculations, and both thus

[61] The 1790 ed. (p. 131) replaces "cognition and worship of the deity" with "the basic truths of Christianity."

[62] This is presumably the circle involved in deriving religion from a divine-command morality only after already assuming God as the source of that morality.

fetch the cognitive grounds of their religion from principles that are wholly different from the principles of the moral law. The influence of these two grounds of cognition lies openly and clearly enough in the enormous confusion that rules among the concepts of both factions concerning the relationship of morality to religion. The hyperphysicists feel themselves compelled to accept two different moral laws – a natural one from reason, and a supernatural one from their faith, which is entirely independent of reason. And depending on whether a metaphysician believes that he has found in his speculations reasons for [15] God's existence or against it, he either calls his morality "religion" or refuses it this title. That is, he either negates religion as something essentially distinct from morality, or he negates it straight away – and thus in both cases negates its very substance. Some have tried, of course, to be neither metaphysicians nor hyperphysicists, yet in doing so they have simply taken up into their own accounts the contradictions of both factions without knowing it. Just recently we witnessed the example of a famous writer who denied all assent to metaphysics yet who at the same time not only conceded to it, but also sought to prove through it, that "every path of demonstration ends up in fatalism."[i] He wanted to know nothing of the orthodox or of blind faith in miracles,[j] yet still grounded religion on a faith that reason cannot provide. If an eclectic of this sort can scarcely explain the connection between religion and morality without contradicting himself – if he sometimes takes the former to ground the latter, sometimes the latter to ground the former, and sometimes fetches both from wholly [16] different sources – then you will no doubt warn me, dear friend, against placing the blame on philosophy. But I will not concede to these writers the innocence of their friend [philosophy] in this dreadful state of affairs until they show me a philosophical work that would eliminate rather than favor the complete disparity between the sources of cognition of religion and morality. Or do they call it "deriving" religion from morality whenever one demonstrates the so-called duties of religion from the moral law yet seeks the ground of all religion,

[i] [Jacobi,] *Concerning the Doctrine of Spinoza in Letters to Herr Moses Mendelssohn* [, p. 172.] [A slightly different translation is found in *Friedrich Heinrich Jacobi, The Main Philosophical Writings and the Novel "Allwill"*, ed. G. di Giovanni (Montreal and Kingston, McGill-Queen's University Press, 1994), p. 234.]

[j] At least the author of the *Results*, who, Mr. Jacobi assures us, has formulated his true opinion entirely and from the ground up, asserts: "Out of unfamiliarity with the spirit of Jacobi, Mendelssohn understood his faith as theological and orthodox" (p. 10).

conviction in the existence and properties of the deity, outside the field of practical reason? Moreover, do they call it "deriving" whenever one borrows something from a science that because of its ambiguity – by which it proves the existence and the non-existence of the deity with equal ease – in part keeps its most energetic supporters in perpetual conflict and in part draws the indifference[63] and disdain of impartial spectators more and more upon itself? And is it not just this disputed metaphysical ground of cognition that separates religion from morality because of the heterogeneity of its origin as well as of its evidence? Finally, can the philosopher hope to be able to assert the highest criterion of reason against those who want to urge upon him a faith independent of reason as long as he himself is forced to urge upon his opponents a knowledge that [17] is no more universally illuminating in its grounds or necessarily connected with the grounds of morality than the blind faith that it is supposed to displace?

Therefore, in order to ground religion on morality completely and in a universally illuminating way, philosophy would first have to derive the ground for cognition of[64] the existence and properties of the deity from the principles of the moral law and, second, to gain acceptance of this moral ground of cognition as the only ground. The first task will be no more successful than it was previously, and the second task will be absolutely impossible – if philosophy does not clear away at once the two other inadmissible grounds of cognition and, consequently, uncover the misuse of reason in metaphysical claims just as clearly as it has demonstrated an encroachment upon the rights of reason in hyperphysical claims. Hence, the problem that our philosophy would have to solve on behalf of religion would be that of exposing the emptiness of metaphysical proofs for the benefit of – and not merely without detriment to – rational conviction in the existence and properties of the deity. – I think that I am able to claim with the best of reasons that prior to the appearance of the Critique of Reason philosophy had not resolved this problem. Until then, everything that in the name of philosophy supernaturalists, naturalists, [18] and skeptics brought against metaphysical proofs concerned the very content[65] itself as much as the proofs. Because

[63] Reading *Gleichgiltigkeit* as *Gleichgültigkeit*, with the 1790 ed.
[64] The 1790 ed. (p. 134) replaces "ground for cognition of" with "ground of conviction in."
[65] The 1790 ed. (p. 135) replaces "the very content" with "the basic truth of religion."

the logical form of these proofs – without whose correctness they would not have deceived a single thinking deist[66] – stood secure against all dialectics, the objections went straight to the content. And as a result these objections turned into genuine counterproofs, metaphysical grounds for the opposing view, which all amounted to denying reason the capacity to prove God's existence, because one believed that one had found in reason the capacity to prove the non-existence of God. The instructive dispute between Jacobi and Mendelssohn offers us an example of this as well. Here I shall take up the already cited statement that the opponent of metaphysical proofs puts forward: "every path of demonstration ends up in fatalism."[67] If this statement is correct, and if all of these paths of reason that lead to fatalism (or even if just a single one of them) are unavoidable or irrefutable by means of reason, then the contradiction between reason and faith is decided. Then either reason is necessarily faithless[68] or faith is necessarily irrational, and reason would tear down by means of demonstration what it builds up by means of the moral law or – as Mr. Jacobi would have it – what it accepts on the testimony of history. If, however, as Mr. Jacobi himself must presuppose, [19] the fatalistic paths are all formed in such a way that reason can and must recognize them as illusions, then Mendelssohn's deistic proofs stand firm in so far as they at least do not let themselves, even as illusions, be nullified by any other illusion. And why, of the two illusions[69] – one of which contradicts his faith while the other confirms it – should the believer want to attack just the latter and spare the former?

If metaphysical proofs are to be refuted for the benefit of the moral ground of cognition, and not only without detriment to it, then this must happen not by way of counterproofs but by way of reasons that themselves nullify all counterproofs as well as proofs. Because such reasons would rob the deist of his imaginary bulwark, they at the same time would spare him any fear of the equally imaginary weapons of his opponents. But that is not all! If the moral ground of cognition is to be forever guaranteed its singular preeminence, and reason is to be forever suspended from its endless striving for new proofs (a striving that would otherwise be sustained by the mere doubt regarding the undecided

[66] The 1790 ed. (p. 135) replaces "deist" with "*theist*." [67] See above, n. i. [68] See above, n. 7.
[69] *Blendwerk*. This is an illusion that involves something like a mirage, or a conclusion improperly arrived at – but it is not necessarily false.

impossibility of such proofs), then the arguments that uncover the emptiness[70] of metaphysical proofs for and against God's existence must count not only against previous proofs that have been brought forward but also against all possible proofs of this [20] kind – or rather, against their very possibility. Such a state of affairs cannot be conceived until it is apodictically[71] proven "that reason does not possess any faculty for recognizing the existence or non-existence of objects that lie outside the sphere of the world of sense." This, dear friend, was not settled by our previous philosophy. And you readily understand that it could not be settled without going beyond all our metaphysical systems, taking up a new investigation of our entire faculty of cognition, specifying with the highest precision the misconstrued domain and undetermined limits of pure reason, finding the laws of pure reason that were in part misunderstood and in part wholly unknown, and specifying the rules of its use – rules that no logician could have dreamed of until now.

The Critique of Reason has carried out such an investigation of the faculty of reason, and one of its preeminent results is "that the impossibility of all apodictic[72] proofs for or against the existence of God follows from the nature of speculative reason, and the necessity of moral faith in the existence of God follows from the nature of practical reason." Thus, with this result the Critique of Reason has fulfilled the conditions by which alone, as we have previously seen, our philosophy could be put in a position to nullify [21] metaphysical proofs for God's existence for the benefit of the moral ground of cognition, to ground the first basic truth of religion on morality, and to complete thereby the unification of both by means of reason – a unification that was the aim of Christianity and that had been introduced by its exalted founder by means of the heart.

From what has been previously said, I believe that I may infer without reservation that the interest of religion, and of Christianity in particular,

[70] The 1790 ed. (p. 136) replaces "emptiness [*Nichtigkeit*]" with "correctness [*Richtigkeit*]."

[71] The 1790 ed. (p. 136) replaces "apodictically" with "from a universally accepted principle."

[72] The 1790 ed. (p. 137) replaces "apodictic" with "objective" here and elsewhere. Cf. *Critique of Pure Reason*, A828/B856ff., "It is quite otherwise with moral belief [*Glauben*] ... I inevitably believe in the existence of God and in a future life, and I am certain that nothing can shake this belief, since my moral principles would thereby be overthrown ... my conviction is not *logical* but *moral* certainty ... since it rests on subjective grounds (of the moral sentiment) ... Nothing more is required for this than that he [anyone "not completely indifferent with regard to moral laws"] at least cannot pretend that there is any *certainty* that there is *no* such being and *no* such life. Since that would have to be proved by mere reason, and therefore apodictically, he would have to prove the impossibility of both, which assuredly no one reasonably can undertake to do."

accords completely with the result of the Critique of Reason. But this claim seems to me to be so important that I would like to bolster it by the following remarks on the cognitive ground of religion, which that result establishes to the exclusion of all others.

As a first point, this ground of cognition carries with it the significant advantage that it is capable by itself of moving a number of the more astute friends of religion away from taking the matter of metaphysical proofs so seriously, and that it in fact contains the first and most important condition for grounding the universal validity of religion. – This ground of cognition is derived from reason and cannot appeal to either natural or supernatural experience. Kant himself (in one of his essays[73] in the *Berlinische Monatschrift*, [22] October 1786) explained the indispensability and importance of this condition in a way that surpasses anything I could say to you about it and that exhausts everything that can be said about it. Thus, he may speak for himself here:[74]

> The *concept* of God and even the conviction of his *existence* can be met with only in reason alone and can proceed from it alone, and it cannot first come to us either through inspiration or through tidings communicated to us, however great the authority behind them. If I come across an immediate intuition of such a kind that nature, as I am acquainted with it, could not provide that intuition, then a concept of God must serve to gauge whether this appearance agrees with all the characteristics required for a Deity. Now even if I have no insight at all into how it is possible for any appearance to present, even as to quality, what can only be thought but never intuited, this much is still clear: that in order only to judge whether what appears to me, what works internally or externally on my feelings, is God, I would have to hold it up to my rational concept of God and test it accordingly – not as to whether it is adequate to that concept, but merely whether it does not contradict it. In just the same way, even if nothing in what it[75] discovered to me immediately contradicted that concept, nevertheless this appearance, intuition, immediate

[73] "What Does it Mean to Orient Oneself in Thinking?" In this essay Kant directly discusses Mendelssohn, Jacobi, and Wizenmann's *Results* (cf. above, n. a.).

[74] Except for the word indicated in the next note, and the phrase "and can proceed from it alone" (which is omitted in the 1996 Cambridge translation), the translation of this passage is from Kant, "What Does it Mean to Orient Oneself in Thinking?," in *Religion and Rational Theology*, tr. and ed. Allen W. Wood and George di Giovanni (Cambridge, Cambridge University Press, 1996), pp. 10–11 (8: 142–3).

[75] The 1996 Cambridge translation has been modified here by replacing "he" with "it."

> revelation, [23] or whatever else one wants to call such a presentation, never proves the existence of a being whose concept (if it is not to be vaguely determined and hence might be subject to association with every possible delusion) demands that it be of *infinite* magnitude as distinguished from everything created; but no experience or intuition at all can be adequate to that concept, hence none can unambiguously prove the existence of such a being. Thus no one can *first* be convinced of the existence of a highest being through any intuition; rational faith must come first, and then certain appearances or disclosures could at most provide the occasion for investigating whether we are warranted in taking what speaks or presents itself to us to be a Deity, and thus to confirm that faith according to these findings. Thus if it is disputed that reason deserves the right to speak *first* in matters concerning supersensible objects such as the existence of God and the future world, then a wide gate is opened to all enthusiasm, superstition, indeed even to atheism.

The doctrinal principles, then, that reason first secures regarding these objects constitute the theory of pure religion, which must lay the foundations for every positive religion – just as natural law does for positive laws – that is to be true and beneficial to humanity [24]. This is the one truth that today is being subscribed to without reservation by the more enlightened followers of all religious creeds. Agreement exists even with regard to the essential unity, universality, and immutability of this religion of reason – just not with regard to its fundamental concepts. This is especially true of the ground for cognition of the existence and properties of the deity. Name for me one ground of cognition among the many previously taken to be fundamental that would not be successfully challenged and refuted, at least in so far as it was passed off as the first ground. Each one, considered on its own, was neither completely true nor completely false, and all of them awaited their thoroughgoing determination and confirmation from a more fundamental concept that had not yet been worked out – a concept whose absence[76] made it impossible for the rest of them to be connected with one another and unified in one and the same thinking subject. In this way, and by means of the dicta, "reason can only believe in God's existence" and "reason alone can secure true conviction in God's existence," the Christian world became divided

[76] The 1790 ed. (p. 140) replaces "absence" with "confusedness."

into two factions that accused one another of superstition and nonbelief. In so far as it is adopted by one of the two factions as its first principle, each dictum is only half-true and contradicts the first principle of the opposing faction. Yet when they presuppose the moral ground of cognition, both dicta are completely true [25] and must be subscribed to without reservation by anyone who adopts rational faith. Was it not the case that even the most resolute followers of the religion of reason broke up into essentially opposed sects without even surmising how easily their claims might be integrated were the common ground for their misunderstanding to be eliminated? Did not the deist, who believed that he had found the first ground of cognition in ontology or cosmology, regard the theist, who in this case held onto physico-theology, as a fanatical anthropomorphist – whereas he himself passed for an atheist in the eyes of the latter? – Of course, our typical compendium writers were neither able nor allowed to be so particular. For them, any cognition used anywhere at all was welcome as a truth that they considered to be already settled for themselves and their readers at the very start. They thus listed ontological, cosmological, and physico-theological arguments, etc. indiscriminately next to one another in their textbooks of so-called natural theology, convinced that they could not overdo it or overprotect our precious youth against the dangers of a faithless age. Incidentally, they were also quite sure that a grumbler who dared to point out that they [26] had amassed nothing more than blank zeroes must count as an enemy of religion and the state. For all their erudition, they did not see that the true ground of their conviction – the unit that they placed, without realizing it, before their row of zeroes – lay in past persuasion. To be sure, they owed this persuasion first to their catechism and to the collective effect of the chance circumstances that allowed them to remain loyal to their catechism. But ultimately, and in so far as it was supposed to stand up to the test of reason, this persuasion always came down to none other than a moral faith whose grounds were intimated in their textbooks in an equally cursory and distorted fashion – and which earned a place in the very back under the rubric of *rationum moralium*,[77] as a mere addition to the demonstrative proofs. – On this account there is nothing more understandable than how it came to pass that the part of our previous metaphysics with which, for want of a pure rational theology, we had to

[77] Moral arguments.

make do was nothing more than an aggregate of indeterminate and disconnected propositions. What was needed in order for it to become a system, then, was none other than the unity of its various cognitions under one idea,[78] which is the most essential condition for a system. It is equally illuminating, however, that the moral ground of cognition remedies this essential defect when it is adopted, in the meaning supplied for it by the Critique of Reason, as the only one, excluding all others. This defect must be remedied if pure theology [27] is not forever to remain a mere pleasant dream, dreamed in a different way by every one of its followers, and vulnerable to the objections of atheists and hyperphysicists, who – because they all agree to the claim that religion cannot be grounded by reason – can be refuted only by a firmly established rational system of religion.

And, in fact, the moral ground of cognition, which the Critique of Reason establishes as the only one, also has the property of being itself a first fundamental principle[79] of a system: it imparts determination[80] and internal coherence to all the metaphysical doctrinal principles that belong to rational theology. One would very much misunderstand the Critique of Reason if one were earnestly to believe that it crushes everything,[81] indiscriminately tears down what our leading thinkers have previously built, and declares without reservation that our previous metaphysics is useless. It does just the opposite. While it denies this science the capacity to demonstrate God's existence – a capacity that metaphysics asserted very poorly – it assigns to this same science the noble vocation of purifying moral faith of the crude and subtle errors that have clouded it until now and of protecting it forever from degenerating into

[78] *Idee*. The 1790 ed. (p. 142) replaces "one idea" with "one principle." For Kant, an *Idee* signifies not a mere empirical and psychological idea of sense, but rather an absolute concept of reason, involving the notion of something like an unconditioned cause or being. See below, n. 97, and *Critique of Pure Reason*, A 313/B 370.

[79] *Grundsatz*. This term is sometimes translated as "fundamental principle" to indicate Reinhold's growing concern with not just any kind of first proposition but one that might serve as an apodictic first truth in a strongly systematic philosophical science. See Reinhold, *Über das Fundament des philosophischen Wissens nebst einigen Erläuterungen über die Theorie des Vorstellungsvermögens* (*On the Foundation of Philosophical Knowledge, Accompanied by Elucidations of the Theory of the Faculty of Representation*) (Jena, 1791), and Kant, *Critique of Pure Reason*, A 300/B 356.

[80] The 1790 ed. (p. 142) replaces "determination" with "meaning, thoroughgoing determinacy."

[81] A reference to Mendelssohn; cf. above, n. 24 and n. 42. The metaphor of building or destroying a structure was also central to Masonic literature, which Reinhold knew well, especially from Lessing; cf. above, n. e.

superstition or nonbelief. This is a vocation for which previous metaphysics became all the less prepared the more it whittled away the powers [28] of the spirit in futile attempts to establish idle pretensions and the more it furthered the misunderstanding that underlies superstition and nonbelief. To bring me back on my course, I can show you an example of how, through the Critique of Reason, metaphysics is made useful for theology. By way of the moral ground of cognition, the Critique of Reason gives theology a first fundamental principle, which metaphysics could not give it, and thereby secures for it everything that metaphysics actually can give it. For, just as the moral ground of cognition stands firm as the only one that survives testing, it gives at once content, coherence, and thoroughgoing determination to the notions that are supplied by ontology, cosmology, and physico-theology for the doctrinal structure of pure theology. As soon as the otherwise indemonstrable existence of a being whose idea these notions fix and help to complete for speculative reason is accepted on the necessary and irresistible demand of practical reason, these notions receive, in a certain way, their actual object – an object that lies outside the idea. To be sure, the concepts of[82] necessary being, first cause, and highest reason have ceased to be the first cognitive grounds of God's existence. But for just this reason they are elevated above all the counterproofs and doubts that they were vulnerable to in that capacity. They have become indispensable to the single [29] true ground of cognition and constitute, together with it, well-ordered parts of a single and complete structure, which from now until eternity will rest upon unshakeable foundations. – It is no wonder that, as long as they had their hands full working on the framework for this structure, metaphysicians were paying less attention to the foundations and even seemed to have forgotten them. But the metaphysicians continued to carry on in this manner until eventually nothing else remained for those who could not construct their structure themselves but to take up residence either next to them, on the framework itself, or among the ruins of collapsing superstition. It was then high time that a building expert come on the scene with the rebuke "that what had so far been built was nothing more than the framework that was supposed to put the workers in a position to order and fix the materials of speculation atop the foundations of practical reason."

[82] The 1790 ed. (p. 143) replaces "concepts of" with "ideas *of the most real thing of all*, . . ."

I have named the moral ground of cognition the unshakeable foundation of religion. And here I appeal to the stability and evidence that it draws from its source, practical reason, and to which no historical or speculative proof can compare. Those who have not yet felt this have either not thought about the ground of rational faith at all or have only thought about it in a cursory manner; [30] they have neglected it because of the pseudo-grounds with which they have gotten by until now, allowing themselves to be deceived by the indeterminate concepts of moral certainty[k] that have been common fare in the scholarly world. The evidence of the moral law is the only thing that could be compared with the mathematical. Whereas all the ideas of speculative reason are without exception void of all intuition – that is, they have no object that could be found in an actual or possible experience, which are the only grounds of cognition of anything existent – the ideas of pure practical reason are thoroughly determined, for they have objects in an actual experience (in the moral actions of human beings). And just as the principles of the moral law can, on the one hand, be discerned in the essence of reason itself, so, on the other hand, they can be rendered perceptible to the senses by their influence on the heart and presented in true intuition. The ground of cognition that they contain for the existence and properties of the deity is thus not only as secure and unchanging as the essence of reason itself, but also as intuitive and illuminating [31] as the self-consciousness that a human being has of its rational nature.[83] Of course, what is always presupposed here is that the false grounds of cognition will be cleared away – grounds that have been urged upon the understanding partly through thoughtless superstition,

[k] Isn't this like many a theologian who was afraid of betraying the substance of religion by conceding that there could be no greater certainty for its basic truths than *moral* certainty – by which he was used to thinking of nothing but a kind of *probability*?

[83] Reinhold here is claiming a very striking and bold link between what many interpreters believe is the first and most certain feature emphasized in Kant's system, namely the awareness that we have of ourselves as rational beings, and the last and most controversial feature emphasized in Kant's system, the affirmation of God as characterized in the postulates of pure practical reason. It is not easy to see how the certainty of the final main claim of a complex system, which must rest on all the claims that have come before it, can have anything like the certainty of the most basic claims in the system. Not surprisingly, Reinhold himself – like the later post-Kantians – soon moved away from a system claiming that the postulates can be immediately certain in this way, and many of them moved toward a new kind of system that attempted to work all the more exclusively from the notion of self-consciousness as such. Cf. K. Ameriks, *Kant and the Fate of Autonomy* (Cambridge, Cambridge University Press, 1987), ch. 2.

partly through carping scholastic wisdom, and that have deranged its true perspective.

As much as the beneficent influence of the moral ground of cognition has suffered on account of the other grounds of cognition, the existence of the other grounds still counts very little against the universal validity of the moral ground. For they actually place it in a most striking historical light. Those pseudo-grounds changed with every age and climate and were literally in contradiction with one another not only at different times and with different peoples but even at the same time with one and the same people. And while those pseudo-grounds changed, rational faith, which propagated itself always and everywhere alongside them, remained in its essence completely the same. It always presupposed an otherworldly seat of judgment that cognizes the morality of human actions, or a higher being that has enough power, wisdom, and will to determine the fate of human beings according to their present conduct. One could go through the religious systems of all ancient and modern peoples in so far as they [32] are familiar to us, and in each of them one will come across the same more or less mythological tales and – in many cases – metaphysical arguments. Whereas the latter have come to be accepted as philosophical grounds of cognition, the former have come to be accepted as historical grounds. If one leaves undecided the credibility of these tales and the evidence of these arguments and compares them amongst themselves according to their content, holding miraculous appearance up against miraculous appearance and scholastic proof up against scholastic proof, then one will find that they cancel each other out purely on their own. Moreover one will find that, taken collectively, all traditions, like all demonstrations, agree on no other point than that they have either grounded faith – for which reason itself bears responsibility – on facts or transformed it into knowledge[84] through demonstrations and, consequently, have misunderstood reason. One will find that everything

[84] *Wissen*. German terms that are often translated as "knowledge" can designate various kinds of cognitive states that need *not* be true – whereas in English, to say that "*x* knows *p*" *is* to imply that "*p*" is true. (Hence *Erkenntnis* is translated as "cognition," i.e., as signifying a cognitive state but not necessarily a state of knowing the truth.) In this context, however, although Reinhold says *Wissen*, which ordinarily signifies knowledge in a strong truth-implying sense, here he has in mind a particular kind of merely formal cognitive process that involves demonstration or inference but has limited significance. Sometimes he also mocks formal systems by characterizing them as "empty knowledge." See below, n. 86.

unfitting and corrupting of morals[85] that one comes across in the various theological systems is based either on a so-called fact, event, appearance, revelation, or testimony[1] – or on metaphysical pseudo-arguments. In contrast, everything true and beneficent connected with these systems [33] reflects the role that morality had in the ground for their cognition. In the end, one will find that the only thing that stood firm throughout the unceasing modification of all their other components was whatever degree of moral faith these systems carried with them.

What is true of the ground for cognition of the existence and properties of the deity is also true of religion. Isolated sensibility, feeling without reason, and blind faith pull inexorably toward fanaticism; isolated reason, cold speculation, and the unrestricted desire to know lead at best to icy, carping, inactive deism. Yet when they are unified, reason and feeling – the elements of morality – give rise to moral faith and constitute, if I may help myself to this expression, the only pure and living meaning that we have for the deity. As I conceive of the universal history of religion, it seems to me to indicate step by step the course of development that this meaning has taken. I discern three main epochs in this course. The first two epochs designate periods during which one of the two aforementioned components that comprise this meaning was always further developed than the other. In the third epoch the higher culture of both begins simultaneously. In each of these periods [34] rational faith reflects the cultivation of its essential predispositions. And just as at first feeling, then reason, and finally the unification of both determined more and more precisely the ground for cognition of the existence and properties of the deity, there existed historical, philosophical (hyperphysical and metaphysical to be precise), and, finally, moral religion.

In earlier periods of the human race, when feeling spoke very loudly and reason very softly, the voice of moral reason, when it proclaimed faith in the deity, could become properly perceptible only through the medium of sensory presentations, instructive examples, and striking facts. In those days the deity revealed itself, for example, through the blessing that followed on the heels of the righteous and through the curse

[85] *Sittenverderbliche*. See above, n. 59.

[1] The author – or authors – of the *Results of Jacobi's and Mendelssohn's Philosophy*, p. 184, call the existence of God a *fact* and believe that we cannot become certain of this fact except through *appearance*, *event*, *revelation*, and *testimony*.

that followed on the heels of the wicked. And these events – which without moral reason would have been just as unintelligible as the religious doctrines drawn from them would have been without the events – gave content to the traditions on which religious teaching was based. Given the dominance that raw sensibility asserted over undeveloped reason, and that must have increased rather than diminished with the passions that were awakened in the first advances of civic life, misunderstood religious events and degenerate [35] traditions were unavoidable. Historical religious systems (mythologies) multiplied themselves in these traditions, and the common ground for cognition of the existence and properties of the deity expanded into a faith whose blindness and aversion to investigation continued to increase the more reason's role in it became lost in a crowd of miraculous tales. Yet scarcely had the cultivation of spirit become an occupation of its own through the emergence and expansion of the sciences, when one went to the other extreme. The role of reason in the conviction in God's existence was now as exaggerated by philosophers as it was neglected by common theologians. If, earlier, dreams of sensibility had been hypostatized, this fate now befell the rules of reason. Notions of the deity that indicated nothing more and nothing less than what the deity could not be were accepted as positive features of the existence and properties of the deity. And because the logical consistency of certain theological ideas of reason could be demonstrated, it was thought that the actuality of their object had been demonstrated. Next to the historical ground of cognition, blind faith, one now had a philosophical ground of cognition – empty knowledge.[86]

Both grounds of cognition survive among us even today, and if the latest advocates of the [36] historical ground do not press entirely for religion without morality, and the friends of the philosophical ground do not press entirely for morality without religion, then we have the beneficent influence of rational faith to thank, which is misunderstood equally by both. Apart from this influence, the deity of historical religion is to this moment still as immoral as it must be whenever reason is excluded as a ground for its cognition. Even according to its present-day apostles this deity is still in conflict with its own work: nature. It still thinks of nothing but mysteries, performs nothing but miracles, hates what humanity loves

[86] By "empty knowledge" Reinhold means not a genuine mode of knowing but a pointless cognitive effort that has no content. Cf. above, n. 84, and below, n. 99 and n. 161.

and loves what humanity hates, looks upon reason with indignant eyes as a foreign and hostile being, and frustrates reason's deliverances with countermands. – The deity of typical so-called philosophical religion, however, is not immoral. For, upon close inspection, it actually has nothing at all to do with morality, and its supporters have religion in common only in so far as they attend to rational faith, whose persuasive power they credit to the account of their metaphysics by a very natural subreption. In fact, the theology of the more consistent deists, like their ground of cognition, is wholly speculative, a thing of thought without connection to their morality. They must rest satisfied with a most real being whose idea [37] they compose from purely logical affirmations, with the most absolute necessity that can be thought, and with a cause about which one knows nothing more than that it cannot be an effect. They must rest satisfied without being able to decide from these concepts whether they should seek this being inside or outside the universe, whether they should ascribe to it a mere natural necessity or freedom, or whether they should make it matter or spirit – in a word, without knowing what they should think under such an idea. The physico-theologian, who builds his ground of cognition on the regular course of nature and on the order visible in the arrangement of the world, need only come up against an astute opponent of final causes and anthropomorphism in order to get tangled up in endless quarreling. He need only forget his moral faith, which he in no way owes to his conception of the world, in order to let himself be tempted by thoughts of Calabrian earthquakes, Icelandic geysers, churches that have the sole power of salvation, canonized good-for-nothings, Tahitian human sacrifices, and a thousand other such facts from his age alone – thoughts that would at least tempt him to look upon the order and regularity of the world as neither more nor less likely than its opposite. – In general we must seek out the perpetual objections to which every proof borrowed from speculative reason is vulnerable and which are not without secret influence even on the most resolute defenders [38] of these proofs. We must seek out as well the nature of the speculative ground of cognition, which necessarily leaves the heart cold and is one of the main causes of the ever-increasing indifference to all religion in general – that irreligiosity of which one can accuse the thinking minds of our age just as little without cause as without exception, and which has become popular, especially among the fashionable crowd, to the same degree that respect for a thinking mind has begun to rise.

In vain, therefore, are all the efforts of the few for whom true religion lies close to their hearts and who, by means of the pure morality of reason, are busy with so much zeal bringing light to the darkness of historical religion and warmth to the iciness of philosophical religion. Forever will their morality be darkened by the one and frozen by the other. Forever will it have to be adjusted to the historical deity; forever will it remain indifferent to the metaphysical deity. And no other end is in sight to the conflict between a religion and a morality that have such heterogeneous grounds of cognition save that the one be driven out by the other. And in that case either we shall return again to times of religion without morality when universal superstition ruled, or we shall come to a time of morality without religion when universal nonbelief will rule.

[39] In the old days the gospel of the pure heart unified morality with religion through the establishment of a single mediating concept that leads from religion to morality by means of the heart. At present, religion has been degraded to a metaphysical thing of thought by philosophers and to mythical nonsense by enthusiasts. And thus at a time when this sad state of religion leaves us nothing less than a fear of universal nonbelief, we have received a gospel of pure reason[87] that will save religion by unifying it with morality through the establishment of the only ground of cognition that leads from morality to religion by means of reason. It is the only ground that raises God's existence above all the objections to which previous historical and metaphysical proofs were vulnerable. It is the only ground that rectifies and preserves all religious traditions and gives to all metaphysical notions of the deity a coherence, character, and interest that has equal importance for the mind and heart. Finally, it is the only ground of cognition that secures the unity of a system for the pure religion of reason, which it unshakeably grounds. This ground promises for the pure religion of reason the very same broad dissemination that the pure doctrinal concept of Christianity provided for morality, because this ground is made for all human beings – for the most elementary as well as for the most enlightened understanding.

[87] *Evangelium der reinen Vernunft.*

[117] Fourth Letter: On the elements and the previous course of conviction in the basic truths of religion

By means of proofs[m] whose thoroughness you yourself, dear friend, will examine in due time, the Critique of Reason [118] has shown "that it is just as impossible for speculative reason to demonstrate the immortality of the soul as it is for it to demonstrate the existence of the deity," and "that practical reason, on the contrary, through the same postulates by which it presupposes a highest principle of moral and natural laws, also makes necessary the expectation of a future world in which morality and happiness must stand in most perfect harmony according to the determination of that highest principle." In my next letter, I shall more closely elucidate this result, which contains the final and forever decisive answer to the second main question[88] with which our speculative philosophy has occupied itself until now. In the current letter, I mention it merely as a sample of the most striking fruitfulness [119] belonging to the moral ground of cognition and of the admirable simplicity that religious

[m] It is not without cause that the author issues a reminder here that he wants to consider the results of the Critique of Reason only in regard to the important needs of our philosophical and moral world, which, according to his conviction, are met by these results. He is thus content if his readers postpone their judgment on its *internal* grounds until that examination to which he wishes to invite and prepare his readers. The unphilosophical – and philosophical – prejudices that oppose these results, and with which the author is actually concerned, are less and less capable of being refuted by *internal grounds* of the *Critical system of reason* the more that they, in part, make the will averse to, and, in part, the understanding more or less incapable of, getting involved in the examination of those *internal* grounds.

[88] *Hauptfrage*, a term often used by Reinhold to signify one of the two defining metaphysical questions in his discussion of religion. Cf. below, n. 89 and n. 125, and Appendix, n. 48.

conviction obtains through it. Assuming the correctness of this cited result, we not only gain a rational system of pure theology that grounds the entire doctrine of the deity on a single, first, and unshakeable principle of rational faith – which was the subject of discussion in my previous letter – but we also gain a true and systematic philosophy of religion. This philosophy encompasses the doctrine of the actuality and nature of the future life as an equally essential component of theology next to theology proper, and derives the doctrine along with that theology from one and the same principle.

It strikes me, dear friend, that speculation has never before justified itself better to common sense, that the deliverances of the latter have never before agreed more closely with the results of the former, and that philosophy and history have never before been so united on a more important matter than in the present case. An investigation, whose depth is as unprecedented as the astuteness with which it was carried out, has derived the highest principle of all philosophy of religion from the nature of pure reason. And this principle contains nothing more and nothing less [120] than a formula expressing the need that has all along obliged reason to prescribe for itself two[89] articles of faith. When we extract from mythological and metaphysical frameworks that which all religions, no matter how varied, have from the most ancient times been in agreement about and credit it, however rightly, to the account of common sense (*sensus communis*), then what remains for this purpose is exactly those two articles of faith. And when we inquire into the ground upon which common sense, which neither believes blindly nor reasons subtly, could have built this ancient and universal conviction – that is, into the reason why philosophy began its first and oldest preoccupations with the properties of the deity and the nature of the future life, and why the existence of both, presupposed in these preoccupations, found such an early and universal acceptance and was maintained so long and so widely until the present day, even with the dubious state of its assumed proofs – then it turns out that this ground could consist in nothing other than the feeling of the moral need, which the Critique of Reason has resolved into distinct concepts and elevated to the single and highest philosophical ground for cognition of religion.

[89] This word is put in bold by Reinhold, presumably as a reminder of his theme that there are two main questions in the metaphysics of religion.

[121] There had to be previous ages when humanity was as little receptive to the distinct cognition of that need as this cognition was indispensable to humanity, when the mere feeling of this need gave rise to a conviction in the two basic truths of religion, and when much less weight was placed on the cognition of the grounds of this conviction than on the utilization of its consequences for morality. Christianity, which was given to humanity for no other purpose than to secure for it these beneficial consequences, thus presupposed – and always presupposes – that conviction to be already present. The intention of its exalted founder was not to reform either the philosophy or the theology of his time. He therefore rested content with the deliverances of common sense in both disciplines, and, without getting involved in the proofs of religion, he extracted the purest and most powerful religious grounds of motivation and presented them in their necessary connection to morality. In this way he grounded that pure practical religion which – through the general dissemination of moral concepts and the higher interest that it urged reason to take in them – has done so much to further not only the moral cultivation of humanity in general but also the scientific cultivation of morality itself.

[122] Both species of cultivation, which cannot be separated from one another, had to be driven to a high degree of development before it was to become possible, and in the end even necessary, for religion to build the ground of its conviction on precisely that morality which was, at least in large part, indebted to the motives of religion for its establishment and dissemination. Before the basic concepts of morality were purified, conviction in the basic truths of religion would have been undermined if one had shown that it had no other proofs for itself than the ground of a moral need. Hence, Christianity was as little able to establish or prescribe the true and moral ground of cognition as it was able to establish any one of the other grounds, i.e., pseudo-grounds. Instead, it had to leave both the development of the one and the clearing away of the others to the advances of the human spirit, which it was determined to guide and accelerate through its active influence.

In the meantime – that is, during the protracted period that was necessary for the human spirit to move from an indeterminate feeling to a distinct consciousness of the moral need – mistaken explanations of that feeling were inevitable. At a certain stage in its development, reason found itself forced [123] to give itself an account of its convictions. It found itself forced to seek out grounds for truths that urged themselves upon it without its being able to know whence these truths were coming; and it found itself forced to accept these grounds – which at some point became just as indispensable to reason as those truths themselves – in the form in which they were able to present themselves to it given its state at the time. Consider the nature of these truths. They are just as incapable of being intuited as they are necessary according to concepts, just as wholly inaccessible to sensibility as unavoidable to reason, just as foreign to one of our cognitive faculties as intimately intertwined with the other, totally incomprehensible from the one side and perfectly comprehensible from the other: an insoluble problem for reason,[n] standing in the way of its complete self-cognition! In its childhood reason could, and had to, connect immediately to experience every non-intuitive concept as soon as it reached consciousness. It could do this because, prior to the complete development of the theological concept of reason, the contradiction between this concept and intuition – the essential condition of all experience – was either not at all apparent or not striking enough. It had to do this, [124] for how else, without intuition, could it have held the concept fast? The earliest cognition of God thus certainly came from history. Yet just as in the mythologies of prehistoric times the philosopher can hardly question the dominance of irregular and wild fantasy over reason, so too in those same mythologies he will hardly be able to mistake traces of the religious concepts of reason[90] and to deny that it was actually these concepts of reason from which fantasy borrowed godliness for its ungodly dreams, even if only in a twilight fashion.

When at some point reason was far enough along in its advances that it could and had to question itself about its religious conviction, the traditions that had emerged in this way had to serve as the first available grounds of explanation, even if they were lacking in any immediate revelation (which is in no way the topic of discussion here). This conviction thus became faith, which reason projected from itself onto miraculous events, facts, and appearances. We therefore explain belief in miracles in a very one-sided manner when we derive it, after the fashionable philosophy of our neighbors,[91] from mere ignorance or unfamiliarity

[n] Unfortunately we have only a single word *reason* for its *subjective* and *objective* senses, which the author, in order not to go too far afield, uses first in the one sense and then in the other, trusting each time that he might presuppose his readers' attentiveness to the context.

[90] The 1790 ed. (p. 157) replaces "religious concepts of reason" with "metaphysical notions."

[91] E.g., radicals in France.

with nature. In so doing, we overlook the remarkable fact that the non-intuitive rational concept of a higher being, which occurs to some degree in every hyperphysical explanation of nature, [125] can be something more than a consequence of ignorance. In the most ancient belief in miracles, it was actually reason that was compelled to seek outside itself grounds for its conviction that it could not find in itself. After all, reason already had at that time the very same cause for its faith that is the cause of its faith today and will forever be its cause – namely the fact that it cannot support its necessary religious concepts with any intuition.[92] This lack of intuition (which the Critique of Reason explains to us in such a satisfying way, and which can have no other consequence for us than that of forcing us to be content with a faith that we credit to our practical reason) was in those days simply an unexplainable incomprehensibility of religious truths, which forced reason to ground its faith on[93] intuitions that likewise had to contain something incomprehensible so that they could testify to the existence of incomprehensible objects. The facts that the so-called historical ground of cognition still refers to nowadays are miracles through and through![94]

Who can deny that this ground of cognition provided the basic truths of religion with a universal and living interest for humanity that reason could not give them? Relying on this fact, the defenders of historical [126] faith admonish their opponents with a triumphant air without thereby considering that this interest – in so far as its vivacity depends on a satisfied penchant for the miraculous – is in no way preferable to that less universal and less vivid interest which the moral ground of cognition affords. And in any case, this latter interest will increase in universality and vivacity at the same rate that rational faith displaces blind faith. – Nevertheless, in those days the advantage of the historical ground of cognition was decisive. On the one hand, it could and had to summon all the powers of sensibility and fantasy for the interest of religion so that, given the state of the higher mental powers at the time, the attention of human beings could be steered from the visible to the invisible. On the other hand, however, there was nothing more natural than the fact that,

[92] The 1790 ed. (pp. 157–8) replaces "support its necessary religious concepts with any intuition" with "*relate its necessary religious concepts to any intuition*, and that, consequently, its conviction *cannot* be *cognition*."

[93] The 1790 ed. (p. 158) inserts "unexplainable, extraordinary."

[94] Cf. David Hume, *An Enquiry Concerning Human Understanding*, section 10, "Of Miracles."

precisely by giving priority to the invisible over the visible, the historical ground had to make religion into the first and oldest object of investigations for thinking minds. In this way, the historical ground of cognition was indispensable as preparation for the philosophical.

As long as it, too, was still bound down to the imagination, philosophy could occupy itself with religion only in so far as religion had a comprehensible side [127] to offer it. To be sure, all that was able at first to fall upon its eyes from this side was a kind of twilight. But with every advance of philosophy, this twilight brightened more and more into the red of dawn; with every advance, philosophy distanced itself from the blind faith that stared over into the night of the incomprehensible on the opposite side. The light of that red dawn was a reflection of pure reason, which was drawing nearer to the horizon of the human spirit. Who can fail to notice in the remnants of the most ancient philosophy features of the ontological, cosmological, and physico-theological concepts of reason, concepts that became more visible and determinate over time? And how is the history of philosophy proper much different from the history of the varied, colorful, and fantastic shapes in which, during the struggle of pure reason with the fog of sensibility, those concepts of reason had to appear to the eyes of the human spirit before they could gradually emerge in their distinctive, determinate, and unchanging form?

The first involvements of philosophy with religion concerned the properties of the deity and the nature of the future life. The existence of both was therefore presupposed.[95] If the most ancient thinkers owed their conviction in that existence to revelation – whether one calls it natural [128] or supernatural – then this revelation of the unknown object's existence should have instructed them by means of its properties and consequently should have revealed these properties to them in the very process. And in this case, of course, these thinkers would have been spared the many serious errors they fell victim to while inquiring into these properties – errors that brought the reproach of atheism[96] upon so many of them. Yet just as their conviction was the result of a felt need that was grounded on undeveloped concepts, their errors concerning the object of their conviction were not only possible but also inevitable prior

[95] The 1790 ed. (pp. 159–60) inserts: "The most ancient philosophical inquiries were investigations into the nature of the cause of the world in which one encounters no trace of a proof or even a question regarding the existence of this cause."

[96] The 1790 ed. (p. 160) replaces "of atheism" with "of either superstition or nonbelief."

to the development of those concepts. Their first theological strayings could not arrive at the existence of the deity precisely because this existence, on account of its incomprehensibility, lay wholly outside the path on which they were guided in their investigation of the divine properties by the light radiating from the concepts of reason. Each step along this path was a more approximate, more or less fortunate determination of those concepts of reason, and in the glorious era of Greek philosophy the metaphysical ideal of the deity was developed in at least all of its essential outlines.

The discoveries regarding the object of faith that were made on the path of reason [129] were projected onto the ground of faith at the same rate that the evidence of those discoveries, on the one hand, and the need to give oneself an account of the ground of faith, on the other, increased with the cultivation of spirit. Compelled by this need, and blinded by that evidence, one inferred from the attributes of the deity in the idea[97] to their existence in an object, presented as an object of knowledge[98] what was an object of faith,[o] and took oneself to have proven something of the object that could only properly hold true of the idea. The philosophical ground of cognition of empty knowledge,[99] which established itself ever more firmly in this way, was thus as inevitable for reason on its way to the moral ground of cognition as the historical ground was.

[130] To the extent that the historical ground of cognition remained dominant, the contradiction between it and the philosophical ground was less able to emerge. Even in the eyes of many philosophers, inferences of reason seemed to be made only to confirm the result of religious traditions. And even in the epochs most favorable to philosophy, the lines of demarcation between knowledge and faith, and

[97] An "idea" is what Kant calls pure reason's transcendental ideal of a perfect being (A 571/ B 599f.). See above, n. 78. Reinhold is alluding to Kant's critique of the ontological argument for God, which infers God's existence from the idea of a perfect being.

[98] See above, n. 37.

[o] In the conviction of God's existence, the necessary and unchanging concepts of reason, from which the idea of the highest being emerges, are wholly objects of *knowledge*. The concept of *existence*, in contrast, belongs according to its nature not to reason but to the understanding and has objective validity only in experience – that is, when it can be supported by an intuition. It can in no way be used as either a subject or predicate of those concepts of reason if faith does not first supply the understanding with the object that is lacking. Hence, here it is merely the object of faith.

[99] By "empty knowledge" Reinhold means not a genuine mode of knowing but a pointless cognitive effort that has no content. Cf. above, n. 84, and Third Letter, p. 35, and below, n. 161.

between the natural and supernatural, were not everywhere determinate and visible enough either to prevent the two cognitive sources of religion from flowing together again into a single one, or to prevent religious conviction from necessarily gaining the appearance – even in the eyes of the more enlightened – that it borrowed its matter from history but merely its form from philosophy.

This[100] at least was the case when philosophy soon thereafter became corrupted at the hands of the Neoplatonists and gradually degenerated into a theory of blind faith. In the following centuries this faith attained a monopoly of power that gradually put it in a position to give back to fallen Rome, through superstition, the scepter over the world that it had lost through despotism. This monopoly of power made blind faith into the highest principle not only of theology and [131] morality but also of positive and natural law and of the political and military sciences – in a word, of all the remnants of human knowledge that blind faith could not extirpate because of their extreme indispensability. Suppressed reason, which had nothing else to do during this entire period of bondage than to pander to its despot, brought about the grand system of religious infallibility – the only doctrine of religion, of all those built on an historical basis, that deserves the name of a "system" because of the coherence and homogeneity of its parts. In this grand system reason exhausted everything it could for the benefit of blind faith, inferring everything it could – and was required to – from its principle. Since then, every disciple of blind faith has had no other choice than to assent to this creed or to become entangled in far greater contradictions. And with regard to this matter the Christian world might well have human inconsistency chiefly to thank when, at least regarding one of its halves, it no longer stands under the commands of an infallible judge of faith. Allow me to remark in passing, dear friend, that the seductive charm that the religion of the new Rome can acquire in the hands of a skillful advocate lies mainly in its systematic foundation. And [132] perhaps the Protestant enthusiasts who may be the least protected against this charm are precisely those who cannot comprehend how a rational Catholic can live peacefully and comfortably in a finished building, while Zion, which they believe they must watch over, consists of nothing but the fragments of that building.

[100] Namely that philosophy was thought to provide only the form and not the content of religion.

For thinking minds, in contrast, consideration of the still erectly standing system of infallibility can and must afford the advantage of showing with a most striking example where, with regard to the cognitive ground of religion, the misunderstood incomprehensibility of divine existence can lead. As a first point, when this incomprehensibility is not derived from the lack of an intuition that could support our rational concepts of the deity,[101] then it is projected entirely from a subjective inability on our part onto an object of our concepts. Modified by their incomprehensible object, these concepts cease then to be concepts of reason,[102] and the deity comes to be represented by properties that are all just as incomprehensible as its existence – in a word, by various mysteries. – Second, if the intuition that is lacking for concepts of reason is not replaced by a faith that reason prescribes for itself, then it must come to be replaced by a faith that an external [133] testimony of facts urges upon it. And these facts must be just as incomprehensible to reason as the truth that is first proclaimed and testified by them – in a word, they must be miracles. Now,[103] if these mysteries and miracles are to lose nothing of their credibility with all the advances of the human spirit – or rather, if they are to have any credibility whatsoever for all those who could not themselves witness these supernatural events with eye or ear – then the witness who does vouchsafe their truth must be infallible. And, as a dead letter gains life only from the concepts of its explicators, that infallible guarantor must be a visible and audible explicator of the meaning that corresponds to the formulas of the mysteries and the original records of the miracles.[104]

The fact that these mysteries and miracles[p] stand and fall with the infallible tribunal of faith is demonstrated by the fate that many of them

[101] The 1790 ed. (p. 163) inserts a footnote: "Intuition is possible only of that which can affect our *sensibility*. *Understanding* thinks the *intuited*, and *reason*, in contrast, thinks that which defies the form of all intuition."

[102] The 1790 ed. (p. 163) replaces "then it is projected entirely from a subjective inability on our part onto an object of our concepts. Modified by their incomprehensible object, these concepts cease then to be concepts of reason" with "then it is projected from the feature of *existence*, to which it belongs, onto the features of the mere *idea* of the deity, to which it does not belong – [thus] from the existence of the object of this idea onto the object itself, which in that case is determined no longer by the pure idea of reason and its thoroughly comprehensible features. Instead, the representation of the deity now begins to be modified by its incomprehensible object and ceases to be an idea of reason."

[103] The 1790 ed. (p. 164) replaces "Now" with "*Third*."

[104] The 1790 ed. (p. 164) inserts: "There must be an *infallible church*."

[p] In order to guard against an all too anxious misinterpretation, the author explains that the discussion here has to do with only those mysteries and miracles that would divest reason of its

have experienced since the impolitic conduct of the infallible ones forced one part of Christendom to protest against their infallibility. To be sure, [134] blind faith still rules in this part as well, and will continue to rule as long as one has faith in the incomprehensible for even more incomprehensible reasons. But what became of those remnants of the Roman system that our reformers retained, intentionally or not, once they handed down to their followers the right and precedent to do to the remnants what they had done to the system as a whole? What is the difference between a Catholic hyperphysics that remains completely unchanged, preserves the essential structure of its system intact, and in all of its reformations uses its secular arm only to embellish its outer appearance – and a Protestant hyperphysics that not only lies open to attacks by reason from all sides but is even abandoned to the imagination of its own apostles, and that would not have been able to prevent itself by any community of pure doctrine from necessarily being worn down in the end from internal divisions among its supporters, had it not been that these supporters were forced by an outside conflict to make common cause against common opponents?[105] – This is the conflict between the hyperphysicists and the metaphysicians.

Reason had scarcely regained some use of its freedom as a result of the revival of the sciences in the West [135], and philosophy had scarcely taken up again its long-interrupted preoccupation with the cognitive ground of religion, when it began to appear that the philosophical grounds for the existence of God and the future world could no longer be so easily reconciled with historical grounds. In what followed, the contradiction between the two grounds of cognition became more apparent the more the dominion of blind faith dwindled.[106] Reason needed to be led through two extremes to the middle path of truth. During its golden age, hyperphysics had taken the incomprehensible side of religion so far through its multiplication of miracles and mysteries that the human spirit, desirous of light the moment it felt itself free, turned

divine right *to have the first say* concerning religious conviction. [The 1790 ed. (p. 164) adds: "To be sure, experience has shown how little this protest among our philosophizing hyperphysicists helped me. But by gladly renouncing the conviction of incurable metaphysicians and hyperphysicists, I wish to be misunderstood all the less by *my* audience, whose current numbers are admittedly still quite small."]

[105] The 1790 ed. (p. 165) inserts "(the *naturalists*)" and deletes the following sentence.

[106] The 1790 ed. (p. 165) inserts "largely as a result of various external inducements and political revolutions."

toward the comprehensible side with a kind of passionate warmth. The theological concepts of pure reason were now eagerly sought after and, especially from the time of Descartes until our own, developed to a completeness that left even the Critique of Reason with little more to do in this regard. One became more closely familiar with the conditions of rigorous proof, and the observation that agreement between the features of the theological concept of reason was capable of the most rigorous proof completed the metaphysical ground of cognition for which all the materials had already been present in Greek philosophy [136]. And one fancied oneself on account of this ground to be just as exempt from all faith in religion as one felt oneself bound, on account of the hyperphysical ground, to renounce all knowledge.

Scarcely had Descartes appeared to have put the finishing touch on the metaphysical system of theology in setting down the ontological proof, when Spinozism – which stood in opposition to this system – offered the most visible proof of how closely putative demonstration borders on nonbelief, which, no less than superstition, was supposed to be made impossible by demonstration. In one and the same concept of the most perfect being, one master thinker had found necessary existence while the other discovered the one and only substance.[107] Both were mistaken about the concept of divine existence. One believed that he could prove divine existence of an object for which no intuition is possible, and the other believed that this concept had to be supported by intuition,[108] which is necessary for any proof of the actuality of an object. Spinoza was mistaken in insisting on an intuition for a concept of reason, for this intuition would necessarily destroy a concept of reason. But he was right in thinking that he could not prove the existence of anything without extension. Kant has irrefutably shown that the concept of existence is an [137] original basic concept of the understanding, which is entirely empty without possible intuition in space (extension) and in time – that is, is without an object.[109] Should not this have been an occasion for several half-witted thinkers to declare the author of the Critique of Reason a Spinozist?[110]

[107] I.e., René Descartes (1596–1650), in his ontological argument for God, and Benedictus de Spinoza (1632–77), in his argument for monism.
[108] The 1790 ed. (p. 167) inserts "of filled space (extension)."
[109] The 1790 ed. (p. 167) inserts "for our faculty of cognition."
[110] Reinhold is playing on the fact that Jacobi had recently created a sensation by calling Lessing a Spinozist, thereby generating the Pantheism Controversy.

Spinozism is to the field of metaphysics roughly what Catholicism is to the field of hyperphysics. It is the one system that has the most coherence and highest plausibility among all the pseudo-systems of nonbelief.[111] Moreover, it can do for the supporters of the metaphysical ground of cognition precisely the same service that I have asserted of Catholicism with respect to the more enlightened defenders of the hyperphysical ground – namely helping them open their eyes to their first principles. Confusing the deity with the world of sense is inevitable for the metaphysician when, on the path of demonstration, he sooner or later discovers that he cannot think of the concept of actuality without intuition.[112] And here lies the basis for the domestic quarrel that divides our metaphysicians, and that had to be exacerbated rather than settled with every advance of our previous philosophy. The concept of divine existence was used by some in their proofs to the exclusion of all intuition, and [138] thus in its merely logical meaning, while by others it was used inclusive of intuition and thus in a physical or real sense.[113] Both could and had to refute one another without thereby being able to establish their own claims. The deist could not dismiss the reproach that his entirely correct concept of reason lacked the essential condition under which alone an existence is at all demonstrable; and his opponent had to be convinced that his correct concept of existence could not be applied to the concept of the deity, for otherwise it would necessarily destroy the strictly demonstrable concept of reason.[114] The Critique of Reason steps

111 The 1790 ed. (p. 167) replaces "that has the most coherence and highest plausibility among all the pseudo-systems of nonbelief" with "that is the most consistent and most complete among all the systems of the faction to which it belongs."

112 The 1790 ed. (pp. 167–8) replaces "that he cannot think of the concept of actuality without intuition" with "that logical actuality must be distinguished from real actuality and the merely thinkable from the cognizable, that the distinction between thinking and cognizing consists in intuiting (which takes place in the latter alongside thinking), and that the feature of an intuitable-actual object which is not a mere representation must be *persistence in space*, extension. *Thus, Spinoza assumed* only *two* attributes of the real, persisting, and substantial: *extension*, through which substance discloses itself as that which endures in space, as *extended* (for outer sense), and *representation*, through which substance discloses itself as the *power of thinking* (as that which endures and is representable through inner sense)."

113 The 1790 ed. (p. 168) replaces "in a physical or real sense" with "in that sense in which *existence* becomes a feature of cognizable – yet for that very reason only of *intuitable* – objects, and consequently contradicts the idea of an object that is *separate from the world*, thinkable only through reason, and incomprehensible to the *understanding*."

114 The 1790 ed. (p. 168) replaces "for otherwise it would necessarily destroy the strictly demonstrable concept of reason" with "for then the strictly demonstrable concept of reason would necessarily be destroyed by a feature that contradicts it, one that applies only to objects of sensibility."

in the middle between the two and finds the true point of contention already clarified to such an extent through the transactions of the factions themselves that its verdict can hardly be unintelligible to the brighter minds on both sides. This verdict is contained in the following result of its investigations: "The idea of an infinite being, which is inseparable from the theological concept of reason, contradicts that of intuition, which is equally inseparable from the real concept of existence." It follows from this that the pantheist was just as entitled to argue for the conditions of his existential concept as the deist was for the conditions of his concept of reason. But the pantheist was just as wrong about refuting the theological concept of reason with his existential [139] concept as the deist was wrong in believing that he had demonstrated the existential concept from his theological concept of reason. For the impossibility of intuition, which is at the root of the contradiction between the existential concept and the concept of reason,[115] can just as little disprove the possibility of the object in itself as the non-intuitive concept of reason can prove the actuality of that object. For the sake of the theological concept of reason, the deist must thus concede the incomprehensibility of divine existence. But his opponent must confess that this incomprehensibility is due in no way to a contradiction on the part of the object but rather to a mere lack of intuition on our part. And, in this way, as the one faction must be content with the demonstrability of the concept of reason while the other can no longer object to it, nothing else remains for the two of them than to heed practical reason, which requires them to believe what they cannot comprehend.[116]

When everything contradictory, then, is removed from the previous grounds for cognition of religion, the following three elements of religious conviction remain: first, the necessary concept of reason, or the metaphysical ideal of the deity; second, the incomprehensibility of divine existence; and, third, the command of practical reason, [140] which makes moral faith necessary. These are the elements of rational faith, or of the distinct insight into the need that requires us to presuppose the

[115] The 1790 ed. (p. 169) replaces "between the existential concept and the concept of reason" with "between the concept of cognizable existence and the idea of the deity."

[116] Presumably for Reinhold to say here that something cannot be "comprehended" (*begriffen*) is to say that it cannot be demonstrated to *exist* from concepts (*Begriffe*) alone – but this is not to say that it is entirely nonsensical. See below, n. 120 and n. 130.

existence of God. Prior to their development they constituted the feeling of this very need[117] and in that sense contained, without it being recognized, the true ground of all religious conviction all along. – That feeling awoke together with moral feeling, of which it is a necessary consequence, and with which, on the whole, it always experienced a similar fate. Hence, through the voice of moral feeling, the command of practical reason[118] was the first summons to faith in the deity. But because the development of the moral concepts, which was supposed to be furthered by this faith, had to proceed before this command could be clearly recognized, it is understandable enough why precisely the same element of religious conviction that was the first element in terms of its effectiveness had to be last in the order of evidence gained for it by rational insight. – First in this order was the incomprehensibility of divine existence. We have seen how, given the indistinctness of the two other elements, this incomprehensibility necessarily produced the hyperphysical ground of cognition; and we have seen how this ground of cognition could not, however, prevent the metaphysical ground of cognition from [141] opposing it once reason had distinctly developed, in its necessary concept of the deity, the other element of religious conviction. – The reason why these two grounds of cognition can neither be integrated with nor displaced by one another lies in the nature of the two elements from which they have arisen and which, without mediation of a third element, necessarily exclude one another without thereby annulling[119] one another. As long as the irresistible command of practical reason is not recognized, the incomprehensibility of divine existence is not compatible in one and the same representation with reason's necessary concept of the deity. This command requires connecting the concept of existence, which cannot be proven in this case, with the concept of reason, which certainly

[117] The 1790 ed. (p. 170) replaces "distinct insight into the need that requires us to presuppose the existence of God. Prior to their development they constituted the feeling of this very need ..." with "*clear insight* into the thoroughly determined nature of reason, through which the human spirit must *believe in* the existence of a merely *thinkable* deity, an existence that is in no way *cognizable* by *him*; and this belief cannot be grounded more firmly than in the necessary and unchangeable essence of reason itself. *Prior to* their development these elements constituted the *feeling* of the necessity of this belief."

[118] The 1790 ed. (p. 170) replaces "the command of practical reason" with "the spontaneous efficacy *of practical reason* (the *divine within us*)."

[119] *Aufheben.*

must be proven,[120] and it completes the ground of conviction in religion by making up, in a satisfying way, for that which must forever remain indemonstrable in this ground. – The unavoidable dispute between the hyperphysicists and the metaphysicians – which at present is causing less of a stir only because it is being brought before the seat of judgment of reason rather than before the petty tribunals of superstition and nonbelief – is thus bound to make ever more visible both what is true and what is false in the two presumed grounds of cognition. And just as in this way [142] the genuine elements of religious conviction that are individually contained in each of these grounds of cognition are bound to gain in evidence, their incompatibility – without the third element that binds them together – is also bound to become more and more obvious. – Thus, we can explain with considerable certainty the course of religious conviction as well as the natural purpose, fate, and manner of emergence of those two grounds of cognition: the hyperphysical and metaphysical grounds of cognition had to prepare the way for the moral ground; supernatural religion and natural religion ought to dissolve into ethical religion; and superstition and nonbelief will give rise to rational faith.

120 For Kant theoretical reason and intuition cannot prove the actuality of God's existence, but the content of reason's concept of God can be proven in the sense that its meaning can be made determinate through the notion of a perfect being. See above, n. 0.

[167] Fifth Letter: The result of the Critique of Reason concerning the future life[121]

As I mentioned in my last letter, the Critique of Reason has discovered and forever established the highest basic principle of all philosophy of religion in that postulate of practical reason which makes necessary both the expectation of a future world and the presupposition of a highest principle[122] of moral and natural laws. I believe that I have so far shown you, dear friend, "that the recognition of that highest basic principle – in so far as it determines the sole secure[123] ground for cognition of the existence and properties of the deity – must be brought about by the course that, in accordance with its nature, the human spirit must take with regard to religious conviction," and "that the reconciliation and unification of religion and morality, on which more depends at present than ever before, completely hinges on this recognition."[124] Both claims must be able to be shown from one and the same highest basic principle [168] in so far as it also contains the sole secure ground for cognition of a future life. Reason's two articles of faith[125] are so intimately tied up with one another, so perfectly of one nature, and have experienced such very

[121] See Appendix, section F for Reinhold's heavily revised version of pp. 167–72 of the Fifth Letter from the *Merkur*. The revised text begins here and ends on p. 172 with the sentence that concludes, "imposed themselves from the invisible world."

[122] *Princip*. The term that is translated in this paragraph as "basic principle" is *Grundsatz*.

[123] *Probehältigen*, literally "holding up through examination."

[124] Cf. above, Third Letter, pp. 11 and 14.

[125] I.e., the two basic doctrines of pure practical faith: a future life and God's existence. Kant is also committed to a third basic pure practical idea, namely freedom, but belief in it requires no prior commitment to religion.

similar fates, that almost everything that I have asserted until now regarding the one can be applied to the other. There thus remains little left for me to do at present than to lighten the small task of this application by means of a few suggestions.

The thought of an unbounded continuance of our existence has a double interest for us: a sensible one and a moral one. The former requires no explanation. It is a necessary consequence of the natural drive for life that – at least in a healthy body and mind – can neither be denied nor restricted by itself. Yet this interest can scarcely be accepted as a ground of conviction in the continuation of our existence after death when from time immemorial this interest has demanded of human beings – and still demands of them – that the grounds for this conviction be sought. The moral interest, in contrast, which was first resolved into its pure elements by the Critique of Reason, is grounded on a need that is either felt or distinctly cognized. This need requires reason, on behalf of its moral law, to assume a world in which morality and happiness stand in most perfect harmony [169] and to expect an intuitive cognition of this harmony in the future. Hence, here we are not dealing with the satisfaction of a drive that has no more necessity than our existence itself – with which it would at the same time cease – and that would have fully achieved its entire aim by continuing to contribute to our self-preservation for as long as we ourselves exist. What we are dealing with is nothing less than the interest of the moral law itself, which must either count as a mere ideal or presuppose a future life. Consequently, this interest urges us not merely to wish or hope for something but commands us utterly to expect it;[126] and this interest carries with it the strongest ground of conviction in the second basic truth of religion – and, as we shall see in what follows, the only ground that is fully valid.

Both types of interest are grounded in the essential constitution of human nature and cannot be separated from one another. Nevertheless, as a consequence of that same constitution, the moral interest could not possibly proceed at the same pace as the sensible interest in the course of its development. Before the moral interest could be even vaguely discerned, moral feeling (the indistinct expressions of practical reason) first had to be awakened into a certain measure of activity. Before it could be traced back to determinate and distinct concepts, the scientific

[126] I.e., a future life (believed in on the basis of an argument involving pure practical reason).

cultivation of morality had [170] to advance fairly far. And before the moral interest could be derived apodictically – as far back as the limits of the comprehensible reach – from its first source, the nature of practical reason, there first had to be that unexpected self-cognition of reason which we owe to the Critical investigation of our entire cognitive faculty.[127]

Similarly, the moral interest could not awaken in the slightest degree of consciousness until the rational concept of the deity had already become visible in the dawning of moral feeling. The crude powers of spirit of the young child of nature were fully occupied with sensory impressions of all that was visible and present; and only in the bosom of society were moments of leisure reserved for these powers to elevate themselves to that which is invisible and in the future. Only social life could introduce that succession of experiences out of which the concepts of good and evil actions, of right and wrong, of reward and punishment, and finally of an invisible bestower of both could gradually develop. The events by which these concepts were explained, confirmed, or rendered more genuinely perceptible – for example, the blessing that followed on the heels of the righteous and the curse that followed on the heels of the wicked – announced nothing but temporal reward and punishment from [171] the powerful and invisible one. Hence, for a time just about everything that one hoped and feared in regard to the deity was restricted to the present life. And it becomes easily understandable why one finds in the remnants of the most ancient history such exceptionally old and frequent traces of moral faith in the deity rather than of the moral expectation of a future life. Perhaps in this regard those [scholars] might not be all that mistaken who have long noted, as an historical finding from the most ancient religious history of the Hebrews, that faith in the deity is much older than belief in the immortality of the soul.

The expectation of reward and punishment presupposes faith in a judge. And, before they had contrived for themselves the late emerging metaphysical concept [of immortality], future rewards and punishments were the first and only possible representations under which human beings could think of survival after death, an existence after the disintegration and destruction of their visible and tangible selves. The thought of a life after death, of a being without a body – a thought that even today has to struggle with so many difficulties – was completely unthinkable at a time when one

[127] Presumably the investigation begun in Kant's *Critique of Pure Reason*.

had not yet dreamed of a distinction between soul and body. Even the sensible interest in the continuation of our existence [172] after death needed for its own awakening and development the earlier, or at least contemporaneous, concept of future rewards and punishments. For if the drive for life were to open up prospects beyond the grave, something had to exist for human beings to think of in place of that life which ceased with death. This something was and is in no way present in the visible world. But concepts of a grand rewarder and punisher, and of retribution for all that the departed had not yet received in life, imposed themselves from the invisible world. For the human spirit there was now a determinate form under which humanity in its youth could think without difficulty of precisely that same concept of existence after death which would cost it so much trouble and strife in its more mature years, after it had attempted to think of it under other forms. The hope and fear that necessarily accompanied this concept under that form weighed very heavily upon the feelings of the human spirit. Both emotions were the natural consequences of the consciousness of good and bad actions; they were expressions that in all of their self-interestedness still presupposed actual activity of moral reason – activity to which belief in a future life owed its growth no less than its origin.

[173] Suppose we separate from the various old folk stories and the oldest philosophical hypotheses about life after death everything contained in them that is obviously mythical and contradictory, and suppose we extract anything and everything that lies at the basis of all these stories and hypotheses – or what amounts to the same, abstract whatever they have in common – and credit it, however rightly, to the account of common sense. Then surely this portion of common sense will retain nothing more and nothing less than the concept of a good or bad fate after death that is determined by the moral course of one's life prior to death. However much those fables and hypotheses have distorted this concept, it is still obvious enough that they owe to it alone the appearance of truth that each of them claimed for a period of time. It is likewise obvious enough that they could not contribute in the least to that evidence upon which the dissemination and survival of this concept had to depend – evidence which extended further than any individual folk religion or philosophical sect, and outlived them all.

This concept, whose moral origin can hardly be subjected to doubt, thus underlies the conviction in a future life that was present prior to all historical traditions and metaphysical speculations, remained undisturbed amidst their unceasing changes, and must [174] outlast them all once it has climbed to that degree of universal evidence which it can reach only by standing on top of their ruins.[128]

All historical traditions and metaphysical speculations began from that conviction. The first revelations of the prophets as well as the first investigations of the philosophers concerned merely the *nature* of the future life; they thus presupposed its *actuality*.[129] This presupposition had no other basis than the felt need of reason to assume future rewards and punishments. For even all the messages of prophets from the other world and all the conclusions of philosophers concerning the future state of the soul once again presupposed future rewards and punishments as something already familiar, and anything new that they produced consisted in nothing other than various manners of representing the specific nature of this retribution beyond the grave. The actuality of this retribution was so settled that no prophet undertook to reveal it and no philosopher undertook to prove it – until those very revelations and proofs concerning the nature of the future life prompted and introduced doubts regarding its actuality. But just as the preoccupations of the human spirit concerning this important [175] matter began with the presupposition of the actuality of a future life and with the investigation into its nature, they will conclude, by means of the Critique of Reason, with the conviction that this nature is and must remain incomprehensible,[130] and that this presupposition is and must remain both legitimate and necessary.

Just as the human spirit was directed by the laws of its nature even before it had become acquainted with them – as, for example, human beings drew rational inferences long before they knew what a rational inference was – so too moral interest in the continuance of our existence gave rise to a conviction in immortality without it becoming regarded as the genuine and sole secure ground for that conviction. This most important discovery[131] was not possible – or at least had to remain a mere supposition – as long as the evidence of the moral law had not

[128] The 1790 ed. (p. 179) replaces "their ruins" with "the ruins of hyperphysics and metaphysics."

[129] Reinhold's extensive use of italics on this page and elsewhere in the *Merkur* text is not reproduced in this translation. In this case, however, "nature" and "actuality" appear not only in italics but also in bold-faced type, and therefore are presented in italics here.

[130] The 1790 ed. (p. 180) replaces "incomprehensible" with "thinkable only through reason and in no way *cognizable* through understanding and sensibility."

[131] Kant's proof of immortality as a postulate of practical reason.

reached, through the advances of moral cultivation, the degree of strength that the sole ground of conviction in the basic truths of religion must have. Moreover, it was not possible as long as speculative reason had not come far enough in its self-cognition for it to gain insight into the impossibility of historical as well as speculative proofs regarding the existence and nature of objects lying outside the world of sense.

[176] The two illegitimate grounds of cognition with which religious conviction had managed during this long interim were absolutely indispensable for the preparation of that notable discovery. In so far as the historical ground of cognition derived the ground of conviction in a future life from a supernatural revelation, it made superfluous the proofs to which those ages were not in the least receptive, replaced them with the weight of an unerring authority, and thereby succeeded in propagating and disseminating the basic truth of religion to a degree that otherwise would not have been attained. Who can deny that in this regard moral cultivation has the historical ground chiefly to thank for the many and important advantages that it has drawn from the hope and fear of heaven and hell? The metaphysical ground of cognition helped to propagate religious conviction through the apparent evidence of its proofs, defended it against the attacks of the doubters on the one hand, and secured reason's influence over them on the other – an influence that otherwise would have been entirely taken away from reason by the historical ground of cognition. Finally, through the disputes that it occasioned, the metaphysical ground promoted the development and self-cognition of speculative reason, without which the discovery and recognition of the sole, true ground of cognition would forever have had to remain an insoluble puzzle.

[177] But the two pseudo-grounds of cognition were just as unavoidable as they were indispensable on the way to that discovery and recognition. The necessary connection alone between God's existence and future rewards and punishments makes it understandable enough why the ground for cognition of the latter had to become historical to the same extent that the ground for cognition of the former did. The deity, which had already revealed its existence, revealed itself all the more as judge of the living and the dead. And one found this supernatural instruction to be all the more necessary the less one knew how to explain the true origin of a conviction that, for all its striking indispensability and dissemination, had either no comprehensible ground at all, or at most only proofs that in part had to remain completely unintelligible to the great masses and in part gave rise

to endless quarreling even among the few who could concern themselves with them. – Both[132] were and are the case with the metaphysical grounds for the continuance of our existence, regardless of the fact that they flowed from a source that had to leap to the eye of any thinking person. The striking difference between representations of inner and of outer sense, between thoughts and sensations, and between consciousness and movement made unavoidable that distinction between body and soul on which [178] metaphysics grounded its well-known demonstrations. In what followed, these demonstrations had to become all the more important and illuminating because they were the only weapons with which the doctrine of a future life could be defended against the opponents of revelation, as well as against all those who believed that they had found in the incomprehensibility of a simple being adequate reason for placing the soul in a class with its body and predicting a common fate for them both.

The emergence and dissemination of the two spurious grounds of cognition was just as indispensable and unavoidable for the previous cultivation of practical and speculative reason as their clearing away is for the rightful future use of practical and speculative reason. Or, to speak more precisely, what largely depends on this clearing away are, first, the reconciliation and unification of religion and morality and, second, the rescue of the basic truths of religion from present-day attacks and their establishment for all future ages.

If you consider, dear friend, that one and the same guideline in the art of educating that is indispensable for handling an infant can be corrupting for a boy and even more for a young man, then perhaps you will find it [179] less paradoxical when I assert that precisely the same grounds of cognition that for a period of time were indispensable for securing for religion its beneficent influence on moral cultivation would necessarily deprive religion of this influence at a later time. Let me demonstrate this first with regard to the historical ground of cognition.

In order to shorten for myself the path to this goal, I distinguish the following two statements: "the moral law must be observed because future rewards and punishments are determined by it," and "because the moral law must be observed, future rewards and punishments are determined by it." Conviction in the first of these statements can certainly produce actions that in and of themselves have all the outer

[132] I.e., general unintelligibility and "endless quarreling."

appearance and all the beneficial external consequences of being completely moral; in general, it can contribute as a preparation for moral cultivation. I say it "can" do this – but only on the presupposition that the external action, by means of which the believer wants to purchase for himself heaven and to ransom hell, actually fits the moral law. But this conviction necessarily makes any genuine moral action impossible because it suffocates the unselfish disposition that is essential to morality. The conviction that lies at the basis of the second statement, in contrast, unites the moral disposition[133] with the expectation of future rewards [180] and punishments, subjects the external motivating grounds of hope and fear to the internal bindingness of the moral law, and vindicates this internal bindingness without robbing it of the support that external motivating grounds can and must provide it. Let us see, dear friend, which of these two convictions is to be found with the historical ground of cognition. We shall assume that the source of conviction in a future life lies wholly outside the domain of reason – and we must assume this if we want to derive its origin from a supernatural revelation. In this case, there is no necessary connection, illuminative to reason, between the moral law and future rewards and punishments. The revealed connection between the two depends solely and entirely on the will of the deity and, moreover, on a will that does not proceed by way of any maxim of reason, for otherwise its determination would have been able to be specified by just this maxim and, consequently, also without revelation. If you wanted to object to me here that divine reason cannot be judged by the standard of human reason at all and that its rules must remain absolutely incomprehensible to us, then you would be meeting my view halfway. For, if the lawgiving that we call moral is the product of an incomprehensible understanding [181] and an inscrutable will, then the internal necessity, illuminative to reason, through which moral laws distinguish themselves from positive laws is a mere illusion. And, in our observance of the moral law, we would in no way be following our own conviction, the direction of our reason, or the inclination of our rational will. Rather we would be following the superior force of a foreign will, a will that must forever remain incapable of convincing us of its legitimacy – precisely because it determines itself through incomprehensible grounds – and that must be content with forcing us into self-interested and slavish obedience

[133] The 1790 ed. (p. 184) inserts "which is already firmly established on its own."

through hope and fear. Hence, if morality is not to be wholly eliminated rather than supported by revelation, revelation must presuppose the reasonableness of moral lawgiving and, with it, a necessary connection between the moral law and future rewards and punishments that is comprehensible to reason and therefore provable as well. Moreover, revelation will have to concede to reason the right of having the first say with regard to the conviction in a future life, and it will in no way be able to provide the first and highest – in a word, the sole[134] – ground for cognition of this basic truth of religion.[135]

Wherever and whenever it was esteemed as such, religion was separated from morality, [182] or rather, there existed two different moral laws – a natural one and a supernatural one – that were in unceasing conflict with one another. As a necessary consequence, the religion of those who called themselves Christians commonly stood in an inverted relation to their morality. And there were times when the teachers of Christianity solemnly declared that even the most innocent and righteous course in life, if it had proceeded under the instruction of the deliverances of reason, could not save one from the eternal flames, let alone warrant the expectation of future happiness. Christian morality truly became as incomprehensible as the will of the deity from which it was derived, and it was believed that one could experience this will only through immediate illumination coming down from above or in the religious books of the Hebrews.[136] Who can count all the inconsistencies and abominations that the historical ground of cognition has brought upon the admirable doctrine of the Gospel through these two channels! One renounced the use of reason in religion – that is, in precisely that matter where it was most indispensable – elevated nonsensical scholastic formulas to the rank of basic truths of religion, raised a blind faith in obvious contradictions to the first condition for pleasing the deity, forswore matrimony and along with it all other duties [183] toward society, punished the diversity of religious opinions with fire and sword, etc. The ground of conviction for having to do all of this was the incomprehensible will of the deity, and the motivating ground for actually doing it was the hope for

[134] The 1790 ed. (p. 186) replaces "sole" with "genuine."

[135] The 1790 ed. (p. 186) inserts a footnote: "Thus, we are *not* concerned here with the possibility and indispensability of *revelation in general* with regard to a future life. *A note for my hyperphysical opponents.*"

[136] The 1790 ed. (p. 187) replaces "or in the religious books of the Hebrews" with "or at least as much from the religious books of the Hebrews as from the four evangelists, as interpreted by the infallible Church."

heaven and fear of hell, without which it would have seemed quite gratuitous to direct oneself according to that incomprehensible will.

Under the heading of the Ten Commandments, there were some laws of nature that, while they certainly did not count as moral, did at least count as positive. They owed their preservation in large part to their extreme indispensability and perhaps also to the spiritual judge and jury presiding over consciences. This spiritual court drew its best revenues from transgressions of these laws but thereby deprived humanity of even the external advantages that the blind and amoral observance of those commandments would otherwise have afforded it. The doctrine of the power of the keys[137] and the doctrine of satisfying works of atonement, by means of which one could settle up with the priests, privileged all evil deeds by making unnecessary the fear of future punishment. And yet these abominable doctrines are anything but absurd if one presupposes the historical ground of cognition as the sole secure one. For why should an inscrutable will, which does not act according to any law of reason familiar to us, not be able to suspend, as often as it wishes, a connection between [184] law and retribution that rests merely on its arbitrariness?[138] Why should it not pass the full authority for this suspension on to those who are appointed to announce to us its mysterious decrees – decrees which we could never experience without an announcement? Why should the conditions that those in power place on the abatement of punishment even be rational if reason has had no role in the connection of law and retribution?–

Ever since Protestants managed to free themselves from subordination to the infallible explicators of the incomprehensible will, their religious morality has drawn closer to the morality of reason with giant strides. Since that fortunate epoch those among them who have advocated the historical ground of cognition have obtained the right to seek out for themselves what the incomprehensible will demands of them. By means of a subreption that was as natural as it was beneficial, they gradually foisted upon the dead letter of the sensory[139] document of that will the results that their heterodox brothers had found in their investigations

[137] A reference to the Catholic doctrine that the authority of its church is based on "keys" to its leadership passed on by Jesus to St. Peter (Matthew 16:17–19).

[138] The 1790 ed. (p. 188) inserts "just as in miraculous works he suspends the physical laws of nature in order to achieve his supernatural intentions."

[139] *Sinnlich*, i.e., the Bible as object of sense perception, the literal written word.

into the comprehensible, i.e., rationally determined, will of the deity. But apart from the fact that under the cover of the historical ground of cognition every enthusiast is at liberty to allow the deity to will whatever his sick fantasies [185] find to be good, it is also the case that the observance itself of the purest doctrines of the Gospel is moral only in so far as it is unselfish, or, a consequence of internal conviction. And this conviction can withstand the external forces of fear and hope only when reason itself unites the ground of fear and hope with the inner bindingness of the moral law – or what comes to the same thing, when the ground for cognition of a future life is built directly upon morality.

(To be continued.)

[67] Sixth Letter: Continuation of the preceding letter: The united interests of religion and morality in the clearing away of the metaphysical ground for cognition of a future life

I feel, dear friend, the difficulty of my undertaking, in which I pass from the historical to the [68] metaphysical ground for cognition of the immortality of the soul in order to demonstrate precisely the same incompatibility of the metaphysical ground with the common interest of religion and morality that I have perhaps only too hastily indicated with respect to the historical ground. You need worry very little about this hastiness in regard to the proofs that lie ahead since the very reason why I believed that this hastiness should be permissible in the one case summons me to a more rigorous investigation and more detailed elucidation in the present case. I have not been concerned with a hyperphysicist who accepts absolutely no other source for his religious conviction than a supernatural one,[140] and for whom every pronouncement of reason on the basic truths of religion is suspicious precisely because he recognizes it as a pronouncement of reason.[141] Rather, I know from your spoken and written remarks that you are all the more willing to grant reason its innate right to have the first say regarding those basic truths precisely because you are

[140] There is a single quotation mark here that has been taken out of the translation. Presumably Reinhold means that he has not been "concerned with a hyperphysicist" in so far as he has been simply thinking of the viewpoint of the hypothetical enlightened friend to whom the letters are addressed.

[141] The 1790 ed. (p. 190) replaces "recognizes it as a pronouncement of reason" with "considers it to be the pronouncement of an oracle that he cannot consult in any matter of religion without thereby making himself guilty of irreligiosity."

used to thinking of religion as a moral matter, and because you cannot think of any moral matter that could not and would not have to be decided before the tribunal of reason. "In the entire domain of moral lawgiving," you write to me on another occasion, "nothing can present itself that is incomprehensible in itself – no law that is not [69] immediately prescribed by reason itself, no sanction that is not recognized by reason as necessary, and thus no sanction that is not both announced by reason's own voice and settled by its lawgiving power.[142] Without it even the deity would not have a language for us that could avoid remaining a dead letter forever. – Every revelation that does not survive reason's test is dismissed; and none survives this test whose content is found not to be consonant with reason's own pronouncements.[143] Therefore, everything that is beyond the rational is irrational, and, in so far as it has any influence on morality, immoral." – Yet I also know that precisely these principles, which for you deprive the historical ground of cognition of all respect – at least in so far as it is passed off as the first or sole ground – have until now, anyway, given support to the metaphysical ground. I know that, along with so many other enlightened friends of religion, you are more inclined to heed the proofs with which rational psychology attempts to demonstrate the immortality of the soul. And you are so inclined precisely because you believed that in these proofs the rights of reason were demonstrated by reason's actual possession of them, as it were, and because you believed that the hyperphysicists, who deny reason the capacity to convince itself of the basic truths of religion by means of its own powers, were refuted in their opinion. This time, therefore, I have something to take up with you directly. [70] I must prove nothing less than that the interests of religion and morality would, in truth, be no less divided and opposed to each other by the very ground of cognition that seems to you to establish at once both the conviction in a future life and the reputation of reason – and consequently to unite the interests of religion and morality – than they would be by the opposing

142 The 1790 ed. (p. 190) inserts ", and no observance of a law that is not carried out by its spontaneity," and replaces "it" in the next sentence with "this *spirit* of our soul."

143 The 1790 ed. (p. 190) replaces "and none survives this test whose content is found not to be consonant with reason's own pronouncements" with "and none can pass that test if it denies reason the right to judge what is revealed according to its own necessary and universal laws; if it forces upon reason, as the will of the deity, a demand contradicting reason's nature, or even one foreign to it; or if it denies reason the status of being the voice of God *within us*."

historical ground, which was supposed to have been made superfluous by this metaphysical ground.

Before all else, let us be in agreement about what we ought actually to think here under the term "metaphysical ground of cognition." I understand by it not just any form of conviction that is based on grounds of reason in general and is thus set in opposition to blind faith. Conviction based on grounds of reason is absolutely indispensable to the morality of religion, and the moral faith that the Critique of Reason establishes is built entirely on grounds of reason. Rather I separate from the metaphysical ground of cognition itself the actual role that reason had in it, the role on account of which this ground of cognition was not only a result of the legitimate endeavor in which the human spirit struggled for its own inner conviction but also the only means for asserting the independence of reason during that period when reason had not yet been developed enough to recognize the moral ground of cognition. [71] It was the only means for keeping reason itself in the actual possession of those rights without whose use its true nature and the entire extent of its domain would have necessarily remained unknown to it.[144]

I also do not mean by this term every use of reason's psychological concept of a simple thinking substance – and least of all that use which is made of it in defending against its opponents the basic religious truth of a future life. Since these opponents take to the field with nothing but metaphysical weapons,[q] the use of this kind of weapon for resistance will remain not only legitimate but even necessary as long as the feud itself lasts – or what comes to the same thing, as long as, on account of its previous weaknesses, philosophy of religion will incite attack. The psychological concept of reason, which represents our thinking I as a simple and indestructible substance, is certainly irrefutable if it is supposed to express nothing more and nothing less than that the subject of our thoughts, entirely unknown in itself, is, in so far as it thinks, not an object of outer intuition – i.e., not a body – and that therefore destructibility, which is a predicate [72] that can be attributed only to bodies, cannot be asserted of a thinking subject. Yet this concept contradicts itself as soon as its meaning

[144] See Appendix, section G for the heavily revised and expanded version of the text that begins here and ends on p. 79 of the Sixth Letter from the *Merkur* with the sentence that concludes, "must remain unimportant for him."

[q] The dress and trappings do not change anything with regard to the matter itself: the *blade* is metaphysical every time, or the weapon, like the sword of some short rifles, has no blade at all.

extends beyond the distinction between soul and body that arises in experience and that no materialist can rationalize away. It contradicts itself as soon as it is supposed to express more than the mere difference between predicates of inner and of outer sense, or as soon as it is supposed to express the absolute subject of our thinking I, the genuine and incomprehensible essence[145] of our soul. And it does this by making a mere predicate of intuition into a subject in itself, by attaching a known nature[146] to a wholly unknown thing – in so far as it is unknown – and by transforming an empty concept into an actual object. The advocate of the moral ground for cognition of a future life thus renounces all advantage that he could draw for his conviction [in immortality] from the concept of incorporeity – as long as an opponent does not intrude to attack that concept at the expense of this conviction. For then, of course, the advocate feels himself compelled to offer proof that the distinction between soul and body – to the extent that we are acquainted with both – cannot be abolished without contradiction. But mindful of his own conviction that this distinction – in so far as it is supposed to refer to the actual essences of body and soul – can be just as little asserted without contradiction, the advocate is content with having deflected the presumption of his opponent [73] without making himself guilty of a similar one. And he is modest enough to admit to himself that, while he refutes the objections to his claim, he is very far from having proven the claim itself. In a word, he uses the psychological concept of reason as a mere bulwark[147] for his conviction in a future life.

The contrary use – or rather misuse – of that concept, which is still very widespread today, and which turns that concept from a bulwark into a foundation,[148] is what I understand then by the metaphysical ground for cognition of immortality. Speculation has extended the undeniable distinction between the representations of inner and outer sense to the objects in themselves of these representations and on this basis has constructed the familiar demonstration of the future survival of our soul, which, because of its seeming plausibility[149] as well as the universality of its use, is held in high esteem – and not merely by a majority in the philosophical world.

[145] *Wesen*, a term that Reinhold sometimes uses interchangeably with *Beschaffenheit*, signifies a thing's nature, constitution, or properties.

[146] *Beschaffenheit*. [147] *Schutzwehr*. See above, n. 16. [148] *Grundfeste*.

[149] *Scheinbarkeit*, an appearing with a suggestion of deceptiveness, is translated as "seeming plausibility." It is related to the German term *Schein*, which can connote something's lustre but also carries a suggestion of illusion. In philosophical contexts, this term contrasts with *Erscheinung*, which can simply mean something that really appears and need not carry a suggestion of illusion.

At present I will consider this form of conviction in a future life less in respect to its validity than in respect to its influence on the common interest of religion and morality. But I would be committing a grave error if I could not convince you that as a result of the metaphysical ground of cognition the influence on morality of the basic truth concerning a [74] future life must become either ineffectual or wholly damaging, as it degenerates into either irreligious frigidity or mystical enthusiasm – and that, consequently, either the religiosity of morality or the morality[150] of religion must suffer from that ground of cognition. Yet you may judge this for yourself.

Granted that, in itself, the soul is actually a spirit[151] – something which I would never think of denying – then, as such, it is a mere being of the understanding. That is, it can be thought only through the understanding and never perceived through sensibility. Even if the understanding distinguishes the intuitions of inner sense from the intuitions of outer sense and declares the former to be simple because they do not occur in space, this simplicity refers only to perceived representations and not to their subject. The understanding can certainly think of this subject as something in general, but can never cognize it as something determinate because it lies outside the horizon of all possible perception. "But," you might object to me here, "do I not already by thinking it cognize something quite considerable about this otherwise unknown subject, such that my reason feels compelled to attribute to it the predicates of substance and the simple?" – I reply that the attribution of these two predicates has [75] much more likely distanced you from a familiarity with this subject than brought you closer to it. For, now, what is this subject, which, as a result of those alleged new insights, you may never think of as a predicate of another subject and to which you must deny all extension? Has it ceased being a mere empty concept on account of these two determinations? Has it been given an actual object to which the concept could be applied? Or has it not rather been excluded thereby from the sphere of all things that, for us, are more than mere thoughts? All actual objects to which we grant a subsistence outside our concepts must exist somewhere – that is, in space – and all that can be cognized with regard to these objects are mere predicates. The concept of

[150] Reinhold uses the two terms *Moral* and *Moralität* in this sentence, but he does not make a systematic distinction between these two terms or *Sittlichkeit* (which, especially after Hegel, is usually translated as "ethics" or "customs"), so they are all translated here as "morality." See above, n. 59.

[151] *Geist*. See above, Note on the texts and translation, and see below, nn. 154–7.

the simple contradicts one of these criteria of actuality, and the concept of a subject that cannot be a predicate contradicts the other. – Perception alone can teach me whether an actual object corresponds to one of my concepts. I am convinced through it alone that the concept of the simple with respect to the objects of my inner intuition and the concept of substance with respect to the objects of my outer intuition (everything that persists in space) are not mere forms of thought without content. Perception, then, and it alone, can supply me with the content of these concepts – namely [76] the actual representations that inner sense presents to me in the one case, and the objects in space that outer sense presents to me in the other. For then the concepts of the simple as well as of substance no longer designate a mere something, a [something] $= x$; rather, the one designates actual representations that succeed one another in time, and the other designates actual empirical objects that persist in space. But as soon as the concept of the simple is projected from the form of representation belonging to inner sense, while the concept of substance is projected from the persisting thing in space, onto the unknown subject of thoughts, the matter for perception falls entirely away. For the matter of perception concerned only the given representations of inner sense and not their subject; it concerned only the persisting thing in space and not something that cannot occur in space. And no other determinations remain for the subject that I wish to cognize in this way than the empty concepts of substance and the simple – determinations by which reason certainly prohibits me from regarding my thinking self as a property[152] (an *accidens*) of my body but in no way announces to me what the subject of my thoughts might be in itself. Hence, cognition of this subject, in so far as it is more than a mere concept, does not gain anything when we seek to extend it without intuition by means of the concepts of substance and the simple; [77] to the contrary, it loses something, for we augment what is lacking in it by tacking on two unknown properties.

If after repeated readings, dear friend, you should find my elucidation thus far not to be entirely satisfactory – one which, to be sure, had to distance itself somewhat from the customary manner of representation and for which I ought to have requested twice as much of your attention – I suggest to you the following shorter route.[153] Hold yourself to a strict

[152] *Beschaffenheit.*

[153] Reinhold often proposed "short" arguments (which proved to be very influential and controversial) that he thought could be used to reach Kant's conclusions. See K. Ameriks, *Kant and the Fate of Autonomy* (Cambridge, Cambridge University Press, 2000), chs. 2 and 3.

account of the representation that you have made for yourself until now of the soul as a spirit. Because I know how much you are able keep a tight rein on your fantasy, I can easily predict the result of this investigation. Spirit is for you an unknown and incomprehensible something, of which you know nothing more than that it is the subject of your thoughts. You think of it as simple merely because you must distinguish it from all bodies – and as a substance because you must distinguish it from the properties of your body. You and every spiritualist are also in agreement with me that this substantial, simple, and thinking something can indeed be thought of as existing but can never be perceived. For is not perception the exclusive occupation of sensibility, or of the faculty of intuition? And is not a spirit, which, [78] according to the universal admission of all spiritualists who are not spirit-seers,[154] can only be thought by the understanding, infinitely elevated beyond this kind of cognition? In any case, this deficiency, or rather impossibility, of perception is indeed the true and genuine cause why the something thought of as a spirit is for us an unknown something $= x$, and why all of its determinations – substance, simplicity, the power of thinking, etc. (the coefficients of this x) – must forever remain empty and without content.

And now let us see with regard to the basic religious truth of a future life what necessarily follows from the foregoing explanation of the nature of the concepts that make up the idea of a spirit and constitute the entire subject matter of rational psychology. I indicated it earlier, but only now can I hope that it will appear less strange to you; what follows is none other than indifference or fanaticism, depending on whether one thinks of the psychological concept of reason in its natural emptiness and lack of content or fills it in through non-natural intuitions with the help of the power of the imagination.

To the extent that a speculative mind[155] is in harmony with itself, thinks more consistently according to its principles, and knows how to protect its concepts from heterogeneous additions, it will also keep pure its concept of reason regarding the nature of a spirit – that is, [79] it will keep this concept of reason free from all illusions of the imagination just as it has found it empty of all intuitions of sensibility. But to that same extent, this

[154] Kant began a sharp attack on "spirit-seers," such as Swedenborg, in his *Dreams of a Spirit-seer Elucidated by Dreams of Metaphysics* (Königsberg, 1766).

[155] *Kopf*, literally "head," a common term that Reinhold uses frequently with this meaning.

concept of reason that the speculative thinker cannot apply to an actual object, this spirit that can only be thought of – this mere thing of thought – must hold less interest for him. He distinguishes the something in him that thinks from all his representations[r] precisely because he must, on account of its spiritual nature,[156] think of it as something that is present as an absolute subject. And he distinguishes it from everything actual that he is acquainted with outside himself because he must think of it as simple. In a word, this thinking, simple, and substantial something = *x*[157] can have as little of an effect on him as he can have on it. It intervenes in none of his actual representations and is an object neither of his hate nor of his love precisely because for him it is [a something] = *x*. However important his I may be to him, to that same degree every unknown property of this I that is elevated beyond all possible perception must remain unimportant to him. Now, if he knows of no other ground for cognition of a future life than that which is fetched from those unknown properties of simplicity, substantiality, etc., then he who thinks sharply and correctly can promise himself a continuing existence after death only inasmuch [80] as he is the aforesaid something – a something to which applies none of the determinations of actual objects with which he is familiar. In regard to this something he can think of nothing but the subject of those representations which he has perceived over the course of his life; and, with regard to those representations, he cannot know if he will still perceive them once the particular thing persisting in space to which the empirical consciousness of his personality is bound will have fallen away with his body. Since, therefore, the metaphysical demonstration of survival after death concerns only what he does not know about himself, while everything that he has become acquainted with over the course of his life either excludes his future existence straight away or at least leaves him in uncertainty with regard to it, a consistent thinker must be just about as indifferent to a future existence in an invisible world as to a former existence in the realm of possibilities.

One complains not entirely without cause that the influence of religion on morality is decreasing at the same rate that the enlightenment of the

[r] That is, from everything actual regarding his soul that he can perceive.

[156] *Geistigkeit*.

[157] Cf. Kant, *Critique of Pure Reason*, A346/B404: "Through this I or he or it (the thing) which thinks, nothing further is represented than a transcendental subject of the thoughts = *X*."

age increases, and that the basic truths of religion – which used to be the noblest object of all speculative philosophy and must forever remain its noblest end – are often doubted by the best philosophical minds of our time and even more often passed over in complete silence. Above all, [81] one complains not entirely without cause that the lofty and important thought of a future life generally appears least of all in the writings and discussions of those who are the most capable of this thought and who have the most suitable profession for obtaining the highest degree of possible evidence for it. Indisputably, the strangest part about this is that the cause of all this complaining in the philosophical world has become rampant mainly since the time Descartes purified reason's concept of the spiritual nature of the soul and, with it, put the finishing touch, as it were, on the demonstration of the soul's immortality. But this very situation, which at first sight appears to create an even deeper puzzle, will upon closer examination offer us its own solution.

As long as the concepts of reason out of which the idea of spiritual nature is composed were not yet completely developed, this idea could not be thought, even by the most acute of thinkers, in its distinctive purity – or rather in its emptiness, without any matter of sensibility and imagination. It was precisely this incompleteness of the undeveloped concepts of reason that made their supplementation with representations of sensibility and imagination at once both possible and necessary, and the two otherwise very different forms of representation flowed together into a confused whole without allowing the contradiction between [82] them to become visible. So, for example, while before Descartes the concept of the simple was distinguished from the concept of the composite, it was not yet clearly enough distinguished from the concept of the extended. Because one did not therefore think of spirit entirely without extension – or at least did not straight away exclude extension from it – persistence in space, without which no actually existing[158] substance can be thought, let alone proven, was not omitted from the substantiality of spirit. If, on the one hand, reason's concept of a simple substance gained its completion through the metaphysical discovery of Descartes, it lost, on the other hand, the last support that it had been receiving from sensibility until then. For from now on the soul could no longer without contradiction be thought of as something persisting in space. The last rule regarding how one ought to

[158] The 1790 ed. (p. 205) replaces "actually existing" with "*actually cognizable.*"

think of spirit had now been found; yet at the same time the last thread had been cut by which fantasy had held the idea of spirit bound to the order of actual things.[159] One had not yet dreamed on that account, however, that no actual[160] object can be thought through pure reason alone, and thus reason's pure concept of the soul was still hypostatized as before – but with very different results. The pure form of reason's concept no longer applied to any matter whatsoever in the entire realm [83] of experience, and, in place of all the content that one had been able to ascribe to it without contradiction, nothing now remained except the similarly empty concept of a something $= x$ – a something which did not cease to be a true *x*[161] simply on account of being taken as an existing *x* in a demonstration.[162] Thus, considered from this perspective, the cold attitude of philosophers with regard to a future life is not wholly without an excuse. More often perhaps than they themselves realize, this attitude is a very natural effect of the actual *x* that every thinking mind on the path of demonstrative conviction in the immortality of the soul must more or less stumble upon according to the degree of precision with which it adheres to the rule of pure reason in the determination of its concept of spiritual nature.

You may now decide for yourself, dear friend, the extent to which I was right in claiming that the demonstrative form of conviction in a future life would deprive the basic truth of religion of its influence on morality. The very considerable restriction that my claim admits of is of so little aid to the connection between religion and morality that it actually undermines it from another, much more dubious side. The common interest of religion and morality suffers just as much when the concept of reason,[163] on which [84] the basic truth of religion is built through demonstration, is filled in by fantasy as when it remains empty.

159 The 1790 ed. (p. 205) replaces "actual things" with "cognizable objects."
160 The 1790 ed. (p. 205) replaces "actual" with "cognizable."
161 Here "true *x*" means something completely unknown.
162 The 1790 ed. (p. 205) replaces "an existing *x*" with "an *x* that is cognizable with regard to its properties of substantiality and simplicity."
163 The 1790 ed. (p. 206) replaces "You may now decide for yourself, dear friend, the extent to which I was right in claiming that the demonstrative form of conviction in a future life would deprive the basic truth of religion of its influence on morality. The very considerable restriction that my claim admits of is of so little aid to the connection between religion and morality that it actually undermines it from another, much more dubious side. The common interest of religion and morality suffers just as much when the concept of reason, . . ." with "Through this very same *emptiness* of representation by which the metaphysical *ground of cognition*, on the one hand, brings about *indifference* in religious conviction, it generates *fanaticism* on the other. And the interest of moral religion loses *no less* when the idea of reason, . . ."

It is undeniable that only very few people – and even very few among speculative philosophers – are capable of thinking in a pure way about the concepts of reason that compose the idea of spiritual nature. In part, the minds that are in a position to grasp a concept of reason in any disciplined way are not very numerous; and, in part, not all the hearts that belong to such minds are sufficiently inclined to be content with an empty concept of reason in such an important matter. Thus, fantasy continues to create a content with which it either supplements a concept of reason of spiritual nature that is still incomplete or fills in a concept that is complete but on that account also empty: hence, the striking variety of the manners of representation under which the idea of spirit appears even among those writers who cite the same definition for it, agree entirely in their notions of substance, simplicity, the power of thinking, etc., and consequently are in perfect agreement about the rules concerning how one is to think about spirit.[164] The unmistakable uniformity of the metaphysical outlines according to which these psychological ideals are drawn betrays the compass and ruler of pure reason just as clearly as the variety of actual content and coloring betrays [85] the paintbrush of the imagination. Reason, which can sanction nothing in regard to a supersensible ideal that is not its own work, has in the meantime protested ever more expressly and widely against any resemblance of these painted-over outlines to its convictions concerning the nature of spirit. For, in regard to the nature of spirit, reason knows at least this much – that it has nothing to do with anything that can be presented through sensibility or the imagination. But the more reason succeeds, on the one hand, in gaining acceptance for its pure concept of spiritual nature – or rather, for the rules that it prescribes for this concept – the busier fantasy appears, on the other hand, maintaining itself in its old possessions, from which it is being displaced by those rules. Let me state this observation more precisely. The less reason[s] can hide from the emptiness of its developed concepts of supersensible objects – concepts

[164] The 1790 ed. (p. 207) inserts: " – But those writers deviate from one another just as much in the doctrines that they infer from this. And even if they *unanimously* confuse the soul with the person that consists of flesh and soul, and the spirit with the human being, nonetheless, through the variety of features they borrow from the sense organs and apply to the spirit, they posit as many kinds of spirits as they write books – or prepare revised editions of such books – about them."

[s] *Subjective* reason, which is capable of unlimited increase in its approach toward *objective* reason (the perfect ideal). We have been justified in speaking of *objective* reason only since the time when the *Critique* made us familiar with *pure reason*. [This footnote is omitted in the 1790 edition.]

that are becoming more and more disseminated and established – and the less this emptiness is compatible with its other needs,[t] the more reason feels itself compelled to invite fantasy into precisely that domain [86] from which reason had expelled it by irrevocable laws. For examples of this phenomenon I can cite the recent disputes already frequently mentioned in my previous letters.[u] To be sure, these disputes actually concern the first basic truth of religion (the existence of God), on which the contending factions appear to ground the second basic truth (regarding a future life). But they are still relevant here in so far as they are the most lively expression of the perplexity in which reason finds itself when it becomes aware of the incongruity between its essential needs and its previous means for satisfying these needs, and when it is forced to sin against its own laws – laws by which it cuts down fanaticism – in order to set limits to the intrusion of brooding nonbelief. In this way I can explain not only, for instance, the ever more frequent and vehement efforts of obvious fanatics to make whole again what cold reason has corrupted, to cover over what it has exposed, and to fill up what it has emptied; but, above all, I can explain the strange and curious war that men with lively imaginations and the uncommon acuteness of speculative philosophy – or more precisely, of pure reason – have declared without knowing it. The empty concept of reason incites them. They want cognitions with content; they want intuitive concepts [87] of either historical or even physical facts. The agitated genius among them, who is all the less able to lower himself to learn[165] from one of his living contemporaries precisely because he is used to instructing them all,[166] spares them, by means of his plastic power, the following

[t] An emptiness, which, however, can be utterly inconsequential for reason once reason has adopted the *moral ground of cognition*. [Here Reinhold is referring especially to Kant's idea that our *basic rational* "need" is to attend to morality, a need that he calls "subjective" simply because it cannot be known through theoretical faculties alone. Cf. Kant, "What Does it Mean to Orient Oneself in Thinking?" (8: 137): "But now there enters *the right* of reason's *need*, as a subjective ground for presupposing something and assuming something which reason may not presume to know through objective grounds; and consequently for *orienting* itself in thinking, solely through reason's own need." This footnote is omitted in the 1790 edition.]

[u] E.g., the Jacobian, Mendelssohnian disputes.

[165] Reading *leeren* as *lernen*.

[166] The 1790 ed. (p. 208) replaces "The agitated genius among them, who is all the less able to lower himself to learn from one of his living contemporaries precisely because he is used to instructing them all" with "In these discoveries, sometimes even a *poetic genius* comes in handy, to which the *philosophical spirit*, when encountering this genius in one and the same mind, must commonly offer his right hand, . . . " This is one of many places in the 1790 edition in which Reinhold softens his tone against Jacobi.

Critical investigation: Can a supersensible object be proven, or at least illustrated, by sensible events and appearances? And thus can there be intuitive concepts of God and spirits? – For this genius[167] provides himself with whatever concepts he needs and single-handedly changes the long-established and universally accepted meanings of terms. He abolishes the distinction between concepts that arises in the experience of the objects of those concepts and instead makes their common feature into an actual object. He amalgamates concepts and intuitions, notions and images, ideas and things, daring suppositions and insightful analogies, probabilities and demonstrations. – And in this way he obtains that original and magical mass of realities, actualities, and powers with which he stuffs the empty metaphysical form of thought (for unfortunately he, too, knows of no other form of thought, and it always turns out in the end that only the matter is newly created) so forcefully and so fully that it shatters into pieces. – Imagine how much the already decisive dominance of fantasy over reason in regard to religion [88] would be reinforced if writings of this kind were to gain influence on the ruling concepts, and if the obscurity that totally dominates these writings – which is a result of mishandled concepts of reason and is in no way illuminated by the lightning of wit – were not to frighten off the greater part of the reading public already with their first pages!

This is how fantasy[168] proceeds with the first basic truth of religion, and this is how it would also proceed with the second basic truth if it were just as rigorously and universally pressed for a demonstration with regard to the latter as it has been with regard to the former. And in this case the concepts of reason that compose the idea of spiritual nature would become just as visible and effective in their necessary purity and emptiness – that is, they would repel and attract the images of fantasy with equal vivacity and give us the very same show that the theological concept of reason has given us. If at present fantasy is causing less fuss and less of a sensation with the concept of spiritual nature, then this is because it is somewhat less uneasy in its possessions. For by virtue of these possessions, fantasy has been used to supplementing – or more precisely, adulterating – the concept of reason ever since its emergence, and to corrupting the morality of religion through it. The history of the psychological concept of reason, to which I will devote my next letter, will show this in more detail.

[167] Presumably Jacobi.

[168] The 1790 ed. (p. 209) inserts here "even of philosophical minds."

[142] Seventh Letter: A sketch of a history of reason's psychological concept of a simple thinking substance

That the distinction between body and soul belongs among the earliest advances of the human spirit on the path of its development must have struck you long ago, my dear friend, given your close familiarity with the vestiges of the most ancient eras of eastern and Greek philosophy. But even if all of these original records had been lost, this distinction would have emerged simply by a closer examination of the nature of our cognitive faculty. Right at the first dawning of reason, the thinking I, in conformity with the laws of consciousness, had to distinguish itself from every one of the representations it was thinking and consequently also from the body, particularly in so far as this body appeared among those representations. Similarly, the laws of sensibility made necessary the essential distinction between the objects of inner and of outer sense – that is, between representations in [143] us and things outside us. Now, in so far as all representations in us attach to the I as their subject, while the body belongs to the order of things outside us, the distinction that is thought in consciousness between the I and the body – between representations presented through inner sense, on the one hand, and the body that is presented through outer sense, on the other – had to be given already in intuition as well.[169]

[169] The 1790 ed. (p. 211) replaces "distinction that is thought in consciousness between the I and the body – between representations presented through inner sense, on the one hand, and the body that is presented through outer sense, on the other – had to be given already in intuition as well" with "distinction that is unavoidable in self-consciousness between the representing *I* and the

Thus, there was agreement very soon[170] about the fact that the I and the body had to be two very different things. But disagreement arose almost just as quickly concerning the question of what the distinction between these two things consisted in. On one view, it was a necessary consequence of the aforementioned constitution of our faculty of cognition, according to which this distinction had to emerge, even without cognition of its ground. On the contrasting view, this distinction was a no less necessary consequence of an unfamiliarity with that constitution and of the unavoidable misunderstandings that came with it regarding the ground of that distinction – a distinction one felt compelled toward without knowing on what account. Already from the most ancient times there was agreement about the actuality of the distinction between body and soul, but until our day there has been disagreement about the possibility of this distinction. And this single fact is sufficient proof that the human spirit [144] has asserted this distinction without really knowing why and that, consequently, the ground of its assertion lay not in actual insights but rather in laws of its cognitive faculty[171] that were unknown to it. In the meantime, this ground has actually been uncovered in the analysis of the faculty of cognition that has been undertaken by the *Critique of Pure Reason*. And it has been proven apodictically that this ground was, is, and will be none other than the rule that reason prescribes for the concept of the soul in conformity with the laws of inner and outer intuition – a rule that is contained in the following formula: it is not possible to think[172] the subject of the predicates of inner sense by means of the predicates of outer sense. Without my reminder, dear friend, you will recognize in this formula reason's psychological concept of a simple thinking substance, which, in so far as it was taken by our previous metaphysicians to be an *insight of reason*, has served as the bone of contention between the materialists and spiritualists and has left the distinction between body and soul open to a number of disputes. But in so far as this concept was grounded in the nature of the human faculty of

represented *body* – through *representations* that *inner sense* intuits and renders perceptible, on the one hand, and through the *body* that *outer* sense intuits and renders perceptible, on the other – must on this account have also become striking already in the infancy of philosophy."

170 The 1790 ed. (p. 211) replaces "very soon" with "before all philosophical investigation."

171 The 1790 ed. (p. 212) replaces "cognitive faculty" with "faculty of representation" (and often elsewhere).

172 The 1790 ed. (p. 212) replaces "think" with "*represent*."

cognition[173] as an unrecognized *rule of reason*, it brought about a universal and invincible conviction in a distinction between body and soul that could not be demonstrated – that is, a distinction for which no objective ground[174] could be specified. – You [145] also see why I begin the history of reason's psychological concept with that premature epoch in the history of the human spirit which is preoccupied with the distinction between body and soul.

For a very long time, the psychological concept of reason lay undeveloped[175] among the basic determinations of the human faculty of cognition; its individual components emerged only gradually and very slowly, and they obtained their completeness only after long intervals. Millennia had passed from the point in time when the first unambiguous traces of the distinction between body and soul appeared in history to the time when the concept of substantiality – and the concept of simplicity almost two thousand years later – emerged in purity and completeness out of the chaos of varying and indeterminate representations. And it was only six years ago that we came into possession of the work that has exhausted the concept of thinking through the analysis of the faculty of cognition and has fully determined by means of it the meaning and use of the concepts of substance and the simple.[176] Thus, if one accepts these concepts as insights of reason, they are neither as old, nor as widely disseminated, nor as evident[177] as the distinction between body and soul – a distinction which one wishes to demonstrate by means of them and [146] to which they are supposed to have led. As rules of reason, however, they were always included among the many other unrecognized laws of our faculty of cognition and therefore could be as little without consequence as these laws. Much as light rays gave bodies color even before Newton spied

[173] *Menschlichen Erkenntnißvermögens.* This phrase is a precursor to the central term of Reinhold's later Elementary-Philosophy, the human faculty of representation (*das menschliche Vorstellungsvermögen*).

[174] The 1790 ed. (p. 212) inserts "obtained from the *thing in itself*," and omits the following sentence.

[175] The 1790 ed. (p. 212) inserts "with regard to its scientific form."

[176] The 1790 ed. (p. 213) replaces "that has exhausted the concept of thinking through the analysis of the faculty of cognition and has fully determined by means of it the meaning and use of the concepts of substance and the simple" with "that has exhausted the principles of everything comprehensible through a complete analysis of the faculty of cognition and has fully corrected in these principles the ever misunderstood significance and the ever mistaken use of the concepts of *substance* and *the simple*."

[177] *Einleuchtend.* This term is usually translated as "illuminating," but it is translated as "evident" here and on the next two pages.

them out in this beneficent effect, the laws of our faculty of cognition, which the psychological concept of reason expresses, gave rise to the distinction between body and soul before Kant discovered them in this capacity. And just as before Newton one misunderstood light by attributing its color to bodies and crediting it with nothing more than the illumination of those bodies, so too before Kant one misunderstood reason in its psychological concept. For one projected onto a thing in itself the subjective rules[178] according to which and from which reason alone produced this concept, while granting to reason nothing more than a faculty for learning those rules from a thing in itself as laws of the latter – even though those rules are entirely reason's own work.

Had it not been possible to obtain the distinction between body and soul in any other way than through the cognition of what the body and soul are in themselves outside our form of representation, then this distinction would have appeared only with the age of metaphysics and would have to have shared in the gradual progress of this science as well as in all aspects of its fate generally [147]. Moreover, it would have been confined to the metaphysicians alone and, given its supposed ground of cognition, would even have been an object of endless controversies among them. As a subjective law of our faculty of cognition, however, it had to appear right with the first expressions of reason's proper use – hence, its historical antiquity. It had to be more or less evident to all human individuals – hence, its popularity and universal dissemination. Neither substantial nor superficial objections could be established against it, and the objections that later would inevitably result from misunderstandings of its origin never had an effect on anything beyond the confines of the School[179] – hence, the ancient and lasting agreement that assigns to this distinction a permanent status among the verdicts of universal human understanding. Thus, as a natural product of the human spirit, this distinction had all those properties which it had to have in order to be able to serve as a bulwark for the basic religious truth of a future life: antiquity, popularity, universal dissemination, and irrefutability – properties that even the proudest of metaphysicians would hesitate to claim for it given its transformation by the School

[178] The 1790 ed. (p. 214) replaces "subjective rules" with "rules grounded in the constitution of the faculty of representation."

[179] The traditional schools of dogmatic metaphysics, rooted in scholasticism.

into a product of ostensible science and its misuse as a foundation for religious conviction. – Unrecognized [148] and undeveloped, the psychological concept of reason[180] performed for religion the only service that it could render it, when this concept is taken in the meaning supplied for it by the Critique of Reason. This is a service that religion needed from it, and one that this concept was no longer able to provide when it was taken in the more ambitious meaning that metaphysics had supplied for it. That is, the psychological concept of reason gave rise to a distinction – which was just as evident as it was unexplainable – that so invincibly opposed any confounding or conflating of body and soul that even the most plausible and ingenious fallacies could achieve nothing against it. And as a result, the expectation of a future life grounded on moral need was completely protected by it from any possible refutation on account of the death and dissolution of the body.

A complete enumeration and elaboration of the various forms under which in its childhood and early youth the human spirit sensibly represented to itself the distinction between body and soul – and of which we unfortunately have very few and unreliable samples to point to among the materials belonging to the most ancient history of philosophy – is not part of the aim of my present sketch. The forms that will be discussed here do indeed appear among these historical vestiges, but at the same time they receive a perfect confirmation from the nature of the human faculty of cognition.[181]

[149] Besides already having the first role to play in the philosophical domain during the protracted period of philosophy's immaturity, fantasy was left to its own – perhaps more than with any other task – in the determination of the distinction between body and soul. Inner intuition supplies nothing persistent in space and thus no image by which the soul, in contrast to the body, could be represented.[182] And yet, with the continued attention to the distinction between body and soul, such an

180 The 1790 ed. (p. 215) replaces "psychological concept of reason" with "*psychological idea* in its elements."

181 The 1790 ed. (pp. 215–16) replaces "The forms that will be discussed here do indeed appear among these historical vestiges, but at the same time they receive a perfect confirmation from the nature of the human faculty of cognition" with "For my present purpose I can content myself with citing some of those forms as examples of how much the results of the Critical philosophy are in agreement with the results of the history of philosophy in general."

182 The 1790 ed. (p. 216) replaces "the soul, in contrast to the body, could be represented" with "the representing subject (even if it does not have to be distinguished from all the predicates of inner sense) would be capable of intuiting itself."

image was just as indispensable as it was unavoidable.[183] Such an image therefore had to be generated by fantasy, just as the image of the body was given in outer intuition. Granting this presupposition, it seems to me that a hypostatized representation of life served as the most ancient and universal image in which the concept of the soul[184] appeared to the youthful power of imagination of the human spirit, and it was painted with strokes that must have frequently presented to fantasy the very striking difference between an animate and an inanimate[185] body. The sight of a corpse must have shed a sudden and blinding light on the unclearly conceived distinction between body and soul. What this sight brought into view was the former human being's body; what it left out, and left out very strikingly, was the life that had passed from it – the soul.

[150] With every advance of reason, which developed at the same rate as the culture and leisure time of social life, fantasy was forced to make modifications in the aforementioned image, to remove contradictory strokes and to add missing ones. It happened entirely for the satisfaction of reason, which demanded a determinate subject for the hypostatized life, that fantasy sought among its rich supply an image that could represent at least the substratum of the animating forces of a human being. Fantasy had to give into the demands of reason in so far as reason required this substratum to be invisible, for the substratum was supposed to be unlike the flesh. But reason had not yet pressed its demands to the point of requiring that the substratum be fetched from outside the world of the senses altogether. Hence, fantasy sought and found the required image in the only invisible body known at that time – air – and in this way the subject of life (*anima*) came to be an invisible body that appeared only through its effects. It became an airy substance (*spiritus*). Who can fail to recognize in this schema[186] provided by the power of imagination – however crude it is – reason's psychological concept of a simple substance, which expresses the simplicity of the subject of inner intuition by means of its invisibility, and its substantiality by means of a perceived invisible reality (air)?

[151] Here I am skipping over the various modifications that this schema subsequently assumed in the different philosophical schools. Just

[183] The 1790 ed. (p. 216) inserts "to philosophizing reason before it had reached a very considerable degree of development."

[184] The 1790 ed. (p. 216) replaces "concept of the soul" with "the representing substance."

[185] The 1790 ed. (p. 216) replaces "an inanimate" with "a lifeless."

[186] *Schema*. Cf. Kant's chapter on the schematism, *Critique of Pure Reason* (A 137/B 176f.).

as with the world-soul, which came to be conceived in a very early period and almost universally (how this happened does not concern us here), and which was sometimes fused with the deity and sometimes distinguished from it, so too the human soul was sometimes of a godly nature and sometimes of an ungodly nature – but in both cases sometimes airy and sometimes ethereal, sometimes pure elemental fire and sometimes a mixture of fire and ether, etc. The schema of an invisible body was preserved in all of these different hypotheses and defied even the most sublime speculation of a Plato and the astuteness of an Aristotle,[187] as well as the astuteness of all their successors among the Greeks and Romans. The exalted founder of metaphysics struggled against this schema with all the acuity of his piercing glance;[188] he declared the soul to be a simple substance (*haploun ousian*) and an incorporeal thing (*asōmaton ti*). But all the same he could not break away from regarding the soul as something material, as a mass (*ogkos*), as an invisible body. Even in the remarkable passage[V] where he attributes a divine nature to the human soul on account of its understanding and thus draws the conclusion that a human being ought to elevate itself above mere human dispositions (*anthrōpina phronein*) [152] – because its better part, its soul, is far superior to the other parts of its nature – the following remarkable words slip out, which seem to me to characterize very precisely his opinion regarding the simplicity of this better part: "however small it may be in terms of mass" (*ei gar kai tōi ogkon mikron esi*). And similarly, when Cicero[189] subsequently speaks about the nature of the soul with expressions that sound as if they had been interpolated from Descartes's writings into his own (*naturae individuae et incorporae, omnis concretionis et materiae expers*[W]), he immediately raises the question there of whether the soul is fire, air, or water – or as Empedocles had held in this regard, a mixture of the finest parts of the four elements.

Nevertheless, even in those times when one had least disembodied it, and before one had elevated it to a substratum of mental powers – or

[187] Plato (429–347 BC), Aristotle (384–322 BC).

[188] Reading *Blick* in place of *Blut*, as in the 1790 edition.

[V] [Aristotle], *Nicomachean Ethics*, bk. 10, ch. 7 [1177b–1178a]. [Cited by Reinhold simply as "*De moribus*, bk. 10, ch. 7," as short for *Aristotelis Ethicorum, siue De moribus ad Nicomachum, libri decem*.]

[189] Marcus Tullius Cicero (106–43 BC).

[W] [It [a soul] is of an individual and incorporeal nature, and it is devoid of all matter.] *Later Academic Questions*, bk. 4, ch. 39. [This passage is not to be found at the location Reinhold cites.]

more properly speaking, to a pure intelligence – the aforesaid sensible schema had absolutely no influence, or at least no detrimental influence, on belief in a future life. Since the experiences of death and destruction did not extend beyond the visible and – if I may allow myself the expression – corporeal body,[190] the invisible [153] body of the soul remained unbesmirched by the terrifying testimony of those experiences. The invisibility of this body protected it in the eyes of the unmetaphysical child of nature much more effectively against the arrows of death than its simplicity ever was able to protect it in the eyes of the philosophical world. With this [notion of] simplicity the Schools subsequently not only snatched the soul away from these arrows but also transported it beyond the horizon of everything comprehensible. Even if its nature, as it was conceived prior to and outside the Schools, yielded no proof for its continuing existence after death, it still encouraged at least the expectation of such an existence that one had formed because of persuasion by grounds of another kind. For the Greek and Roman populace not only were the shades that represented the souls of the deceased incapable of being seen except by means of a miracle, but they were also incapable of being destroyed by any power of the gods, even at the site of their punishment. And these shades were no more capable of being seen or destroyed than was the extended repository or substratum of spiritual nature, which the most zealous defenders of immortality among the Greek and Roman philosophers were also forced to accept simply because they could not think of an actually existing thing without its persistence in space and, consequently, without extension.

This is how matters stood with the two aforementioned components of the psychological concept of reason, i.e., [154] simplicity and substantiality, until the third – which is actually first and foremost in the natural order of things but which with proper forethought I have reserved for this place in the discussion – had advanced far enough along the path of its development to divide the Schools into two main factions concerning the nature of the faculty of cognition.

This third component is the concept of the power of thinking. It gradually emerged from the confused representation of hypostatized

[190] *Leiblichen Körper*, i.e., the body of mere flesh. *Körper* and *Leib* both mean "body," but *Leib* is used literally only to refer to the body of an animal, and not a supernatural or merely mechanical entity.

life, and, depending on whether it strayed to the right or to the left of the boundary-line that divides and connects the understanding and sensibility, it was either elevated to a pure Platonic intelligence or degraded to an Epicurean modification of sentient atoms.

Since the elucidation of the specific manner in which the human spirit arrived at the distinction between thinking and sensing is not essentially tied up with my present aim, I am reserving it for a more pressing occasion in the near future. Here I am content to remark that even in regard to this distinction, which[191] defines one of the most important epochs in the history of reason's psychological concept,[192] agreement about what the distinction itself was came just as prematurely as disagreement about its explanation. Prior to the appearance of the Critique of Reason, by which [155] sensibility, as the receptivity of our faculty of cognition, was distinguished with complete determination from the receptivity of our sense organs, the true relation of sensibility to the understanding remained a deep mystery. For the Critique of Reason explained for the first time sensibility as an essential part of our faculty of cognition that is present in the mind before all sensation and before all receptivity of the organs (which themselves are perceived only through sensation), and it showed the essential cooperation of sensibility with the understanding in all actual cognition. Given this fact, we should be all the less surprised that in the earlier eras of philosophy sensation was sometimes made into a property of the body and sometimes made into a property of a separate soul that was closely related to the body. The more frequently and extensively one busied oneself with speculation, the more the difference between abstract concepts and sensations was bound to become visible. And the fact that the soul appeared to be working together with the body in its sensations but to be working alone in its abstract concepts must have served as a powerful influence on the explanation of both. The almost complete neglect of empirical psychology and the old original sin of speculative philosophers – that of rushing ahead of experience and observation in their explanations – were the cause of close to nothing significant at all being achieved in the way

[191] The 1790 ed. (p. 220) inserts here "*as fact* [*Tatsache*]."

[192] By "reason's psychological concept" Reinhold means not a psychological concept of reason's powers, but reason's concept of a psychological being. In the 1790 edition he makes this clearer by speaking of reason's psychological "idea" of the subject, in Kant's sense of a transcendental notion that defines a whole rational discipline in a pure way.

of a theory of thinking and sensing even in the best periods of Greek philosophy. [156] Moreover, these two factors were the cause of either assuming two different souls – one thinking and one sensing – in order to explain the distinction between understanding and sensibility, or of abolishing that distinction, on account of the very same hypotheses that had been forged for its explanation, in order to save the unity of the soul.

The mere fact that one had to deny the sensing soul all cognition of truth (even of its own representations)[193] in order to endow the thinking soul with this cognition brought the designation of irrationality upon the sensing soul. In what followed, the age-old and forever misunderstood doctrine concerning the relativity of the sensible properties of external things sanctioned a far worse meaning for that designation. At a very early stage common experiences of differences in taste, smell, touch, etc. in different human beings – or even in one and the same human being at different times – must have already occasioned in thinking minds the entirely correct observation that our representations of sensible properties depend just as much on the constitution of our sense organs as on the effects of the things outside us.[194] With a leap that even the more cautious reason of modern philosophers[x] has [157] frequently ventured, one was taken beyond this observation to the more or less distinctly conceived proposition that all sensible properties are merely relations of things[195] to our sense organs[196] (not to our faculty of intuition in general). Already with the Eleatics it was asserted that actual things could not at all be as they appear

[193] The 1790 ed. (p. 222) replaces "(even of its own representations)" with "(even with respect to sensible representations)."

[194] The 1790 ed. (p. 222) replaces "on the effects of the things outside us" with "on the distinctive natures of things in themselves."

[x] Most recently *Weishaupt* in his remarkable writing, *On Materialism and Idealism* [(Nuremberg, 1786)]. [Adam Weishaupt (1748–1830) was a leader of the Illuminati, a radical secret society. For recent research on the relations between Weishaupt and Reinhold, see two essays in *Philosophie ohne Beynamen. System, Freiheit und Geschichte im Denken Karl Leonhard Reinholds*, ed. M. Bondeli and A. Lazzari (Basle, Schwabe, 2004): Sabine Roehr, "Reinholds *Hebräische Mysterien oder die älteste religiöse Freimauerei*: Eine Apologie des Freymauertums," pp. 160–4, and George di Giovanni, "*Die Verhandlungen über die Grundbegriffe und Grundsätze der Moralität* von 1798 oder Reinhold als Philosoph des gemeinen Verstandes," pp. 380–7.]

[195] The 1790 ed. (p. 222) replaces "things" with "external things."

[196] *Organisation*. Reinhold uses this term sometimes to mean the sense organs themselves, and sometimes the distinctive way in which they are organized.

and that, consequently, judgments of reason, in so far as they are grounded on the testimony of the senses, must necessarily be false.[197] Before the famous distinction that Locke established between the *qualitatibus primariis* and *secundariis*,[y] variability in the testimony of the senses and, along with it, the deceptiveness of the senses had been taken much too far in general. And even after that distinction was established, this variability and deceptiveness were kept within only very indeterminate bounds until the Critique of Reason specified more precisely the aforementioned distinction between the receptivity of the sense organs, which itself is only a perceived representation, and the receptivity of sensibility in general,[198] which first makes all representations possible. For only after presupposing this distinction does it emerge in a sufficiently illuminating way that while the subjective [158] constitution of the organs is certainly subject to variations, sensibility (the faculty of intuition in general) is not at all. In so far as the sensible properties of things outside us refer merely to the constitution of the sense organs (*qualitates secundariae*[199]), they can be called variable illusions;[200] but, in so far as they are grounded on the laws of sensibility, they are invariable appearances[201] and thus carry with themselves the very same truth and credibility[202] that one rightly presupposed beforehand, though vainly sought, in things in themselves.

I return now to the object of my study. – One very natural consequence of the misunderstood doctrine concerning the deceptiveness of sensory cognition was that the philosophers who subscribed to this doctrine, without however adopting completely skeptical *akatalēpsian*[203] (as

[197] The 1790 ed. (p. 223) inserts: "It was a doctrine that, to be sure, has been modified, abridged, and expanded in very different ways by the *skeptics* and *idealists* of modern times, but which, taken on the whole, has not been raised to a higher degree of evidence and determinacy than that which it had already reached among the Greeks according to the report of *Sextus Empiricus* [c. AD 200]."

[y] *Descartes*, in his *Principiis Philosophiae* part IV, §198, had already noted this distinction [between primary and secondary qualities] very clearly where he states, "*Nihil a nobis in objectis externis* sensu *deprehendi praeter ipsorum* figuram, magnitudinem, *et* motum." ["By means of our senses we apprehend nothing in external objects beyond their shapes, sizes and motions." Translation from Descartes, *Principles of Philosophy*, in *The Philosophical Writings of Descartes*, vol. 1, tr. J. Cottingham et al. (Cambridge, Cambridge University Press, 1985), p. 284. Cf. Locke, *An Essay Concerning Human Understanding*, II.viii.9. Reinhold's 1790 ed. (p. 223) replaces "very clearly" with "rather clearly."]

[198] The 1790 ed. (p. 223) replaces "of sensibility in general" with "*of the faculty of representation.*"

[199] Secondary qualities. [200] *Schein*. See above, n. 149. [201] *Erscheinungen*.

[202] The 1790 ed. (p. 224) replaces "carry with themselves the very same truth and credibility" with "contain the very same necessity and universality, and, hence, *objective truth.*"

[203] Incomprehension, a term from ancient skepticism signifying a lack of comprehension of matters beyond phenomena.

Pyrrho and Arcesilaus[204] later did), not only excluded sensibility from the cognitive faculty of the rational soul but directly opposed it. That is, they asserted two souls that were opposed to each other, and not merely distinct from one another, and they declared the reliable ideas[205] of rational souls to be innate in order to exempt them from a suspect origin in deceptive sensibility. Plato's innate concepts certainly must be distinguished from the concepts of the understanding and the pure intuitions of the Critique of Reason, which, as conditions [159] of cognition, refer to experience. Plato's concepts were representations of things in themselves, representations which that great man[206] allowed the understanding to have not only in thought but also in intuition, and which he derived from a former supernatural life of the soul. For him, all cognition of truth in the present life was thus a mere recollection of the previous one, just as every error of the understanding was a consequence of the connection of the thinking soul with the sentient soul and the body, which he looked upon as a prison and as a natural antagonist of the thinking soul.

Because Aristotle very much distanced himself from the opinions of his teacher with regard to both the deceptiveness of sensory cognition and the origin of concepts, his distinction between the rational and the sentient souls, which he took to be two wholly different beings with wholly different lines of descent, is all the more striking. To be sure, his explanation of the faculty of cognition comes closest to the truth of all those among his predecessors and contemporaries. He not only grants to the rational soul a faculty for judging the similarities and differences between sensible representations (*koinē aisthēsis*) as Plato had already done, but he even concedes to it the representation of sensible objects and, to a certain extent, sensation by [160] distinguishing a passive and an active understanding (*nous pathētikos* and *poiētikos*) and by declaring the former to be a distinct faculty for comprehending sensible images. Moreover, the production of these images itself presupposes a power of representation in addition to the effects of external objects and of the sense organs – organs which themselves belong among those objects. Yet despite all of this, this production was credited by him, just as by Plato, to the account of a distinct sensible and irrational soul, which he took to be

[204] Pyrrho of Elis (365–275 BC), Arcesilaus (316–242 BC). [205] *Ideen.*

[206] The 1790 ed. (p. 224) replaces "that great man" with "this great predecessor of our celebrated *Leibniz*."

part of a distinct animal power that, according to his view, was spread throughout the whole world as the principle of life and sensation in all living creatures. His rational soul, in contrast, was taken from a fiery or ethereal nature that was entirely different from both the four bodily elements and that animal power; and this soul came from somewhere outside to its punishment in the body, from which it also became separated when it left behind the sentient soul and even the passive understanding in order to continue its life in another state.

What was not at all grasped was how understanding and sensibility were supposed to be essentially different and yet essential parts of one and the same faculty of cognition. For Aristotle, the passive or sentient understanding was supposed to explain the unity of the faculty of cognition, and the two different souls were supposed to explain the distinction between [161] thinking and sensing. In all the other philosophical schools – schools that did not adopt the expediency of two souls – this distinction disappeared. Epicurus, who was likely misled by the entirely correct observation that the understanding needs sense experience for its development and that abstract representations are derived from those of sense, traced back to sensation all the powers of the soul, understanding and reason, and made sensory evidence (*enargeia*) into the source of all conviction and certainty.[z] Zeno,[207] in contrast – or more properly, the Stoic school – seems to have excluded sensible intuition from any distinctive cooperative role with the understanding in the cognition of truth, or rather, seems to have traced this cognition back entirely to the understanding. For he derived the effects of sensibility, the stirrings of the faculty of desire – the affects and passions – from the judgments of the understanding, and he allowed everything to be truly or falsely cognized by means of the understanding alone. Hence, both schools, the Stoic as well as the Epicurean, did not recognize any distinction between the rational and sentient souls. [162] As a negative consequence of conflating essentially different modes of cognition, morality turned into a mere unattainable ideal of reason in the Stoic system and into a wholly calculated system of self-interestedness and refined sensibility in the Epicurean system. And as a further negative consequence, the doctrine of

[z] For Epicurus [341–270 BC], both *prolepseis* [anticipations] and *kataleipseis* [comprehensions] belonged to sensibility. They were *representations of absent objects*, acquired from previous sense impressions, and the criterion of their truth was their agreement with new sense impressions.

[207] Zeno of Citium (334–262 BC).

immortality disappeared in both. Nothing survived eternally but prime matter and the substance of the deity in the one system, and atoms and the void in the other. In both systems, the soul came into and passed out of existence with the body – a fate with which it purchased the salvation of one part of its faculty of cognition at much too high a price.

The Stoics as well as the Epicureans elevated sensibility to the point of making it the source of all concepts. Like present-day followers of the celebrated Locke, they believed that they could show how truths of experience emerge from a multiplicity of homogeneous sense impressions, how universal concepts and principles emerge from truths of experience, and how reason emerges from all of these taken together. Now, what was more natural than their view that whatever had emerged with and through the use of the sense organs had to end with the sense organs? They would have had to deny the indispensability of the latter in sensation in order to allow their sentient understanding, or [163] their comprehending sensation, to survive the destruction of the sense organs. Aristotle, in contrast – while holding that for the rational soul all concepts, including even those most proper to the soul, are owed to the senses – helped himself to an animal soul, which he then placed in immediate communion with the senses through sensation and left to share in their fate at death.

Regardless of the fact, then, that all of the aforementioned philosophical schools were in agreement amongst themselves that the material of the soul[208] was of a different and finer kind than flesh, the variety of their views on the sensible and rational faculties of cognition still had an unmistakable influence on their ideas concerning the very nature of the soul's material[209] itself. Those who adopted a sentient soul alongside a thinking soul derived the latter from a nobler part of the world-soul, or directly from the deity, and granted it immortality without exception. Others abolished the distinction between the two souls and either, like Epicurus, denied the world-soul or, like the Eleatics, Heraclitus, and the Stoics, regarded the soul as nothing more than mere matter, air, fire, or water. And they asserted its mortality directly. The sentient soul – whether or not one immediately recognized in it the faculty for thinking [164] – was too narrowly tied and too closely related to the flesh to be capable of the better fate that only the supersensible power of

[208] The 1790 ed. (p. 228) replaces "soul" with "soul's substance."

[209] *Seelenstoff*, not literally matter but the content that makes a soul whatever it is.

thinking[210] had, thanks to its spontaneity and affinity with the first spontaneous cause. In this way, through the misunderstanding of its proper ground of explanation, the distinction between thinking and sensing occasioned spiritualism and materialism almost two thousand years ago, when the pure concept of spirituality was developed and established. One half of the philosophical world at that time directed its attention more to the co-presence of sensibility and understanding in one and the same faculty of cognition. For those philosophers, sensibility and understanding were thus taken to be attributes[211] of one and the same[212] subject, and they (like the Stoics) declared sensibility to be a modification of the understanding or (like the Epicureans) the understanding to be a modification of sensibility. The subject[213] of this soul, however, which was taken to be immediately connected to the flesh through sensation, was declared to be of a material similar in nature to flesh. And this material was subjected to a constant ebb and flow just like the particles of air and fire that either constituted the world-soul or were composed of the finest atoms of Epicurus – particles that more or less penetrated the flesh or, after its destruction, had to cease penetrating it. – The other half of the philosophical world, in contrast, [165] which had the essential distinction between understanding and sensibility more in view, found the co-presence of these two properties in one and the same subject contradictory and thus inferred the existence of two different souls. Only one of these souls (the sentient soul) was composed of the ebbing and flowing particles of fire that belonged to the cruder world-soul, and it perished with the flesh. The other (the thinking soul), in contrast, was an immutable, enduring, and indestructible essence that was taken from the divine part of the world-soul, an emanation from the deity itself. Both factions, the materialist as well as the spiritualist, inferred the mortality or immortality of the soul more from the concepts they formed of the faculty of cognition than from those they formed of the substratum of the soul. – I shall have to reserve the further course of the fate belonging to reason's psychological concept for my next letter.

[210] The 1790 ed. (p. 228) replaces "only the supersensible power of thinking" with "the supersensible power of thought in the Aristotelian and Platonic systems."
[211] The 1790 ed. (p. 229) replaces "attributes" with "predicates."
[212] The 1790 ed. (p. 229) inserts "logical."
[213] The 1790 ed. (p. 229) replaces "subject" with "substance."

[247] Eighth Letter: Continuation of the preceding letter: The master key to the rational psychology of the Greeks

Thank you for the direct communication of your doubts concerning the latter half of my previous letter, or more precisely, concerning the elucidation of the materialism and spiritualism of the ancients that I attempted there and whose grounds I, admittedly, have not so much developed as merely indicated.

The reply to your objections lies so little outside the path that I have struck upon with you in my history of the psychological concept of reason that, rather than merely sparing me the danger of perhaps continuing on this path presently without your company, this reply will take us both a considerable distance further along it.

You are, then, in agreement with me regarding at least the following results that emerged from my last two letters:

> [248] If the subject[214] of our representations (or the soul, in so far as it is more than the mere faculty of cognition) is as unknown today as it was six thousand years ago and must remain unknown as long as humanity remains humanity; if the idea of a simple substance can in no way designate[215] actual properties[216] of the thinking subject that have been discovered through a gradual acquaintance with it; if this idea contains nothing more and nothing less than the rule of the logical distinction between the unknown subject of inner sense and

[214] The 1790 ed. (p. 230) replaces "subject" with "substantiality of the *subject*."
[215] Reading, with the 1790 ed., *bezeichnen* for *bezeichen*.
[216] The 1790 ed. (p. 231) replaces "actual properties" with "a *cognizable property*."

the known objects of outer sense; and if this rule of reason has not been extracted from things in themselves but rather drawn from those laws of our faculty of cognition which lie at the basis of the ancient, enduring, and popular distinction between body and soul – then it is evident that the forms of representation that have emerged in the history of philosophy concerning the soul's simplicity and substantiality, as well as its thinking and sensing, must have been determined by the current degree of insight into the nature of the faculty of cognition. Right with the first use of reason – and even without being recognized as such – the natural laws of the faculty of cognition alone could and had to give rise to the distinction between body and soul. But the true significance[217] of this distinction [249], the cognition and use of the rule of reason that serves as the genuine ground for it – in a word, the meaning[218] of the psychological concept of reason by all means presupposed cognition of those natural laws and was therefore relative to the degree and state of this cognition. The faculty of cognition was bound to be misunderstood for a long time and in a variety of ways before the simple, yet on that account no less deeply hidden laws could be discovered that tie together the distinction and connection between sensibility and understanding, between inner and outer sense, and between understanding and reason. And since these laws (like every other law of nature) necessarily had their effect even without being recognized, they themselves were also the ground for seeking outside their domain[219] the distinction between body and soul that they had generated; moreover, they were the ground for believing that this distinction could be explained by any one of the many hypotheses about the objective nature of the soul. And because the principal question here always concerned none other than the subject of the faculty of cognition,[220] the views concerning the nature of the faculty of cognition had to have a decisive influence on these hypotheses.

Thus, you also found it very natural, dear friend, that I attempted to derive the materialism and spiritualism of Greek philosophy – that [250] is, its division over the transient or intransient nature of the soul – from a misunderstanding regarding the distinction between sensibility and

[217] *Sinn.* [218] *Bedeutung.*

[219] The 1790 ed. (p. 232) replaces "outside their domain" with "in things in themselves outside the faculty of representation."

[220] The 1790 ed. (p. 232) replaces "cognition" with "*representation* (the *representing thing*)."

understanding, a misunderstanding that was common to and unavoidable for all schools. The reason, you write, why my attempt did not entirely satisfy you lies partly in your previous conviction that the materialism and spiritualism of the ancients can be explained even more succinctly and naturally by their views on the nature of the world-soul, and partly in your conjecture that the misunderstanding that I have turned into my ground of explanation amounts to a mere dispute about words. For you suppose that the confusing of sensibility with understanding, by which I sought to explain materialism, and the separation of sensibility and understanding, by which I sought to explain spiritualism, would much more likely be found in the expressions than in the concepts of the ancients.

I happily concede to you, dear friend, that with your two objections you also have on your side the authority of the most preeminent philosophical writers, and especially of the more recent historians of philosophy. Because in the previous state of speculative philosophy it was simply impossible to combine the views of the Greeks on thinking and sensing or to bring them under one viewpoint, the only two options open to previous historians [251] of philosophy whenever they dealt with those views were either to charge the most sophisticated minds of antiquity with the crudest of contradictions[221] or to suppose a hidden agreement of concepts beneath their diverse claims.[222] This slashing[223] of the knot, of which our philosophical compendiums of history have furnished so many examples, was thus also the usual way of pulling oneself out of the quandary into which one was propelled after perceiving the strange fact "that two thousand years before Descartes – and hence two thousand years before the development of the concept of a simple substance – the Greeks inferred the mortality or immortality of the soul directly from the corporeal or incorporeal nature of the soul."[224] It was impossible to hide

[221] The 1790 ed. (p. 233) inserts a footnote here: "E.g., Mr. Meiners. See his *History of the Sciences.*" [Christian Meiners (1747–1810), *Geschichte des Ursprungs, Fortgangs, und Verfalls der Wissenschaften in Griechenland und Rom* (*History of the Origin, Growth, and Decline of the Sciences in Greece and Rome*) (Lemgo, 1781/2).]

[222] The 1790 ed. (p. 233) inserts a footnote here: "E.g., Mr. Platner. See the remarks concerning Greek philosophy that accompany his *Aphorisms.*" [Ernst Platner (1744–1818), *Philosophische Aphorismen nebst einigen Anleitungen zur Philosophiegeschichte* (*Philosophical Aphorisms Accompanied by Introductory Observations on the History of Philosophy*) (Leipzig, 1776, 2nd ed., 1784).]

[223] The 1790 ed. (p. 233) inserts "or tightening."

[224] Inserting closing quotation mark, as in the 1790 ed.

from the fact that the Greeks thought about the nature of the simple in an essentially different way than we do, that even those who held the substance of the soul to be indivisible were far from the idea of regarding it as unextended, and that they therefore no more grounded the indestructibility of the soul on the absence of all parts (or even on homogeneous parts) than they grounded its destructibility on its extended[225] nature. So, whence arose this transient or intransient nature of the soul, which was not inferred from the necessity or[226] impossibility of the extension of [252] the soul, but was nonetheless attributed to its substance? – The more recent philosophical writers whom I have consulted on this matter have replied with an almost unanimous voice: "From the various concepts of the destructible or indestructible nature of the world-soul, from which the ancients derived the substance of the human soul." And I, like you, my friend, have for a long time allowed myself to be content with this answer. But let us see whether the genuine difficulty has been thereby denied rather than cleared away. First of all, it is not even the case that all philosophical schools sought the origin of the human soul in the world-soul. The Epicureans did not recognize a world-soul at all, and Aristotle distinguished the fifth nature – from which he had the human soul emerge – not only from the substance of the deity but also from the animal power, which, as the universally disseminated principle of life and sensation, took the place of the world-soul for him. But let us assume – as I myself conceded in more than one place in my previous letter – that the influence of views about the nature of the world-soul on views about the nature of the human soul in all the other systems was always more far-reaching than it actually was.[227] But whence then, according to this presupposition, were the ideals taken for the faculty of cognition with which one endowed these various [253] world-souls, and through which alone they acquired the name "souls"? Whence, I ask, could these ideals be taken other than from the archetype

[225] Reading *unausgedehnte* as *ausgedehnte*, as in the 1790 ed.

[226] Reading *auch* as *aus*, as in the 1790 ed.

[227] The 1790 ed. (pp. 234–5) replaces the following two sentences with: "On account of this very presupposition the following questions are raised: How did the idea of the world-soul itself arise? And whence were the features taken with which one had to endow the common principle of all appearances of *life* in the whole of nature in order to be able to refer to it by the term '*soul*'? The answer to this question is then necessarily traced back to the concept of the *human soul* as the only possible archetype for all representing powers, souls, and spirits thinkable by us – excluding not even the divine."

of the human being, the only possible archetype for all faculties of cognition, souls, and spirits thinkable by us – excluding not even the divine? Whence the thinking and intransient, or the sentient and transient world-soul? Whence the elevation of the pure power of thinking, of intelligence, to the eternal nature of the deity, and whence the degradation of the faculty of sensation to the perishability of the bestial body? – Thus, you see our question here again – and it is provoked by the very same answer through which earlier it was believed to have been necessarily done away with. My answer, which I have attempted to offer in terms of an ancient and universal misunderstanding of the distinction between thinking and sensing, has then only your second objection still left against it, which supposes that whole misunderstanding to be merely apparent and seeks to trace it back to a difference in expressions rather than in the concepts themselves. Your opinion is that:

> However much he otherwise opposes sensibility to understanding, even Plato in no way directly denies sensibility to the rational soul; he concedes to the rational soul not only the faculty [254] for distinguishing similarities and differences between sense impressions but also a faculty of intuition, which belonged to it even prior to its connection with the body.[aa] From the opposite perspective, Epicurus, while tracing the concepts of the understanding back to sensation, does not on that account deny either the understanding or its distinction from sensibility. And this is evidenced already by the simple fact that this philosopher confers upon the understanding the faculty for checking, reporting, and confirming the testimony of the senses. It can be shown even more easily that Aristotle's division of the faculty of cognition into a rational and an irrational soul was merely figurative, and that while the Stoics confused some of the operations of the understanding with those of sensibility, they otherwise distinguished the two sources of cognition very precisely, regardless of the intimate connection they asserted between them. From all of this it follows that the Greeks were at bottom just as

[aa] One of our philosophical historians has *Plato* claim that *the senses are in the soul* and cites the words, "*he aisthēsis (esi) dynamis psychēs, to de organon sōmatos*" [the sensory powers (are in) the soul, but the organ is in the body], which *Plutarch* puts in the mouth of *Plato* (*The Tenets of the Philosophers*). [This work is now ascribed not to Plutarch of Chaeronea (c. 46–120) but to Pseudo-Plutarch, *Placita Philosophorum*, bk. 4, ch. 8. Reinhold cites it simply as "*de Placit. philos.*, bk. 1, ch. 20."] Regarding whether Plutarch has correctly understood Plato here, and whether "*psyche* [soul]" here means *rational* soul, the text of this philosophical historian remains silent.

> much in agreement as our present-day philosophers regarding both the unity of the human faculty of cognition and the diversity of its essential components. [255] And, consequently, it follows that the diversity of their views on the duration of the soul had to be derived from grounds entirely different from the ones found in their supposed separation of the power of thinking from sensibility or in their confusion of the two sources of cognition. –

I am entirely of your opinion, dear friend, that, with regard to their views on the nature of the faculty of cognition, our modern philosophers have until now had little over the Greeks. Moreover, I share your opinion that probably more than one thread can be found that would tie together the hypotheses of the Greeks as well as the systems of the moderns. I have also never thought that the ancient spiritualists completely denied the unity of the faculty of cognition or that the materialists completely denied the distinction between its components. There is a connection as well as a distinction between thinking and sensing about which Plato was just as much in agreement with Epicurus, and Zeno with Aristotle, as Leibniz later was with Locke, and Mendelssohn with Helvétius.[228] But there is also a connection and a distinction between these two sources of cognition that Plato, Epicurus, Zeno, and Aristotle conceived differently, no less than Leibniz, Locke, Helvétius, and Mendelssohn did.[229] There is a difference of opinion regarding the nature of thinking and sensing that is a consequence of the [256] different, correct viewpoints from which different thinkers considered the faculty of cognition. But there is also a difference among those opinions that is a consequence of a single point of view not having been discovered yet, one by which all other viewpoints can be united. We shall examine more closely these two kinds of differences among the views of the ancients regarding the faculty of cognition.

Epicurus' point of view was psychological.[230] Guided by the healthy and lucid spirit of observation that constituted the character of his philosophy, Epicurus found that all the materials of thinking were produced by the senses, and that consequently both the subjects and

[228] Claude-Adrian Helvétius (1715–71). The 1790 ed. (p. 237) inserts: "In order to presume this, to presuppose it as settled – indeed even to confirm it with passages from the writings of the ancients – neither extraordinary astuteness nor any great exertion [of mind] is required."

[229] The 1790 ed. (p. 237) inserts "and whose elaboration *previous* philosophy, even with the support of all the astuteness of its representatives, had to leave unattempted."

[230] The 1790 ed. (p. 238) replaces "*psychological*" with "*empirical-psychological.*"

predicates that occupy the understanding, in so far as actual[231] objects and properties are supposed to correspond to them, must be presented entirely in sensation. Yet by stopping at the contribution that sensation makes to cognition, he failed to recognize the role in it that belongs to the understanding. For him the concepts of the understanding were therefore nothing more than left-behind impressions of sensations, and thus, in the search for truth, scarcely a task was left to the understanding besides that of holding together old impressions with new ones and observing the agreement or conflict between them. In so far as this agreement – [257] the highest criterion of all truth according to Epicurus – depended solely on the testimony of the senses, it was in no way generated by the understanding according to its own laws. Rather it was given to the understanding from the outside, just as sense impressions were given to the senses.[232] In this way Epicurus certainly conceded not only a connection but even a distinction between understanding and sensibility, for he took them to be different kinds of receptivity of one and the same soul; but he also thereby abolished the genuine and essential distinction between the two sources of cognition by confusing the spontaneity[233] of the one with the receptivity[234] of the other and by subjecting the understanding to sensibility not only in regard to its content but also in regard to the form of its concepts.

The point of view of the Stoics was moral. This school had made the grounding of morality, which it took to have been undermined by the Epicureans, into the principal end of its philosophizing. The consequence of its persistence in this viewpoint, which it pressed too far, was that it modified even its psychology according to its moral system, just as its opponent had derived its moral system from its psychology. Whereas this opponent allowed even the activities of the understanding to emerge from the source of empirical representations (sensation), the Stoic school traced even the representations of sensibility back to the source [258] of moral actions – to reason. Moreover, the latter believed that it had found the sole cause of emotions and passions in the

[231] The 1790 ed. (p. 238) replaces "actual" with "*cognizable*."

[232] The 1790 ed. (p. 238) inserts "and with regard to the form as well as the matter of its activity the mind depended wholly on sensations and things outside of it."

[233] *Selbstthätigkeit* (*Spontaneität*). Reinhold gives the German term here, followed by a Latinate equivalent in parentheses.

[234] *Empfänglichkeit* (*Receptivität*). Reinhold gives the German term here, followed by a Latinate equivalent in parentheses.

judgments of the understanding, and it declared the thinking part of the soul, *to hegemonikon*,[bb] to be the principle and seat of the sensing part[235] rather than, for instance, a mere contributing faculty of the soul. Thus, regardless of the fact that the Stoics still left room for the distinction as well as the connection between understanding and sensibility in so far as they took sensations to be effects of the sense organs[236] on the understanding and the stirrings of the faculty of desire to be effects of the understanding on the sense organs, it remains just as undeniable that they also failed to recognize the genuine and essential distinction between the two sources of cognition. That is, they imposed on the understanding, in addition to its distinctive activity of thinking, the distinctive properties of sensibility – sensing and desiring. Or, as I have already expressed it above, they made sensibility into a modification of the understanding, just as their antipodes, the Epicureans, transformed the understanding into a modification of sensibility.

The point of view of Aristotle was, at least in part, logical. With his acute analysis [259] of the faculty of cognition, he was the first to arrive at a clear and determinate distinction between the judgments of the understanding and its concepts and between these concepts and the mere representations of sensibility. As a result he was also put in a position to cross over to the viewpoint of Epicurus, in so far as it was correct, and to derive the content of the concepts of the understanding from sensibility without thereby abolishing the essential distinction between the two sources of cognition. He sets down a detailed account of this distinction on very many occasions in his writings, but principally in the third chapter of the third book *On the Soul*, where he wholly occupies himself with the proof of the proposition, *hoti ou tauton esi to aisthanesthai kai to noein*.[cc] In other places (e.g., *Posterior Analytics*, bk. 1, ch. 25) he declares even more expressly that there is no sensation of the universal and that sensibility can supply only the particular (*to kathalou adunaton aisthanesthai ouk esi tou kathalou hē aisthēsis*), from which the understanding separates the universal and thinks it according to its own laws. Who,

[bb] More properly speaking, the ruling part.

[235] The 1790 ed. (p. 239) replaces "the principle and seat of the sensing part" with "the ground or the substratum of all the other [faculties]."

[236] *Organisation*.

[cc] That sensing and thinking are not the same thing.

then, will dispute the claim advanced, my friend, by you and by the historians of philosophy that Aristotle taught the distinction and connection between understanding and sensibility? But concerning this claim have you also closely considered the nature of this connection as Aristotle himself explains it? [260] As has already been mentioned, he distinguished between the active understanding, which thinks the universal,[237] and the passive understanding, which receives the particular, or the matter of sensibility. From a logical perspective, this passive understanding constituted, as it were, the bond with which Aristotle joined the spontaneity of the understanding to the receptivity of the senses; from a metaphysical perspective, this was, as it were, the point of division by which he not only distinguished the one from the other but also essentially separated the two, and assigned them to different subjects. From the latter perspective, then, the passive understanding was for him not the cause but the mere effect of the connection between understanding and sensation, or more precisely, of the connection between the thinking and sensing soul that ceased with death. According to the opinion of Aristotle, only the active understanding survived the cessation of this connection; the passive understanding, along with the sensing soul, shared in the fate of the sense organs.

And here we catch Aristotle at the same time with the point of view of his profound teacher, which was metaphysical. Plato's investigations into the soul were not so much logical analyses of the laws of thought or psychological observations regarding the subjective constitution of the faculty of cognition as they were metaphysical considerations of [261] the nature, origin, and objective properties in general of the thinking and sensing being in itself. He confused the faculty of cognition with its unknown subject, or if you prefer, he inferred from the nature of the one to the nature of the other.[238] But in so doing, of course, he allowed himself neither more nor less than what all the dogmatists after him – materialists as well as spiritualists – allowed themselves. Indeed, they were utterly forced to make such inferences until the Critique of Reason demonstrated from the very nature of the faculty of cognition that, for us, the subject of that faculty necessarily is and must always remain

237 The 1790 ed. (p. 241) replaces "thinks the universal" with "represents the *universal*, which is grounded in *things in themselves*."

238 The 1790 ed. (p. 242) replaces "from the nature of the one to the nature of the other" with "from the misunderstood nature of these faculties to the nature of the substances to which they belong."

[a something] = *X*. For the time being, I will restrict myself merely to that part of the Platonic theory of the thinking and sensing soul which was retained by Aristotle – or rather, which Aristotle amended and determined more precisely – and thus I will remain silent about Plato's doctrine of innate concepts and his doctrine of the deceptiveness of sensory cognition, however important their influence was on his view of the nature of the rational soul, as we shall subsequently see. Both philosophers were in agreement that the faculty of cognition behaves actively when thinking and passively when sensing, and that it absolutely requires the instruments of the senses in order to be capable of the latter state. Moreover if, as our historians of philosophy would have it,[239] they took the sensing soul [262] to be the organization and excitability, or receptivity, of the sense organs – a soul which they both very often referred to as "irrational" (*to alogon*) – then this fact itself already makes manifest that they had distinguished its subject from the subject of the rational soul. For them, the rational soul was the efficient cause of thinking, and the sensing soul was the efficient cause of sensing. Thinking belonged to the one as the expression of its own proper power, whereas sensing belonged to the other only on account of the influence of something else, a foreign power. Supposing too, finally, that they believed the cooperation of the rational soul to be indispensable to the functioning of the organs in sensation, it is in any case not subject to doubt that they took the cooperation of the sensing soul to be quite dispensable to the life and continuing existence of the rational soul in its most proper activity. The sensibility belonging to the power of thinking – or as Aristotle called it, the passive understanding – was so inessential to the rational soul that the soul left the passive understanding behind with the body at death and continued living and thinking better without it. Plato's sensing soul, which was essentially distinguished from his rational soul, has been interpreted as a merely poetic manner of representation.[240] But this is without considering that the unpoetic Aristotle – who indisputably advanced furthest among all the philosophers of antiquity with regard to logical and psychological insights into the nature of the faculty of cognition [263] – straightforwardly declared the sensing soul to be the

[239] The 1790 ed. (p. 243) replaces "as our historians of philosophy would have it" with "as some recent writers claim."
[240] See below, n. hh.

power of a separate subject and not something like a modification of the rational soul, and that he assigned to each of the two souls a unique nature and origin of its own. To the rational soul he assigned a fifth species of being, different from the four known elements, for which he invented its own name "entelechy," and which he held to be part of the ethereal substance[241] that constituted the stars.[dd] To the sensing soul, in contrast, he assigned that animal power which, according to his view, was spread throughout the whole of nature as the principle of life and sensation – a power common to human beings and animals, and one that both developed with the body from the seed and disintegrated with the body back into its former components.[ee]

The most distinguished Greek schools thus failed to recognize either the essential distinction between the two components of the faculty of cognition (the Epicureans and Stoics) or their essential connection (the Peripatetics[242] and Platonists). – This common result of my historical-critical presentation of Greek psychology will be even more illuminating for you once I have shown you the necessary [264] ground of its origin in the ancient and universal misunderstanding regarding the nature of the faculty of cognition. This misunderstanding was unavoidable until the human spirit had continued exercising its powers long enough to become capable of an analysis of its faculty of cognition as precise and complete as that which the Critique of Reason has supplied.

In this work Kant discovered a new, or at least heretofore wholly unrecognized, source of human cognition – pure sensibility.[243] It is neither the activity of the sense organs nor their excitability, but rather the faculty of the soul for being affected in general, and it consists in the conditions present in our faculty of cognition that lie at the basis of every intuition (immediate representation) of an object. It is the subjective constitution of the faculty of intuition, and it is called its universal form because all intuitions are determined through it. It is the receptivity of

[241] The 1790 ed. (p. 244) replaces "he held to be part of the ethereal substance" with "he took to be of one nature with the ethereal substance."

[dd] Aristotle, *On the Generation and Corruption of Animals*, bk. 2, ch. 3.
[ee] Aristotle, *On the Soul*, bk. 3, ch. 5. – Cicero, *Tusculan Disputations* I.10.26.

[242] I.e., the followers of Aristotle.
[243] See Appendix, section II for the heavily revised and expanded version of the text that begins here and ends on p. 266 of the Eighth Letter from the *Merkur* with the sentence that concludes, "and sensing part of our faculty of cognition."

the soul, which must precede all impressions from the sense organs because it is presupposed by each of them. But precisely because it is a mere faculty, a mere subjective form, a mere receptivity, objects must be given to it – or rather, it must be affected by objects. And the affecting of pure sensibility by objects is what Kant calls sensation, empirical [265] intuition. Now, because pure sensibility provides the form while sensation supplies the matter for empirical intuition, there can be no sensory cognition, no immediate representation of an object, without pure sensibility and sensation. A representation of an object mediated by a feature of it or by a predicate (a concept) is essentially different from intuition and is an effect of the understanding in the widest sense, the spontaneity of the soul, the faculty for thinking and even generating representations. Because these representations that are to be generated can only ever be predicates or features of objects, they presuppose given objects and thus also the faculty for being affected by objects – pure sensibility and sensation. In its most essential operations, the understanding thus relates to pure sensibility and sensation, just as sensibility and sensation relate to the understanding, in so far as objects are not merely to be given through them but also cognized. Hence, pure sensibility supplies the form of intuition, and sensation its content; intuition supplies the content of the concept, and the understanding its form – so that without the cooperation of pure sensibility, sensation, and the understanding, there can be no cognition of an actual object. And this, in general, is the result of the Critique of Reason regarding the connection [266] and distinction between the thinking and sensing part of our faculty of cognition.

Prior to this theory – which restricts our cognizing to only those objects that can be given to sensibility and, consequently, declares as impossible all cognition that is of things in themselves and that goes beyond sensory representation – the genuine distinction as well as connection between thinking and sensing was necessarily misunderstood. As long as one believed that one cognized things in themselves; as long as one projected the predicates of intuitions onto subjects beyond intuitions; and as long as one confused what in representations is merely the form of understanding or of pure sensibility with what can be given only through sensation – one was also forced to allow the understanding to be given its concepts, as well as sensibility its representations, by objects. Hence, the understanding had to have receptivity just as much as sensibility did, and by "receptivity of sensibility" one could think of nothing other than the receptivity of the sense organs, or at least receptivity by means of these organs. Moreover, pure sensibility, or true receptivity, which belongs neither to the understanding nor to the sense organs but rather to the faculty of cognition (the soul), was actually divided between the understanding and what one was used to calling "sensibility." [267] And it was divided in such a way that, of its two forms, the one (inner sense) was taken together with the understanding and the other (outer sense) was taken together with the sense organs – or more precisely, with its five empirical modalities, the five senses. And here, dear friend, you have the thread that will lead you safely through all the labyrinths of Greek psychology, and which I will presently follow only through the confused determinations of thinking and sensing that lead up to the boundary dividing materialism and spiritualism.

For the ancients, then, thinking meant not merely bringing unity and connection to the representations of sensibility, but also intuiting with inner sense.[244] For them, both[245] were one and the same act of the understanding. The understanding did not merely think but intuited either its proper objects, such as the essences of things for Plato and universals for Aristotle, or the objects of sensation, of the outer senses, as was the case for Epicurus and Zeno.[246] But sensing meant not just any being affected of our mind's receptivity, or any empirical intuition, but only the receptivity of outer sense, only intuition through the sense organs. More precisely, sometimes it meant the excitability, receptivity, and activity of these organs themselves, sometimes their effect on the understanding, and sometimes both at once. Thus, the sensation that Plato [268] and Aristotle attributed to the understanding was the mere activity of the sense organs or of the animal power, and the mere passivity of the rational soul. This can be seen easily enough, in Plato, in the confinement of spirit by sensibility and, in Aristotle, in the passive understanding. – Hence,

[244] The 1790 ed. (p. 252) inserts: "They allowed unity as well as the manifold to be given to the understanding by things in themselves."

[245] The 1790 ed. (p. 252) replaces "both" with "thinking and intuiting."

[246] The 1790 ed. (p. 252) replaces the following two sentences with: "But to the extent that it is referred to the subject and is an alteration of the subject's state, *sensation* did not signify just any representation arising through the passive relating of the mind and the manner of its being affected, whether it be from inside or outside; rather it signified only a being merely affected *from outside* – whether this takes place in the sense organs or is imparted to the understanding through the sense organs."

the distinction drawn between understanding and sensibility was, on the one hand, much too weak and, on the other, much too strong. It was too weak in so far as inner sense was confused with the understanding, and too strong in so far as outer sense was projected from the soul onto the body. Understanding, taken together with inner sense, was the rational soul, whereas outer sense, taken together with the sense organs, was the sensing, irrational soul. Precisely for this reason, and according to the unanimous opinion of all philosophers, the irrational soul was mortal in its nature. And it was merely this soul's distance from or proximity to the rational soul – or rather, the different points of view from which one considered its actual relation to the rational soul – that decided the mortality or immortality of the latter. If one found outer sense to be indispensable to cognition, then, when the sense organs disappeared – to which outer sense was attached – so did the entire faculty of cognition and, consequently, the understanding and the very soul itself. This was the case with the Stoics, the Epicureans, and certainly all the other materialists [269] of ancient and modern times. In contrast, if one found the understanding, with the help of inner sense – which was thought along with it – to be sufficient for a cognition on its own, then in its activity as well as its existence it was independent of the sense organs and elevated above their fate in death. And this was the case with Plato, Aristotle, and in general all the spiritualists of ancient and modern times.

From his psychological point of view, Epicurus had observed the course of development of the faculty of cognition from the first sense impressions up to the highest abstractions and had found the matter of sensibility to be indispensable in every act of the understanding.[247] He therefore tied the understanding immediately to outer sense. Similarly, the Stoics tied outer sense immediately to the understanding by insisting too one-sidedly on their moral point of view – from which they correctly subordinated sensibility to the understanding – and by crediting the most characteristic effects of sensibility to the account of the understanding without being able to deny the indispensability of the instruments of the senses in these effects. Thus, regardless of the fact that the Stoics as well as the Epicureans distinguished not only thinking from sensing but also

[247] The 1790 ed. (p. 254) replaces "in every act of the understanding" with "to the validity of the act of the understanding in cognition."

the soul from the body and even assigned to the former[248] a subject that was wholly different from the sense organs, [270] their view on the relation of the understanding to sensibility still made it impossible to grant survival after death to that subject's faculty of cognition. For they held this faculty to be a mere result of the connection of the subject to the organs of the body.

Aristotle understood this point despite his agreement[249] with the Epicureans and Stoics that all concepts obtained their content through sensibility. He was able to unify the psychological point of view, from which he had observed the development of concepts from sense impressions, with the logical point of view, which forced him to distinguish judgments from the mere concepts of the understanding and these concepts from the representations of sensibility. According to this presupposition, he attributed perception of the universal – which was, to be sure, contained in sense impressions but could in no way be cognized through sensibility – exclusively to the spontaneity of the soul, to the faculty of judgment, to the active understanding. Now, as he very clearly explains, since the universal existed in things in themselves – or in the objects outside representation[ff] – as their self-sufficient form, its representation, the universal concept, was in no way generated by the faculty of judgment but rather only [271] developed by it; and through the medium of sensibility even the understanding was given its most distinctive concepts, in regard not merely to their content but also to their form, by things in themselves. Thus, it was also the case for Aristotle that the understanding, in so far as it was spontaneous – that is, in so far as it was a wholly different faculty from sensibility – had not only spontaneity but also a faculty for being affected (by the universal). It had not only the power of judgment but also (inner) sense. Now, in so far as this receptivity of the understanding took up and represented the universal from sensible representations – or rather, the predicates of things in

[248] Reading *der ersteren* for *der letzteren*, as in the 1790 ed. (p. 254), which replaces "and even assigned to the latter a subject that was wholly different from the sense organs" with "and even assumed a special body [*Körper*], separate from the visible flesh [*Leibe*], for the substance of the former [the soul]."

[249] The 1790 ed. (p. 254) replaces "Aristotle understood this point despite his agreement" with "In Aristotle's theory, in contrast, this survival contained nothing contradictory, however much this philosopher agreed . . ."

[ff] See Aristotle's *Metaphysics*, bk. 12, ch. 6 and bk. 14, ch. 3.

themselves – it constituted an essential condition, a basic property, of the active understanding itself. Yet, in so far as it could be affected by sensibility, outer sense, and the sense organs, it was receptivity of the particular, of the individual impression; it was the passive understanding. This passive understanding was a mere result of the connection of the understanding to the sense organs, an accidental faculty of that understanding which had a receptivity and spontaneity of its own even without this connection. Consequently, nothing was lacking for the complete faculty of cognition, which, once sensibility had independently supplied the content for it, was raised above sensibility not only in judgment but even in its representations and thus also above the fate of the instruments of sense – death.

[272] Without having carried out an analysis of the faculty of cognition as precise as Aristotle's, Plato nevertheless arrived at the very same result. Even he had confused receptivity with the spontaneity of the soul – or rather, had taken inner sense together with the understanding – in so far as he conceded to the latter the faculty not only for thinking but also for intuiting the essence of things.[gg] In doing so, even he was already forced, like Aristotle, to accept the understanding as a separate, complete, and self-standing faculty of cognition and to attach to it a subject that is different from the body and outer sense.

Even if he had not asserted innate ideas or the deceptiveness of sensory cognition, Plato could have – and must have, in so far as he thought consistently – arrived at his pure intelligence merely by confusing the understanding with inner sense and outer sense with its five empirical modalities. [273] This fact will come to light from the little that I now have to say about the actual meaning of these two views of Plato and their connection to his pure intelligence.

I have already noted that Plato, just like everyone to date who has countenanced cognition of things in themselves, was forced not to allow

[gg] One of the many famous opponents of the *Kantian philosophy* has cited the distinction between *thinking* and *intuiting* as proof of the *scholastic caprice* and *sophistical subtleties* of which the Critique of Reason is supposed to be full – a distinction quite like the one to be found in *Sacculo Distinctionum, Tyrnaviae typis Soc. Jesu.* [Presumably a Jesuit work concerning a collection ("sack") of quodlibetal distinctions published at the press of the Jesuit university in Trnava, Slovakia, i.e., Tyrnaviae, Typis Collegii Academici Societatis Jesu.] For him, the *thing of thought* would no doubt be a *synonym* for the *actual thing*. [Reinhold's "opponent" may be one of the authors translated in *Kant's Early Critics: The Empiricist Critique of the Theoretical Philosophy*, ed. B. Sassen (Cambridge, Cambridge University Press, 2000).]

the concepts of the understanding to be generated in any way by the spontaneity of thinking but instead to have them intuited by the receptivity of inner sense – which was projected onto the understanding – and thus given to the understanding. As already mentioned above, with Aristotle these concepts were given by things in themselves through the medium of the sense organs. Plato, in contrast – and for reasons whose elaboration I must reserve for another place – imputed to matter[250] a certain "evil character" or "evil spirit," as he expressed it, and brought this view into a very natural connection with the old Eleatic doctrine of the deceptiveness of sensory cognition. He thus found things in themselves as well as even the sense organs, in so far as they both contained matter, absolutely unsuitable for giving the understanding its concepts.[251] Whence, then, did these concepts come? A very respectable philosophical writer[hh] has recently expressed the opinion that Plato, [274] either because he had found the solution of this problem impossible or because

[250] The 1790 ed. (p. 257) inserts a footnote here: "To mention only one of these grounds here, I note that the *incomprehensibility of the essence of matter* might have been, according to my opinion, the first prompting of this doctrine in the following manner. In order to represent to oneself matter *in itself – mere matter* – one not merely distinguished it from, but also divested it of *all form*, and thus thought of it as that which is originally *formless*, and, accordingly, as something *evil* in itself. The deity introduced forms into matter by limiting its formlessness. But the deity would have had to *annihilate* matter in order to take away from it all that was formless – hence, the evil character of matter that could never be wholly obliterated, and its resistance even under the almighty hands of the deity that *formed* it, the source of everything physically and morally evil in *Plato*."

[251] The 1790 ed. (p. 258) replaces the following sentence with: "The understanding presents to the soul everything unchangeable, necessary, consistent, and *true*, whereas, through the senses, matter impresses upon it everything changeable, contingent, contradictory, and *false* under an external form – a *semblance* – of the opposite. And, consequently, matter strives endlessly to deceive. How then does the understanding arrive at its representations, which contradict the sensations of sensibility, and to that extent cannot possibly arise from them?"

[hh] Prof. Eberhard in his essay on the origin of contemporary magic, see *Berlinische Monatsschrift*, July of this year [1787], p. 17. [Johann August Eberhard (1739–1809) was a defender of Leibniz, sharply criticized later by Kant in *On a Discovery According to which Any New Critique of Pure Reason Has Been Made Superfluous by an Earlier One* (Königsberg, 1790). Also, the 1790 ed. (p. 258) expands this footnote: "Before him [Eberhard], Mr. *Platner* had already claimed this in §93 of his *Philosophical Aphorisms*, part 1, new edition: '*Plato* combines his otherwise *wholly philosophical* system of the innate laws of reason with a *fictional account*, which was already ascribed to Pythagoras [born 570 BC], of the formerly perfect state of the soul, etc.' Thus, it was in no way the *novelty* of that claim that *astonished* me, as Eberhard seems to want to suggest in the newest treatise inserted in his *Assorted Writings* (*Vermischte Schriften*) (Halle, 1788). It also did not occur to me to charge him with wanting to *blame* Plato. To be sure, I find a refutation of this supposed charge in the aforementioned essay anyway, but not a refutation of my claim that the doctrine of the *pre-existence of the soul* can be thought of as a component of the Platonic system and as a *philosophical theorem*; and *thus*, as long as the opposite is not shown, it may not be called either *fiction* or *myth*."]

the solution had led him too far away from the plan of his dialogues, took refuge in the pre-existence of the soul as a mere myth. [That is,] he did this merely for the sake of the external form of his composition and in order not to leave any remaining gap in it.[252] First of all, however, if one were to consider the Platonic doctrine concerning the pre-existence of the soul more carefully, it would fail to meet the conditions for the concept of a myth that the aforementioned excellent writer has himself laid down in the passage just noted. Moreover, by means of the very artifice with which he would have filled in the alleged gap in his exposition, Plato would have caused another gap just as wide and visible. For, then, another question would have forced itself upon every attentive reader: Whence did the pre-existing soul get its ideas? But even if one were to suppose that Plato had found the pre-existence of the soul already in the philosophy (not the mythology) of the Italian peninsula, this doctrine still has a much too philosophical meaning – especially in the way it was adopted by him – for it to serve as nothing more than a stopgap in his composition. [275] Could it not have been a deeper look into the nature of the truths of reason that led the profound Plato to his view on the origin of the concepts of the understanding and of the soul itself, a view that constitutes the true meaning of his doctrine of pre-existence? I shall explain this as succinctly as I can.

When one abstracts a concept of the understanding from the representation of time – a representation which makes the concept sensible and restricts its meaning to an actual intuition in us – the meaning of the concept becomes supersensible, and its object (henceforth a mere thing of thought) becomes immutable and eternal.[253] You, dear friend, will not fail to recognize here the logical immutability and eternity belonging to the

[252] The 1790 ed. (p. 259) replaces the following two sentences with: "But if we also suppose that Plato was abandoned by his philosophical system in answering the question about the origin of the concepts of the understanding, it still cannot be assumed, at least without proof, that he was also abandoned by his philosophical *spirit* in the choice of the method of exposition that his *poetic* genius offered him. The latter might very well have been the case, however, if *Plato*, by means of precisely that artifice with which he wanted to fill in the alleged *gap* in his exposition, had caused another *gap* that was just as wide and visible."

[253] The 1790 ed. (p. 260) inserts: "If, for example, one combines the pure concept of *substance* with the representation of time, one obtains as a result *that which subsists in time*, which can thus be cognized as substance only in so far as it is *perceived* (*substantia phaenomenon*) as subsisting in time. If, in contrast, one separates time from substance, the condition through which subsistence is restricted to perception falls away, and one thinks of that which subsists *in itself* (*substantia noumenon*) and outside any time."

truths of reason and to the concepts of substances, essences, etc. of the understanding – an immutability and eternity that one has ceased to quarrel about in our schools perhaps only because, thank God, one has found something better to do. That this eternity belonging to the truths of reason did not remain a secret to Plato is something you know, just as well as I, from more than one place in his writings. But that Plato transformed this logical eternity into a metaphysical one comes to light from the fact that he understood by eternal truths not mere subjective rules of thought but rather actual laws of things in themselves, essential properties, essences of things. [276] These eternal truths presupposed an eternal understanding – or rather, constituted an eternal understanding – and, according to Plato's doctrine, they were actually present from eternity in the infinite understanding of God. They were the ideas of the deity and contained the eternal archetypes according to which the creator formed unformed matter, tamed the evil principle in it, and generated the best world. Only copies of these ideas could be projected onto created things, in which they could exist not as something cognizing but only as something cognizable, not as concepts but as properties – as the essential forms of things in themselves. The archetypes, in contrast – the cognizing ideas themselves – could not be imparted to any created[254] thing and, on account of their eternal nature, could not be present anywhere except in the uncreated understanding. – And yet they were present in the rational souls of human beings, whose genuine cognition (the truths of reason) concerns entirely necessary, immutable, and eternal truths. Hence, the subject of rational souls, their substance, could no more differ from the subject of the divine mind, the substance of the deity, than its understanding could differ from the divine understanding. It must be uncreated; it must be an emanation of the deity. In this capacity, [277] before their connection to the body (in their demonic state and thus during their pre-existence), rational souls cognized and contemplated the eternally true, beautiful, and good, which resided in them and in their source, the deity itself. But after their imprisonment in the body by the evil character of their material shell, the true, beautiful, and good were lost from view and had to give way to errors and passions, the effects of sensibility. Nevertheless, rational souls could in no way lose

[254] The 1790 ed. (p. 261) inserts here "– and with Plato, this means brought forth from matter through the forming of it –."

their original nature even in this state of degradation. Thinking and contemplating the copies that were contained in the essential forms of matter itself reawakened in them the innate divine ideas. And abstracting from matter, combating sensibility, and controlling the passions secured for them again the enjoyment of their former happiness, which approached its full extent again only after the separation of the soul from the body.

From this explanation, which, for me at least, seems to illuminate and remove all the obscurities and contradictions in the entire Platonic doctrine of the soul that do not obviously lie in its mere expression, I think I may conclude with much confidence that, first, nothing appears in that entire theory that even remotely resembles a myth; and, second, that the rational soul in Plato is different from the rational [278] soul in Aristotle only with respect to the origin of its concepts and in no way with respect to their essential nature or to the constitution of its faculty of cognition.[ii] Pure intelligence, as it was conceived by the two philosophers and by all the spiritualists after them – and must be conceived, according to the deduction I provided above – was itself a separate and complete faculty of cognition, elevated above sensibility (outer sense). It was the faculty not only for thinking but also for intuiting the form of things in themselves.

I have very little to say concerning the later fate of this concept, which in any case did not obtain a single new and essential determination – until the time of Descartes – among all the countless modifications that it had to pass through. But concerning its influence on religion and morality, which half a millennium after Plato became so universal and decisive, I shall have much more to say in my next letter.[255]

[ii] Even the opinion of *Plato* that the power of thinking, or the rational soul, was confined to punishment in the body was retained by Aristotle. Cicero, *Fragment*, *Editio Ernesti* [*Opera*, ed. Johann August Ernesti (Halle, 1756/7)], p. 1097.

[255] This promised letter never appeared in the *Merkur* but did appear as the Twelfth (and final) Letter of the 1790 edition. See below, Appendix, section 1.

Appendix: the major additions in the 1790 edition

A Preface (pp. 9–13; newly added)

B Selection from the First Letter, "The spirit of our age and the present state of the sciences heralds a universal reformation of philosophy" (pp. 22–44; addition inserted at p. 105 of original First Letter)

C Second Letter, "Continuation of the preceding letter: The need for a highest rule of taste, for guiding principles for positive theology and jurisprudence, and, above all, for a first basic principle of natural right and morality" (pp. 44–74; new letter added at p. 105 of original First Letter, following addition "B")

D Selections from the Third Letter, "The shaking in the domain of the philosophy of religion heralds a reformation of this philosophy: my judgment regarding the Kantian philosophy in general" (pp. 74–7, 84–7, and 90–7; revised and expanded versions of pp. 105–7, 116–18, and 122–3 of original First Letter, respectively)

E Selection from the Fourth Letter, "The result of the Kantian philosophy on the question of God's existence, compared with the general as well as particular results of previous philosophy regarding this subject" (pp. 101–17; addition inserted at p. 132 of original Second Letter)

F Selection from the Eighth Letter, "The result of the Critique of Reason concerning the future life" (pp. 172–8; heavily revised version of pp. 167–72 of the original Fifth Letter)

G Selection from the Ninth Letter, "Elucidation of the metaphysical ground for cognition of the immortality of the soul with regard to its origin as well as its consequences" (pp. 192–203; addition inserted at p. 71 of original Sixth Letter)

H Selection from the Eleventh Letter, "The key to the rational psychology of the Greeks" (pp. 245–51; addition inserted at p. 264 of original Eighth Letter)

I Twelfth Letter, "Suggestions regarding the influence of the undeveloped and misunderstood basic truths of religion on civic and moral culture" (pp. 263–92; new letter added where the last original Letter, the Eighth, concludes)

A[1]

[9] Preface

The man to whom the letters collected here are addressed belongs among the few people for whom philosophy remains close to the heart, and who make up the smallest fraction of the not very considerable number of scholars who occupy themselves with philosophy today. Philosophy is, to be sure, not his business as a civic profession. But perhaps for that very reason it interests him more than it does most professional philosophers; it interests him directly on its own account. To him, philosophizing means seeking the truth for its own sake, which, he is wont to say, is nowhere more misjudged than where it has a market price.

Yet regardless of the fact that philosophy lies quite far outside the sphere of his station in life, it is for him much more than a mere pastime. Rather, as a citizen of the world – an identity that he is able to combine very well with that of being a citizen of the state – he knows of no pursuit more pressing or more serious. He concedes that one does not need philosophy in order to prove church doctrine concerning one of the three confessions that are privileged in the Holy Roman Empire and to refute the others, to administer justice according to the letter of positive laws or according to the mind of the ruler, to come up with successful cures as a doctor, or, indeed, even to play a brilliant role as a minister of finance or war. – But just as little can he be wrested from the conviction that without philosophy the establishment of the duties and rights of humanity [10] in this life and of the ground for our expectations of a future life is absolutely impossible. Here he also deviates from the dominant way of thinking of our age in so far as he holds this *establishment*

[1] This selection from the 1790 edition (pp. 9–13) was added as an entirely new Preface to the letters.

to be the most important of all things that can be important to human beings, and in particular to philosophers. He believes that we would have every reason to wish the *realities*[2] that are nothing more than *non-negations* back into our philosophy if it should come to a point where our philosophers are willing to recognize no other realities than those which can be *grasped with their hands*.

He believes, not without concern, that he has observed the state of our scientific and scholarly culture being determined by an ever-expanding quest for *graspable objects*, the limited enthusiasm of the nation for her poets and philosophers visibly decreasing, morality being degraded more and more widely to self-interested cleverness by teachers of morality, and the rights of humanity being explained by legal authorities more and more expressly in terms of the advantage they offer to a particular state. He believes that he has observed the affairs of religion being set aside by clear-thinking minds and abandoned for the most part to a fruitless struggle between the defenders of superstition and those of nonbelief, and Elementary-Philosophy[3] being corrupted by attempts to bring it closer to the manner of representation of the common man. He believes that he has observed the value of textbooks being estimated according to the degree to which they spare thought, and every writing that advances new ideas being misunderstood, opposed, and decried to that same degree. Finally, he believes that he has observed in the essays that are published here and there, and almost against the appreciation of the public, the few remaining independent thinkers working against one another more than ever before, intentionally and unintentionally, and with such determination [11] that one is always tearing down what the other has built.

According to my conviction, the main source of this dreadful situation lies where my friend least suspected it, in the *internal state* of philosophy itself – that is, in the complete absence of the very principles he assumes were found long ago. Therefore, there was nothing left for me to do to put him at ease than to attempt calling to his attention some of the most

[2] Here "realities" is used in its scholastic meaning, as in the ontological argument, and designates determinate features, not bare existence.

[3] Reinhold gave his own philosophy the title of *Elementarphilosophie*, in *Beyträge zur Berichtigung bisheriger Missverständnisse der Philosophen. Erster Band das Fundament der Elementarphilosophie betreffend* (Jena, 1790) (*Contributions to the Correction of Previous Misunderstandings of the Philosophers*, vol. 1, *Concerning the Foundation of Elementary-Philosophy*).

essential needs of *previous* philosophy and – because I had become familiar with a *new* philosophy that promises to satisfy these needs – to prepare, encourage, and invite him to study this new philosophy. In this way, suggestions arose concerning the shape of present and future philosophy – suggestions that make up the content of these letters.

My friend understood these suggestions. They occasioned in him a critique of the system that he had previously adopted for lack of a better one, but that had not yet in any way become second nature to his reason. To be sure, he had neither invented nor improved that system. For ever since he began thinking for himself about *dogmatic theism*, he was convinced that, while it could perhaps be elucidated better than it had been by others before him, it certainly could not be more firmly *grounded*. Perhaps my letters would have fallen short of their goal if, at the time when he was prepared to begin slowly orienting himself from a wholly new point of view, my friend had been forced by daily lectures on philosophy – in whichever of its previous manners of representation[4] – to turn back daily to the old point of view from which he was used to seeing things in exactly the opposite way. In that case, might he not have refuted by mere thinking – without even wanting to – what he [12] had scarcely begun to examine with silent observations? If my friend had advanced some new metaphysical system as its author or even dressed one up as new, I would have nothing to worry about with him concerning the usual vanity of famous men who believe that they lose something with every alteration in the manner of representation of their contemporaries that is not brought about by themselves; and I would have only very little to worry about concerning the natural, fatherly love of an author for the fruit of his spirit. But perhaps I would have had to worry all the more about a certain strength and evidence in his former convictions that in similar cases can probably be explained just as well by psychological grounds as by the solidity of the system being defended. Finally, it is of no small advantage to me in this case that my friend finds himself right now in the prime of his adult years. This is not just because, were the opposite to be true, it would be said of him that

[4] *Vorstellungsarten*, a variation of the more common phrase, *Denkungsart* (way of thinking), but with a typical Reinholdian emphasis on the notion of representation. In informal contexts like this one, the term carries a reminder of, but does not have the same technical meaning as, Kant's term, "forms of representation" (*Vorstellungsarten*), which designates the *a priori* and transcendentally ideal forms of human sensibility and knowledge in general.

> they hold it a shame to yield to their juniors and to confess in their old age that what they learned in beardless youth should be destroyed.[5]

Rather, it is because he probably would have lacked the time and energy in that case for undertaking an analysis of his doctrinal system in which no stone would be left standing.

Because I composed letters and not a system, suggestions and not demonstrations, intended for an experienced independent thinker and not a beginner divested of prior knowledge or a scholar who has become acquainted with philosophy only through his *memory*, I may – indeed I must – very often leave out elucidations and proofs that would have to have been given in either of the other cases.

In revising the letters that were already printed in the *Merkur*, I sought to remedy some misunderstandings of my opinion that have come to my attention by inserting elucidations, and to prevent future misunderstandings by paying extra careful attention [13] to clarity and precision of expression. But if a defender of mystical theology proclaims me a naturalist, counts me among the newest enemies of revelation, and reprimands me sarcastically and seriously as an enemy of this kind because I have declared myself against supernaturalism – that is, against a *philosophical system* that derives the idea of the deity, which is grounded in the form of reason, from supernatural phenomena – then I confess that it is utterly impossible for me to prevent *this kind of* misinterpretation. Still less would a much greater clarity of thought and command of language than I am in a position to achieve protect me from the doubts and objections of those who, because they seek in my book nothing but weaknesses, will also be able to find nothing but weaknesses in it.

The subsequent volume[6] will deal mainly with comparing the previous manners of representation of *morality*, *freedom*, and *instinct* with the

[5] "Turpe putant parere minoribus, et quae/Imberbes didicere senes perdenda fateri." Translation from Horace (Quintus Horatius Flaccus, 65–8 BC), *Epistle* II.1, in *Horace: Satires, Epistles, and Ars Poetica*, tr. H. Rushton Fairclough (Cambridge, MA, Harvard University Press, 1978), p. 405.

[6] Reinhold, *Briefe über die Kantische Philosophie* (*Letters on the Kantian Philosophy*), vol. II (Leipzig, 1792). This volume contains: (1) "On Some Prejudices against the Kantian Philosophy," (2) "On the Previous Disagreement of Philosophizing Reason with Itself concerning the Source of Duty and Law," (3) "On the Future Agreement of Philosophizing Reason with Itself concerning the Source of Duty and Law," (4) "On the Previous Disharmony between the Science of Natural Law and the Science of Positive Law," (5) "On the Future Harmony between the Science of Natural Law and the Science of Positive Law," (6) "Essay on a New Presentation of the Fundamental Concepts and Basic Principles of Morality and Natural Right," (7) "On the Previously

results that the Critical philosophy has established regarding these important subjects.

Jena, April 23, 1790.

B[7]

Selection from the First Letter, "The spirit of our age and the present state of the sciences heralds a universal reformation of philosophy"

[22] Because the causes and occasions of those phenomena do not in any way lie within the domain of theology alone, I shall admittedly have to cast fairly far afield in order to justify my conviction against yours. I shall have to compare the so-called *signs* of our time that you cite, and that all belong to one class in so far as they concern *religion*, with other phenomena that admittedly belong to other classes but can be called signs of our time with just as much right. In a word, I shall have to repay your depiction of the state of our enlightenment in matters of religion with a portrayal whose object encompasses no less than the *spirit of our age*. In what follows, let us be in agreement above all about the meaning that I wish to adopt for this rather ambiguous and very misused expression.

As a result of a very natural manner of representation – about which even our most famous philosophers are far from a consensus, for they disagree about whether or not it should be declared a mere illusion of *sensibility* – the place to which one usually assigns the *I* is nothing less than the center of the universe. Hence, it comes about that the maxims and prejudices of those trades or classes to which a particular *I* belongs, and which delineate the *closest* circle around that center, are very often designated the *spirit of our age*. With this very significant designation the *professional scholar* commonly certifies the dominant opinions on the

Misunderstood Difference Between Unselfish and Self-Interested Drives, and Between These Two Kinds of Drives and the Will," (8) "Elucidation of the Concept of Freedom of the Will," (9) "On the Incompatibility of All Previous Philosophical Concepts of the Soul with the Correct Concept of Freedom of the Will," (10) "On the Incompatibility Between Previous Philosophical Grounds of Conviction in God's Existence and the Correct Concepts of the Freedom and Law of the Will," (11) "The Basic Outlines for a History of Previous Moral Philosophy in General and, in Particular, of the Stoic and Epicurean Moral Philosophies," (12) "On the Remote Possibility of Future Agreement Between Independent Thinkers Concerning the Principles of Moral Philosophy."

[7] This selection from the 1790 edition (pp. 22–44) is an entirely new addition, inserted at p. 105 of the First Letter from the *Merkur*.

subject of his discipline, as does the *burgher of the grand and sophisticated world* the taste and fashion of his coterie. The scholar seldom succeeds in having his system adopted by the members of his guild, [23] for he has the more numerous or better part of it against him; whereas the burgher is scarcely to be refuted in his conviction that *he* upholds the fashion of his circle wherever he has not already set it. On account of this fact, it can be rather easily understood why the burgher commonly finds the *esprit de son temps*[8] just as enlightened and charming as the scholar finds the *genius saeculi*[9] backward and odious. I seek the spirit of our nation in *its soul*, which in a certain sense, of course, is spread throughout the entire body, but which has its proper seat only in the class of minds that prefers to be called the *thinking class*. For this class is not used to having its power of thinking dulled by a one-sided preoccupation of its memory or its fantasy entertained in a perpetual slumber by dreams, or at best, awakened by games of wit. You, dear friend, who are used to assessing the true value of nations, no less than of individual human beings, according to the constitution and degree of their *living* powers – you cannot possibly be indifferent about having your attention drawn to a point of view from which the *power of thinking* of our nation can be surveyed at one glance in its most vigorous activity, in its most characteristic expressions, and in its most varied occupations. Perhaps my attempt to trace such a point of view may not be wholly unwelcomed by you, in particular as a *word at the right time*. We are beginning the last decade of a century that we take to be exceedingly remarkable – in no way just because it is *ours* – and that is especially remarkable for Germany on account of the higher cultivation of the German spirit, the considerable advances that our nation has made in all fields of the arts and sciences, [24] and the important rank to which our nation has ascended among its sister states, which were cultivated earlier. Whether and to what extent it will preserve this rank – whether it will remain caught at a certain level like every one of its sisters or rise to the dignity of being a school for the rest of Europe – must largely be decided in this decade. That this decision must actually ensue in this period, and *how* it presumably will turn out can emerge solely (and also certainly) from a general overview of the phenomena that characterize the present state of our thinking powers taken as a whole.

[8] Spirit of the age (reading *temps* for *tems*), in the sense of current fashion.
[9] Spirit of the age, in the sense of the world at large.

The most striking and characteristic feature of the spirit of our age is a *shaking* of all previously known systems, theories, and manners of representation, a shaking whose range and depth is unprecedented in the history of the human spirit. The most varied and even mutually contradictory signs of our time can be traced back to this feature – signs that herald without exception an ambition, more lively than ever before, to erect *new* forms on the one hand, and to bolster every *old* form on the other. The impartial, independent thinker considers whether the old forms might ultimately be displaced by the new, or the new by the old, and whether and what humanity might in each case gain thereby. But he is all the less capable of deciding, for he finds neither the old forms to be as wholly unusable nor the new ones to be as wholly satisfactory as they are proclaimed to be by the zealots in both factions,[10] who, in the spirit of our age, prophesy happiness or unhappiness for humanity according to their unconditioned adherence to the old or new forms and according to their enthusiastic hopes or apprehensions.

At all events, the independent thinker is least able [25] to resist this question: Whence did this remarkable shaking come, and what will arise from it? A satisfying answer to this question presupposes an investigation that transcends the limited horizon of individual disciplines. It tracks the power of thinking in the fields that most exemplify its effectiveness, takes the most remarkable events from each of them, and places them *all* under *one* viewpoint that is far removed from the viewpoints of both the praisers and condemners of our age alike. The *pedant* assesses the advances of the human spirit according to his conception of the current state of the individual discipline that he works on, and that, for this very reason, is in his eyes the most important of them all. He congratulates humanity or laments it, depending on whether he believes that what he takes to be theology, jurisprudence, political science, military science, philosophy, etc. is flourishing or decaying. How should he know that the true state of even his own discipline can be correctly judged only by its relation to the state of the human spirit and its needs – just as the entire value of the discipline itself can be correctly judged only by its relation to the proper vocation of man (which, however, must neither be ostensibly presupposed nor vaguely discerned but *cognized*)? –

[10] *Parteien*, usually translated as "factions" in academic contexts, but sometimes as "parties" in more political contexts.

The *shaking* that is being discussed here does not manifest itself only, for instance, in the state of the sciences but also in everything that the power of thinking influences, and it expresses itself everywhere in direct proportion to the magnitude of this influence. It extends as far as European culture, but in such a way that sometimes it appears in scarcely noticeable vibrations and sometimes in violent upheavals. Consequently, the entire range of this shaking will at some point in the history of the human spirit provide a central image [26] that our grandchildren will dwell upon with wonder. But this formidable display of various events, which are in part blinding and in part incomplete, lies much too close to the contemporary viewer for him to be able to comprehend the individual components in their genuine relationship to the whole. The actual role that the *power of thinking* has in the causes of an event – and which alone must determine the more or less significant place that an event should take in that portrayal – can be abstracted from the foreign influence of external circumstances only when the event itself is fully ripe[11] and has obtained its determinate character for *world history* through its effects. Then the many silent and scarcely noticed changes that bear the imprint of the spontaneity of our spirit – changes that were a result of better insights and also disseminated and propagated better insights – will take up their rank far above the shining and admired revolutions in which *one* happenstance overthrows deteriorated constitutions and another reassembles the ruins according to its own caprice. Only then can it be specified with certainty whether and to what extent a developed cognition of human rights and duties was sometimes the cause and sometimes the effect of those events which we are already now used to calling expressions of enlightenment, partly in a positive and partly in a negative sense. Only then can it be shown whether and to what extent [the following events] belong together as effects of one and the same cause: the suppression of the Jesuits; the dwindling ranks of the monks and the fallen reputation of monasticism in several Catholic states; the decline in reputation, power, and revenue of the Bishop of Rome in nearly the entire Catholic world; tolerance, free speech, and freedom of the press in the Austrian monarchy; the abolition now and again of the death penalty; the annulling of

[11] Cf. G. W. F. Hegel, Preface, §89, *Phenomenology of Spirit*, tr. A. V. Miller (Oxford, Oxford University Press, 1977), and Karl Marx (1818–83), Preface, *A Contribution to the Critique of Political Economy* (Berlin, 1859), tr. N. I. Stone (Chicago, Charles H. Kerr and Co., 1904).

serfdom; the limiting of compulsory labor; the North American, French, and Dutch [27] revolutions, etc.

We can already say something more determinate now about the present shaking of the manners of representation within our German fatherland – not only because a more limited domain enables us to survey the whole of this shaking more easily, but also because here this shaking expresses itself most prominently in scientific fields, where it can have a less ambiguous origin in the power of thinking, through which it is a phenomenon of spirit in the strictest sense. Among all other European states, Germany is the most disposed toward revolutions of spirit and the least disposed toward political revolutions. As a result of its fortunate constitution, we, more than every other great nation, are protected against the most corrupt of all sicknesses of a body politic, which lies in the all too extravagant wealth of a few citizens and the all too extreme poverty of many. No excess of goods of fortune excites the imperiousness of the great, no excess of squalor compels the people to rebellion, and the nation's power of thinking, taken as a whole, has not been crippled by either of these opposed ills. No capital city acts as a hothouse, accelerating or slowing down the fruits of our spirit, which are left to themselves in the air of freedom to flourish more slowly but also more vigorously. Admittedly, we shall never experience a golden age of literature like Italy under *Leo X*, France under *Louis XIV*, or England under *Queen*[12] *Anne*, but we shall also never have to survive such an age. Our advances are all the more considerable the less they cause a sensation. Not only do our neighbors, by whom we are used to being misunderstood, scarcely notice it, but we ourselves scarcely notice that the sciences, taken collectively, have not been developed in any other nation either to the extent to which they have been presently developed [28] under us or with the same zeal and favorable results. This fact, however, is little able to be seen, for in our nation all fields of the sciences are without exception being cultivated with nearly equal diligence. And in so far as the relationship of each of the sciences to the rest is becoming increasingly visible through this cultivation, the rigor of the demands that one has learned to make on the contributors to each science is also increasing. Scarcely does one achieve something quite noteworthy when someone else steps forward and calls attention to something much more noteworthy yet to be achieved. Not a

[12] Italics have been added for "Queen."

single one of our disciplines has a dominant system that has been stamped by universal approval with the seal of actual or imagined completion. Everywhere old manners of representation are called upon and defended, and new ones are advanced and combated. A previously popular system, in which one finds essential defects in one place, would be displaced to no avail by a wholly new system because someone else, at another place, is already bringing to light an unrecognized advantage of the old system that is lacking in the new one. New mutually opposed theories are multiplying with new corrections and discoveries, and each one is being contested in vain as wholly unsupportable, and defended in vain as universally valid. No theory can prevail in its claims to have solved the whole problem of science, just as no theory can be convicted by its opponents of not having supplied any usable data for that solution.

Despite all of this irresolution in the present state of our sciences, their influence on the rest of human affairs, and especially on the principles of the rulers, has perhaps never before been so visible. This influence is all the less ambiguous the more that, even among rulers, the wavering between the old and the new – the distinguishing mark of the state of our scientific culture – comes to our attention. One [29] prince, who has a philosophical eye on the positive theology that underlies the prevailing religion of his people, has discovered errors whose inconsistency and harmfulness is recognized even by the most famous theologians in his land; and so he hands this theology over for public examination. Another prince, in contrast, who sees these matters more with the eyes of a statesman, and who knows moreover that the philosophers of his nation are in conflict over the indispensability of positive religion and the inadequacy of natural religion, protects the old doctrinal structure of folk religion against all public attack. The light that has been recently cast on fields such as government or political economy forces its way up to the throne and enlightens the ruler on the essential defects in his form of government and in the administration of the affairs of his land. The ruler[13] abolishes the old constitution and replaces it with a new one *without* the will of the nation – and sometimes even *against* it – and in doing so he believes that he has merely done his duty and has not significantly infringed on the rights of the nation. For he considers the

[13] Possibly a reference to Emperor Joseph II of Austria (1741–90), whose "enlightened despotism" led to problems in Reinhold's early period in Vienna.

interests of the state, which he believes that he understands better than his discontented subjects, to be the highest motive determining his duty as ruler. Presupposing that he actually meant well for his people, is it likely that he would have acted or even thought in this manner if a universal conviction had opposed him – or if at least legal scholars had been in agreement about the inalienable rights of humanity and the principle "that these rights can in no way be determined by *utility* (whether general or particular) and that considerations of utility can be valid only if *right* is determined *first*?" If a ruler in one place abolishes the serfdom of the farmers while generally considering and treating his subjects as an inherited [30] possession; if a ruler in another place wants to dignify humanity by abolishing torture and the death penalty while degrading his subjects to the status of cattle by wholly arbitrary, capricious, and inhuman acts of retribution against crimes; if a third ruler in yet another place recognizes the innate right of his subjects to believe what they can while declaring this very right to be a gift of his grace and its enjoyment a mere toleration that he grants to unsacred opinions in the name of the one and only sacred opinion; if a fourth ruler, in the name of *freedom of the press*,[14] concedes to all people the right to communicate to others their convictions according to the best of their knowledge and conscience while seeking to punish most severely, as *impudence of the press*,[15] the publicizing of convictions that contradict the Symbolic Books[16] (*and so on*) – then it would be just as much an injustice to these rulers to attribute the second half of their *contradictory* behavior to a blind adherence to old customs as it would be to attribute the first half to a mere penchant for novelty. And it would be an injustice in either case if one also did not concede that these rulers could cite decisions of equally famous writers for the one disposition as well as for the other, and that they have acted wholly in the spirit of the age, even to the extent that this age is defined by the state of the sciences.

Although the shaking of old and new manners of representation that characterizes this spirit is spreading across the domain of human knowledge,

[14] *Pressfreiheit.* [15] *Pressfrechheit.*

[16] The creed of the established church in the Protestant lands of Germany. See *What is Enlightenment? Eighteenth Century Questions and Twentieth Century Answers*, ed. James Schmidt (Berkeley, University of California Press, 1996), p. 34, n. 37; and Anton Friedrich Koch, "Die symbolischen Bücher der evangelisch-lutherischen Kirche als Gegenstand der Kritik in der Aufklärungszeit und bei Immanuel Carl Diez," in *Immanuel Carl Diez, Briefwechsel und Kantische Schriften*, ed. Dieter Henrich (Stuttgart, Klett-Cotta, 1997), pp. 924–86.

it is not equally noticeable in all the individual fields of this domain. The law according to which this shaking increases or decreases can be determined by the greater or lesser role that the capacity for the power of thinking called *reason* has in the content and the form of a science. Whoever is not sufficiently familiar with this role [31] need only let himself be guided by the increasing noise and thickening dust clouds, and he will soon be convinced that the *epicenter of the shaking* lies *within the region of metaphysics* and that its outer boundary is determined by the fields of *mathematics*, *natural science*, and *description of the objects of nature*.[17]

That science which, according to its definition, must rank above all others – as the domain containing the first grounds of human cognition, the system of the most universal predicates of things in general, and the science of the *principles* of all human knowledge – is so shaken at present that not only its rank but even its designation as a science is being disputed. And it encounters this [reaction] not only, for instance, from the Critical or so-called *Kantian* philosophers alone (the followers of a new manner of philosophizing that has found only very little acceptance until now and is opposed by the most famous philosophers of our time), but even from *two* factions out of the *four* to which all the previous manners of representation of philosophy can be traced back. The *dogmatic skeptic* disputes the validity of any reference whatsoever of metaphysical predicates to actual objects; the *supernaturalist* wants the validity of this reference restricted merely to the *world of the senses* – or as he prefers to express himself, to *natural* objects – and seeks to derive their application to *supernatural objects* from *revelation*; but both are in agreement that *metaphysics* is the most groundless presumption of a reason that misconstrues its own powers. What the other two factions (the *materialist* and *spiritualist*) concede to metaphysics by awarding it the rank of a genuine science, they turn around and rob [32] from it by making this science into a common foundation for their systems, which stand in direct opposition to one another. And by demonstrating with equal skillfulness – at least in the eyes of impartial spectators – materialism and spiritualism, deism and atheism, fatalism and determinism from one and the same *ontology*, they place the *scientific character* of this ontology in a very questionable light. One of these factions consists for the most part

[17] *Naturbeschreibung*, one of the standard disciplines of eighteenth-century German science, related to what Kant called physical geography.

of public teachers of philosophy – those who practice science as a civic trade and who, because they are committed by oath and duty to present the basic truths of religion and morality, often hold their obligation to extend to the traditional form of lecture that belongs to their charter. These teachers declare the metaphysics of their materialist, fatalist, and atheist opponents to be shallow, long refuted, and unworthy of the name of a science, which they grant only to that exposition of metaphysical formulas from which, according to their opinion, the basic truths of religion and morality can be *demonstrated*. But despite how numerous and even somewhat adept the minds have been that have occupied themselves with the development of such a metaphysical science at our many universities and beyond, despite how much they are even in agreement among themselves concerning its actual existence, and despite how firmly each is convinced of having set it down in his *compendium* – still not one of these men have provided a metaphysics to date that has satisfied even the demands of his own faction, let alone survived the tests of the other factions. There is not a single metaphysics among them that consists [33] in fundamental principles about which the professors themselves would be in agreement – something one is certainly justified in expecting from a science of the first grounds of cognition. Each one of them is refuted in more than one of its most essential claims in the metaphysical compendiums themselves. The possessors and guardians of this science are so far from thinking uniformly among themselves even about its *first principle* that in some well-known and popular textbooks[18] there is not a single discussion about this most essential condition for a science. In other textbooks one divests logic of its first principle[a] and, following an old tradition, establishes a metaphysics with it. In other textbooks, finally, one confuses *principle* and *ground* and directs readers who are curious about the ultimate thinkable ground of metaphysical predicates sometimes to experience and sometimes to a system of a few innate truths. To the same extent that one is busy raising botany, mineralogy, and chemistry to *systems*, one is allowing metaphysics to degenerate into an aggregate of unconnected, ambiguous formulas with

[18] Cf. Kant's criticism of dogmatic discussions of a first principle of cognition in Baumgarten's metaphysics, in *Lectures on Metaphysics/Immanuel Kant*, ed. and tr. Karl Ameriks and Steve Naragon (Cambridge, Cambridge University Press, 1997), p. 111 (29: 749).

[a] Through the misuse of the misunderstood *principle of contradiction*.

which one presupposes as universally accepted what was to be demonstrated, and demonstrates what was in no need of proof. One [author] puts on a façade and gains no small advantage from having hidden the system of his metaphysics, of which he himself has only the vaguest inkling, behind a rhapsodic exterior; while another, with a power of genius in the literary arts, abhors all rules as shackles of the spirit – even if they should come from his own reason – and scorns all systems in general. Since a metaphysical principle can have *truth* only through its connection with *universally valid*[19] grounds of cognition and can have universal evidence only through being traced back to a *universally accepted principle that is evident to all*,[20] [34] it is readily understandable that the popular[21] metaphysicians at our universities are preparing a certain demise for this science – to the extent that it depends on them – by precisely the so-called liberal form through which they fancy that they are procuring its universal acceptance. This result is being accelerated by the best recent writings of those independent thinkers who, because they treat metaphysical objects with high acuity and eloquent presentation and with a spirit free from all constraint of the academic profession, seem to be necessarily helping out metaphysics. To the same extent that they distance themselves from one of the four previously unavoidable philosophical factions, they unwillingly and unknowingly align themselves all the more closely with another faction – and commonly with the opposite one – or even place themselves at that faction's head. Those who want to evade spiritualism speak in favor of materialism (at present most preferably under the consistent manner of representation offered by *Spinoza*); those who struggle against materialism and spiritualism brood over a purified supernaturalism; and others who do not find a satisfying expedient in any of these philosophical formulas slash the knot with dogmatic skepticism. And as a result each one of these writers is causing more massive confusion in the area of ontology the more he places the immense questions concerning God, freedom, and immortality, and those concerning the rights and duties of humanity, in a more original

19 *allgemeingültigen.* 20 *allgemeingeltendes Prinzip allgemeine Evidenz.*

21 A reference to Popularphilosophen, members of a movement in eighteenth-century German that strongly favored anti-systematic approaches at the cost of rationalism altogether. This movement is not to be identified with ideas such as mere respect for common sense or a desire that in some sense philosophy should be popular. Kant and Reinhold shared these ideas, but not the totally anti-metaphysical approach of Popular Philosophers such as Christoph Friedrich Nicolai (1733–1811). Cf. below, Second Letter, p. 66.

light. The more he thinks for himself, the more he takes the metaphysical formulas used by all sects in meanings that distinguish themselves all the more sharply from all previously known meanings. He disputes on all the more striking grounds formulas that are not adopted universally but only, for example, by university philosophers, and he undermines the [35] principles, deranges the point of view, and weakens the reputation of the science of the first grounds of cognition.

Do not these facts explain in a rather satisfactory manner how it is coming to be that even among genuinely philosophical minds the number is continuing to increase of those who loudly and publicly declare the study of metaphysics to be useless, indeed even corrupting? And would it not be untrue to our age if one wanted to explain this phenomenon with that same characteristic shallowness of spirit without considering whether this very shallowness, wherever it actually occurs, is partly a consequence of the condition in which the science that is supposed to constitute the foundation for all other sciences finds itself? Through a further illumination of the present shaking in other scientific fields, it will emerge that there has never been a more universal and pressing need for a *first science*[22] than there is at the present time – a science, whether it is called metaphysics or not, from which all other sciences would await secure principles that in part guide and in part ground. Consequently, it will emerge that the contempt that metaphysics is experiencing is an effect of the unfulfilled expectations that this science has excited at all times by its lofty promises, unfulfilled expectations that had never become as universally conspicuous as they had some time ago, when independent thinkers from all sides were feeling themselves compelled more than ever before to take metaphysics at its word.

The other fields of the sciences are being more or less shaken the more or less remote their domain is from metaphysics proper, and they may be ordered one after another in this regard in roughly the following sequence: rational psychology, cosmology, and theology, philosophy of religion (the science of the ground of our [36] expectations of a future life); the doctrine of taste, morality, natural right, positive jurisprudence and positive theology, and finally history in the strictest sense of the term. The first three fields, which are directly related to metaphysics and usually even count as components of it, share with it the same name and

[22] *Hauptwissenschaft.*

fate, whereas history owes the more tranquil possession and less contested expansion and improvement of its far-reaching domain to its distance from the epicenter of the shaking. The results of modern attempts to reform positive theology and positive jurisprudence were more successful the more the reformers of this science learned to make better use of its proximity to history. It was equally the case, however, that all the attempts of the best minds to come to agreement among themselves regarding the *first principles* of morality and natural right entirely failed because, in the development of the concepts that were presupposed by this principle, it was impossible to avoid the neighboring [field of] metaphysics. Finally, in so far as there is a wavering back and forth between the data of experience and metaphysical notions in the grounding of the philosophy of taste and philosophy of religion, there has yet to be agreement even with regard to the question of whether or not a highest rule of taste or a first principle for the basic truths of religion belong among our conceivable problems.

Under these circumstances the reputation of *history* is rising at the same rate that the reputation of *metaphysics* is sinking. Metaphysics has never before been placed in such stark contrast to history not only with respect to its subjects but also with respect to its reliability, usefulness, and influence. Professional philosophers place history on the throne of the former queen of all the sciences[23] and pay homage to it even in the name of [37] philosophy, as the genuine science of the first grounds of cognition of all human knowledge. "Nature," they say, "always remains the same and is always in accord with itself, whereas metaphysics obtains a new form from every independent thinker and is endlessly caught up in conflict by its solicitors. *Nature* is the *truth* that reveals itself just as little to the pure reason of the metaphysician as it does to the raw sensibility of the thoughtless savage. It speaks loudly and in a universally understandable way through the voice of history, through which it calls common sense back from the empty clouds of speculation to the arena of the actual world where, in its works and activities, it discloses laws that alone can be called universally accepted principles."

Yet, however unanimously our *empirical philosophers* may refer to nature and history, and with regard to whatever important problems of

[23] Cf. Reinhold, "Über den Begrif [*sic*] der Geschichte der Philosophie," in *Beyträge zur Geschichte der Philosophie*, ed. Georg Gustav Fülleborn (Züllichau and Freistadt, 1791), pp. 5–35.

humanity may be under discussion, they are still very little able to agree amongst themselves on how to answer questions concerning what they understand by *nature* and which field of history is to contain the data for such a project – that is, when they are unable either to sidestep this question by a clever move or, as is usually the case, dismiss it out of hand as a metaphysical musing. Only few among the many who frequently carry the terms *nature* and *history* on their tongues have called themselves to account regarding the meaning of these terms. They find such an account all the more superfluous the more the terms have become familiar to them – terms whose ambiguity is quite convenient for anyone used to busying himself more with his memory and imagination than with his reason. Whoever in his excessive seeking and amassing of material about thinking has forgotten thinking itself will adhere immediately to *nature* – or rather, to an indeterminate concept of it – when it comes to those grounds of appearances [38] which he cannot extract from among his collected materials by means of any of his five senses. For this concept of nature is always remote and obscure enough to absorb and hide any inconsistency that one wants to cram into its extension. What a distinction between objects and sciences the empiricist throws into confusion under the designations of *nature* and *history*! He confuses the insights that so-called natural history offers through the descriptions of minerals, plants, and animals with those which become considerably augmented over time through the contrived experiences of anatomy and chemistry; and he confuses the insights that anthropology provides about human beings as a natural phenomenon – whether observed as an appearance of inner sense in the doctrine of the soul or as an appearance of outer sense in physiology – with the insights that the science ordinarily designated by the term *history* (when not used in conjunction with some other term) has so far provided into the civil and moral culture of humanity! The distinction between the previous advances of history in the latter meaning of the term and history inasmuch as it includes natural history and anthropology is nothing less than the difference between the two meanings of the term that our empiricists habitually conflate when they hold their panegyrics for the reliability of history as a foundation for philosophy. While mineralogy, botany, zoology, anatomy, chemistry, physiology, and empirical psychology fetch ever new uncontested gains and deliver them as secure profit into the treasury of human knowledge, not a single one of the decisions about the immense [39] questions concerning the rights and duties of human beings in this life or the ground for their expectation of a future life – decisions that the opponents of metaphysics claim to have found in history – has yet to be accepted universally, and not even among themselves. Moreover, consider how little *historical criticism*[24] is in agreement with itself regarding the value of the raw as well as the already-treated materials of history proper, or regarding the credibility of original sources and historians; and consider how little the philosophy of history is in agreement with itself regarding the form and basic laws for working in this science. It turns out, then, that a shaking is occurring in the field of history as well, which, while less noticeable on the whole, is no less remarkable than the shaking of metaphysics itself; for it is upon the unshakeability of this field of history that the theologians and jurists of positive law believe their improved doctrinal structures are firmly grounded, and the empirical reformers of morality and natural right their principles.

But this shaking must also become more noticeable the more our historical criticism ceases to be an aggregate of indeterminate, wholly unconnected observations and the more it closely approximates the systematic form that at present it is very far from having. The more cohesive and determinate the demands become that this science makes on writers and researchers of history – demands that so far have been very little developed – the more the doubts about the reliability of the previously treated materials of history will necessarily pile up, and the less frequently, and with all the more qualifications, the credibility of previous writers of history will hold up. This is primarily the case with the most noble and instructive content that history has to offer, a content that is also most important for philosophy: [40] namely the events that have had their motives in the spirit and heart of human beings and whose depiction is decisively influenced sometimes by the passions of the narrator, sometimes by his principles, but always by his distinctive manner of representation. A considerable amount of historical reportage regarding such actions of prominent and remarkable human beings has already been proscribed in more recent investigations, and consequently it is becoming increasingly clear that human nature has been misconstrued to the same extent that it has been customarily assessed according to such reports. What important changes ultimately await certain

[24] *Historische Kritik.*

individual fields of history at that point in time when the advances of historical criticism will call into question previously undisputed *original sources* and decide disputes over previously contested ones! Historical researchers as well as even professional theologians are still not at all in agreement about having fully determined the historical value of sacred sources. And even those who take this value to be decided draw directly opposed results from these records – records which are so extremely important for the history of humanity – depending on whether they view them from the standpoint of a reason left to its own resources or from the standpoint of a supernaturally illuminated reason.

The more the materials of history, along with their treatment, multiply the *viewpoints* that provide the *internal form* for any historical composition aimed at being more than a compilation, the more visible the difficulty becomes for our thinking minds regarding a *highest* common *viewpoint*, which would unite all *particular* viewpoints under it and allot to each one its own fixed place. [41] Recent essays on the *history of humanity*[25] demonstrate that the need for such a viewpoint is felt – indeed, even that the effort to satisfy this need is present – just as clearly as they demonstrate that until now no such viewpoint has been found. But the history of humanity in general can and should, entirely on its own, serve as the basis for all attempts to reform the previous state of all *particular* histories. Only through this history can and should there be a correction of the narrowness and one-sidedness of viewpoints from which, for example, one writer in his church history works to promote supernaturalism, and another naturalism; one Catholicism, and another Lutheranism; or from which one writer in his political history works in the service of despotism, and another serves the hatred of princes; or from which one writer places systems of religion in a light that shines upon him from the torch of the chief spiritual ministry of his fatherland, and another places state constitutions in a light that shines upon him from the chief secular ministry of his fatherland. But how is the history of humanity supposed to redress these ills as long as those who treat it are not even in agreement about a determinate concept of this history, or as long as the meanings of the expressions *history of humanity*, *world history*, *history of culture*, *history of human understanding*, etc. unceasingly get

[25] E.g., Kant, "On the Conjectural Beginning of the History of Humanity" (*Berlinische Monatschrift*, 1786).

mixed up with one another? Indeed, how can this happen as long as there is nothing firmly agreed upon even concerning the *characteristic feature* of humanity?

Our empiricists assert in vain that the determinate concept of this important feature must be established through the study of the history of humanity. Far from being made possible by means of this study, this concept must rather be presupposed as already present for the possibility of this study and for each of its even moderately successful results. This concept alone is the basic rule that can safely guide those who treat that history not only in their handling of its materials [42] but also in the very choice of those materials. For only through this concept can the facts that make up the content of the universal history of the human species ever be made determinate from the immeasurable amount of material scattered in the fields of all the particular histories of peoples, states, etc. The lack of such a determinate concept also calls attention to itself conspicuously enough in our compilations and rhapsodies in which fragments from the natural history of human beings as animals are paired with conjectures[26] that are grounded on unreliable results from the barely developed histories of civic culture, religion, and philosophy. They are called "a history of humanity," but these fragments make the meaning of the term *humanity* into a very difficult problem to solve for the reflective reader. Because the *thread* with which each of the historians of humanity strings together his events is determined only by these events themselves – or rather, by the selection and arrangement of them – there is nothing more natural than that an entirely different thread should appear prominent with each. In one case, there appears a gradual and, on the whole, uninterrupted advance toward moral perfection; in another case, the developmental course of human powers tramps onward in various crooked lines sometimes going forward, sometimes backward, in a direction that depends solely on external circumstances; in yet another case, finally, there appears a perpetual standstill with respect to perfection and happiness, a standstill in which the neglect of one capacity is supposed to be tied to the cultivation of another, the decrease of sensation with the increase of reason. Each of these opinions is taken by independent thinkers of nearly the same rank to be an obvious result of the history of humanity. And the defender of one opinion accuses the supporters of

[26] *Ibid.*

other opinions of having imported their opinions into history and [43] of extracting and arranging the facts only according to their arbitrary, preconceived concepts.

The ground of this dispute, *prior* to whose resolution we can in no way boast of possessing a genuine history of humanity, lies in a misunderstanding that is completely hidden to the disputing factions because it concerns a point about which they believe that they are in complete agreement, or of which – as in the case of metaphysical questions – they do not want to take the slightest notice. I am referring to the indeterminate, ambiguous, wavering concept of *reason* and *its relationship to animal nature*. Because this concept concerns the distinctive character of humanity, only through it can the *highest viewpoint* be established. Moreover, through this viewpoint the *internal* form of the history of humanity in general will be made possible, and through this form every particular history will be made possible. This viewpoint cannot possibly be a result of the history that presupposes it, a history that must elucidate and confirm it but cannot first establish it. The data through which it is alone determinable can be given to us only in and through our mind, and it can be discovered only through the analysis of *our mere faculty of representation*.[27] To want to seek it outside ourselves in history is to offer clear proof that one does not know what one is seeking. The universal laws of *intellectual* powers can no more be determined by history than can the universal laws of *physical powers*, and just as scientific familiarity with the nature of movement is absolutely impossible without *mathematics*, so too determinate cognition of *reason's* distinctive *manner of acting* presupposes a science that must be as different from history as mathematics is. Hence, the *shaking* in the field of history that I have indicated [44] must either continue forever, or it must bring about the discovery and recognition of that science from which the highest viewpoint for all history in general is to emerge with universal evidence. And all attempts to give philosophy a better form through history must be entirely futile for, on the contrary, history can receive its form only through philosophy – but only, of course, after philosophy itself has a fixed form.

[27] *Unseres blossen Vorstellungsvermögens.*

C[28]

Second Letter, "Continuation of the preceding letter: The need for a highest rule of taste, for guiding principles for positive theology and jurisprudence, and, above all, for a first basic principle of natural right and morality"

The lack of fixed and universally accepted principles manifests itself not nearly as strikingly in the works of taste as it does in the works of the historical arts. We, and perhaps all of our cultivated neighbors, have many more poets of classical rank to offer than writers of history, and if both were to be judged with equal strictness according to the aims of their arts, the writers of history would probably be found quite a distance behind the poets. Moreover, until now *aesthetic* criticism has been developed among us with disproportionately greater zeal and more favorable success than has *historical* criticism. Through the study of the ancient and modern masterworks of the fine arts in the broadest sense of the term – and even more through their enjoyment – Germany too has finally gained, little by little, that which at the start of our century it still entirely lacked, and that for which even nowadays it is not credited with having the best capacities – *taste*. [45] Whatever objections art critics may properly raise against various particular phenomena in Germany, taken as a whole, German taste is as genuine as the best of our neighbors, and in the last decade it has not only not declined but indisputably increased in its subtlety no less than in its scope. The number of German scholars who no longer regard it as beneath their dignity also to engage seriously in the study of the *beautiful* is not inconsiderable. Our philologists are becoming famous no longer by offering variants of texts, grammatical emendations, and conjectures; not infrequently they themselves censure those in their circle who are always forgetting in the dead letter of the ancient classics the spirit that lives on in their perpetually blossoming beauty. Even those who are not scholars are becoming increasingly familiar with this spirit through translations that far surpass anything of the kind possessed by other nations, and that perhaps display most clearly what the hands of our prominent poets and prose writers have

[28] This selection from the 1790 edition (pp. 44–74) is an addition that constitutes an entirely new Second Letter, following what is translated above as section B.

made out of our native language, a language which until quite recently was very crude and inflexible. Their original works stand up to the most excellent of that which has been left to us from the golden age of Rome and Greece, and they seem to have gradually exhausted all the forms of the beautiful. How much they are being taken up by our reading public and how far this public extends to all classes can be inferred already from the substantial and ever-increasing quantity of *reprints*, whose number in some cases surpasses all belief. Who now does not enjoy the beneficent effect of even a single writer who rivals himself as poet, philosophical spirit, and scholar of the first rank, and who brings together a high degree of clarity and force [46] in his power of thinking with the most subtle delicacy of feeling in his numerous and widely read works, and combines Roman urbanity with Attic elegance in his enchanting language? Our painters, sculptors, and musicians compete with foreigners more zealously for favor the more they can count on their countrymen to participate as spectators and competent judges of their glorious struggle. Among us, the prominent and wealthy are perhaps more content with their *possessions* than in any other nation, and in their opened galleries they share with the public the *enjoyment* of masterpieces of foreign and domestic art. In the hands of the middle class, the more significant features of beauty from works of painting, sculpture, and musical art are reproduced through copperplate engravings, plaster casts, and piano scores. This class is in very many respects the highest on the ladder of human worth, and presently it is being surpassed more in pomp than in culture by that class which stands above it on the ladder of civic status. Finally, we could invoke even the forms of our clothing and household effects, the outward side of our customs and habits, and the tone of our social intercourse in order to deflect the reproach of tastelessness that until only recently we had in large part deserved.

If the arts that can dispense less with an animated public life and a *capital city* – that is, painting, sculpture, and the arts related and subordinate to them – have had less success among us than the literary arts, and less success here than in Italy, France, and England, we have nonetheless made the more important advances in aesthetic criticism. And if our nation is still far from being the arbiter over all other nations in matters of taste, the reason for this is certainly not due to [47] the circumstance that we have not advanced furthest in the *scientific* criticism of taste. Germany is the native land and caretaker of so-called aesthetics, that is, the science that seeks out the principles lying at the basis of all criticism of taste and lays them out in systematic connection. Even if the many attempts that we have so far to point to in this science have not added much of anything new to the original idea of its founder, no thinking mind will be able to deny to the more excellent among them the merit of having brought, ordered, elucidated, and amended a multitude of the most important thoughts that lie scattered in the aesthetic rhapsodies of the Italians, British, and French. The fruitfulness of Baumgarten's principles manifests itself not only in the *general* theories explicitly built upon them but far more, and in a more illuminating way, in the many acute and practical observations by which our *Lessing* and *Engel*,[29] among others, have enriched the materials for future, specialized theories of individual literary genres. Their observations are, to be sure, always traced back to individual cases, but they can be educed from examples only for the most part under the assumption and with the guiding thought of those principles.

One of the most unambiguous hallmarks of our advances in the criticism of taste is the ever more widespread recognition among us that our aesthetics, with all of its undeniable advantages over foreign aesthetics, is still far from fulfilling the demands of a science in the proper sense of the word – demands that we ourselves were the first to make on this science. Our aesthetics has yet to furnish a universally accepted principle for any of the theories of the arts that belong under it. We are still not in agreement even about the fundamental [48] concept of the literary arts or about the distinction between it and rhetoric, and we have been less and less in agreement ever since several of our best minds became preoccupied with firmly establishing these concepts, which are so utterly important for the sciences of the beautiful. If one person takes *vivacity of thought and expression* to be the essence of a poem, then, in order to save the field of the literary arts from the pretensions of *men in power*, he must first add that this vivacity has to be *aesthetic*. And in order to exclude higher rhetoric[30] (which so often elevates itself above many genres of writing on account of its vivacity of thought and expression) from this field, he must first explain that this vivacity has to be

[29] Baumgarten, author of *Aesthetica* (Frankfurt-on-Oder, 1750/8), the work that gave the modern discipline its name and first system; Lessing, author of *Hamburgische Dramaturgie* (Hamburg, 1767); Johann Jakob Engel (1741–1802), author of *Theorie der Dichtungsarten* (Leipzig, 1763).

[30] *Beredsamkeit*, also known as eloquence.

poetic. That is, he must concede that his explanation presupposes the characteristic feature of the literary arts and, thus, in no way contains or provides it. If another person finds this feature in *sensibly perfect speech*,[31] he muddles the boundary between the literary arts and rhetoric; and, if he believes that he is remedying this confusion by declaring a poem to be a speech *through which the highest possible degree of pleasure* is generated, he denies to all past and future masterpieces of the literary arts the right to the title "poem." If a third person finds the character of the literary arts to lie in *fiction*, he can secure this position against ambiguity only by restricting the concept of fiction to the concept of *sensibly perfect speech whose final purpose is that of pleasing* – or what amounts to the same thing, by defining it in terms of a no less ambiguous feature. For is there agreement about what is meant by the *sensibly perfect* or by *the pleasing*? One very respectable party of artists and art experts declares almost [49] unanimously that *pleasing* is the purpose and first fundamental law of all the fine arts and sciences, and that the feasibility of this concept as a first principle is demonstrated by the fact that it is as little capable of an explanation as it is in need of one. But *pleasing* is also the purpose and the first fundamental law of the arts that work on the palate, the nose, and the fifth or sixth sense. And although it is not to be denied that the well-known beautiful spirit of France owes a rather considerable part of the sizable impact it has had on Europe to the use it knew how to make of the *mysteries of the last art* in many of its most popular writings, the less gallant usage of the German language reserves the term *beautiful* exclusively for arts having to do with spirit[32] either directly or at most through the eye or ear. – Another party is united by the claim that the purpose and first principle of the fine arts and sciences is to *please by means of represented beauty* – but only as long as the meaning of the term *beauty* is not asked about. For in that case one person replies that beauty can only be sensed and not thought and that, consequently, it also cannot be explained; and since sensations of it arise only in the actual enjoyment of the beauties of nature and art, the ideal of unexplainable beauty in

[31] In his *Aesthetica*, §14, Baumgarten characterized the perception of beauty in terms of "the perfection of sensible cognition as such." See Paul Guyer, *Kant and the Experience of Beauty* (Cambridge, Cambridge University Press, 1993), pp. 84–6. Baumgarten was honored for establishing aesthetics as a separate philosophical discipline, but he grounded it on neo-Wolffian notions that were rejected by Kant and Reinhold.

[32] *Geist*, here meant not in a metaphysical sense but simply as expressing a "spirit of beauty."

general, which would be destroyed through analysis, can be abstracted only from the impressions of these works. Another person replies, in contrast, that the *beautiful* distinguishes itself from the merely *agreeable* precisely by the fact that, unlike the latter, it is not only sensed but also thought and to that extent must be explainable. Mere sensation cannot possibly be the criterion of beauty, for, [50] if it is not in many cases to remain indifferent to the beautiful and enraptured by the ugly, it must presuppose a certain cultivation, which is called *taste*. Thus, the concept of beauty, which must contain the very *rule of taste*, can in no way be abstracted from that which is merely sensed in the enjoyment of the beautiful, and settling which objects of agreeable sensation are beautiful must be done independently of all sensing. Finally, the feature that expresses the relation of beauty to the faculty of sensation and to the power of thinking is called *sensible perfection*. – Now, if the defender of this opinion is not allowed to be satisfied with mere expressions, he lands himself in new disputes with his own party about the ambiguous meaning of its commonly held formula. One person believes that he has made this formula sufficiently determinate by declaring *perfection* to be the unity of the manifold – without considering that he has thereby specified a feature that must apply to every actual and possible thing, whether beautiful or ugly. Another person thinks that he has adequately characterized the perfection that is being discussed with regard to beauty by declaring it to be that manifold which underlies the *intensity* of the mind's activity, combined with that unity which underlies the *facility* of its activity – or *pleasure* – and which makes the object[33] in which this perfection is being perceived into an object[34] of pleasure. Hence, he even calls pleasure in general the *sensible representation* of perfection, and he forgets that what is at issue here has nothing to do with the object[35] of pleasure in general but rather with aesthetic pleasure; it has to do not with the feature of the *agreeable* but rather with that of the *beautiful*. To be sure, a third party does distinguish aesthetic perfection from sensible perfection in general, but it claims that the feature by which the latter [51] is raised to the rank of the former consists in *purposiveness*. But either he owes all of his readers an account of purposiveness, or he has it consist in the capacity to bestow *pleasure* in general, i.e., that pleasure the concept of which he

[33] *Gegenstand.* [34] *Objekt.* [35] *Gegenstand.*

defines again in terms of purposiveness and, consequently, by means of a circle.

In their dispute over the fundamental concept of aesthetic pleasure, all of these parties are in agreement only about the fact that this kind of pleasure, unlike any other kind, is in no way shared by human beings with their half-brothers, the non-rational animals, and that consequently reason belongs just as certainly to the so-called sense for beauty as sensibility does.[b] Thus, it is evident that this dispute can be reconciled in only one way. The parties must come to an agreement first about the nature of the function of *sensation* that they recognized with regard to *pleasure* in general and then about the nature of the function of *reason* that they no less conceded with regard to *aesthetic* pleasure. Such reconciliation, however, will be absolutely impossible until there is agreement about the essential features of *sensibility* and *reason* and about the *relation* of these faculties to one another – or what amounts to the same thing, until there is agreement about how to determine the concepts of these faculties *thoroughly* by a science of the faculty of representation that rests firmly upon a *universally accepted* principle. Hence, either the shaking in the field of the doctrine of taste, and along with it [52] the absence of a universally accepted *first basic rule* of taste, must continue forever; either aesthetics, with all of its abundant materials, must remain a mere aggregate of mostly unconnected, wavering, half-true observations; either the very possibility of a scientific and reliable doctrine of taste must be denied as before by a large contingent of philosophers themselves; and, finally, either the major and undeniable defects in our theories of the arts will continue to deter our thinking artists from making themselves familiar even with what is feasible in those theories – or that shaking must accelerate the discovery and recognition of a science from which the highest basic rule of taste can be extracted with universal evidence.

The very same shaking that is appearing in the domain of metaphysics and history with regard to all accepted principles of the *true*, and in the domain of aesthetics with regard to all accepted principles of the *beautiful*, is also becoming visible with regard to all accepted principles of the *good*. In the fields of science that concern our *duties* and *rights* in this life

[b] This is also conceded by those who hold that beauty is merely *sensed*. For them, reason itself is only the faculty for *sensing agreement* and *contradiction* and, consequently, is a modification that is *distinctive* of the *human* faculty of sensation.

and the ground for our hopes in a *future life*, these principles have become more shaky the more skilled the contributors in these fields have become. To the extent that our rights and duties in this life and the ground for our hopes in a future life are based in *original* predispositions (not ones that have been acquired) of our nature, they constitute the subject matter of *morality*, *natural right*, and *pure philosophy of religion*. To the extent that they are modified by the facts of outer experience, however, they become the subject matter of *positive lawgiving*, *positive jurisprudence*, *and positive theology*. The claim of the *naturalists* that the moral [53] lawgiving of nature is older than the positive lawgiving of rulers, that the rights of human beings are older than the rights of citizens, and that natural religion is older than all positive religions is no more true than the claim of the *supernaturalists*, who pass the natural off as a mere consequence of the positive and hold it to be valid only in so far as it can be confirmed by the positive. Both manners of representation are grounded on a very unphilosophical confusion of the forms that are determined in the bare original dispositions of humanity with the forms that are recognized and accepted in the world. That the positive forms actually preceded the natural ones is shown by history; that they had to precede the natural ones is shown by the limited nature of the human spirit, which can gradually attain cognition of itself only through a long-sustained use of its powers, aided by favorable external circumstances. From the beginning of civil society, humanity's moral nature was operative through its active rational nature. This nature was operative before all civil and scientific culture, for both of these are possible only through the spontaneity of human nature. But for a long time it had to operate wholly unrecognized – and it had to be *misconstrued* even longer – because a familiarity with it that is grounded on universally accepted principles can be the result only of a late scientific culture that has prospered to a very high degree. Until then, reason was forced to seek somewhere outside itself the grounds of its moral agency – grounds that were unknown to it, or not known determinately enough – and to take the *effects* of its own activity, which appear in experience and are modified, of course, by external circumstances, to be causes of that activity. Reason was forced to explain the meaning of the vaguely discerned demands of its moral nature in terms of *facts* that partly owe their existence to the attempts to validate those demands. If, [54] among all the traces of a moral origin that the philosopher admires in what is *positive* [*law*], he still cannot ignore the mark that it bears of the immaturity of the human spirit, then he can just as little abstain from marveling at how this law is a wise educational institution perfectly suited to this immaturity. Even among positive law that deviates from the laws of reason – where the philosopher meets the same mark of immaturity – he cannot avoid perceiving that beneficent hand, guiding from the *outside*, which is and will remain indispensable to humanity as long as humanity is not able to guide itself according to the inner law of its spontaneous powers.

There are wholly irrefutable grounds for the priority that positive jurisprudence and positive theology have previously claimed over natural right and natural theology, and that is by no means made known by the mere ranking of academic faculties alone. The disciplines of positive jurisprudence and positive theology are accepted in the actual world and are sustained by the power of the state and the needs of its members; whereas the disciplines of natural right and natural theology have not even been universally recognized in study halls and until now have remained problematic even among professional philosophers. The content of natural right and of natural theology is partly scattered in the works of some original minds, mixed in with paradoxical fancies, and partly set down in compendiums that contradict one another, including even the most excellent among them; whereas the content of positive jurisprudence and positive theology remains fixed in the law books and sacred documents of nations. Natural right and natural theology are propagated by the disputed issues of philosophers, and positive jurisprudence and positive theology by education, custom, and public institutions – in a word, by all the mainsprings of political machines. At the universities philosophy has for ages been the indentured maidservant of the [55] positive sciences, which always decided her fate according to the nature of the services that they could expect from her. At the hands of the *scholastics* the misunderstood formulas of *Aristotle* gradually acquired a meaning that was dictated by the needs at that time of the authorities of faith and the law, and they were championed by these authorities against the philosophy of *Descartes* with a pressure that forced many a Cartesian to give up his position or his system. This [battle] raged on until Cartesianism became malleable enough to demonstrate the thoroughgoing reasonableness of the Athanasian Creed, the Council of Trent, the Symbolic Books, the Code of Justinian, the Saxon Mirror,[36] and so on.

[36] *Sachsenspiegel*, the first compilation of German law, edited by Eike von Repgow in 1235.

Cartesianism in turn was subsequently protected with the same zeal against the *Leibnizian-Wolffian philosophy* until this philosophy also gradually succeeded in justifying its orthodoxy to the majority. In the brighter days of this philosophy a remarkable period finally commenced in which positive jurisprudence – and to a greater extent, the positive theology of the Protestants – rose to a respectable degree of perfection through a very zealous, appropriate, and successful use and cultivation of the *ancillary* historical *sciences*; in their current degree of perfection, these sciences have become a point of honor for our age. Philosophy now became *free*, but, because it was thought that *history* could manage matters better, philosophy was for the most part released from the service that from now on it offered voluntarily. Academic philosophers were now no longer forced to adhere to commonly held formulas as fearfully as before, and philosophy gradually discarded its systematic form along with those formulas. It appeared more and more to give up all hopes and aspirations for universally accepted [56] principles, and it adopted a new form that won for it the name *eclectic* among its practitioners and admirers. Many a famous recent theologian or jurist demands nothing more from the philosophy he has relinquished than that it recognize along with him the basic truths of religion and morality as claims of *common sense*. At the same time, he *tolerates* or *ignores* the fact that every philosopher excerpts fragments at will from all the ancient and modern philosophical systems, including even the most ill-reputed of them, and assembles them in his own way into a new whole without thereby allowing himself to be guided by any universally accepted principle other than the principle of *being compatible* with the most indispensable, basic practical truths. This principle is adopted for a very understandable reason, and it is all the more easily adhered to because the total lack of other universally adopted principles allows this one principle to give to basic truths – as well as to fragments lacking any determinately fixed signification – a meaning whereby this *compatibility* is always maintained. Some of our most deserving reformers of positive theology and positive jurisprudence distinguish themselves just as strikingly by the narrowness of their philosophical insights as by the magnitude of their historical erudition; and others among them have even won themselves the honorary title of being philosophers in spirit simply through public proofs of their indifference to philosophy – or as they would prefer to call them, proofs of their tolerant attitude toward the opinions of philosophers.[c]

[57] The first principle of Protestantism declares reason to be the highest arbiter in all matters of religion and the only legitimate interpreter of the meaning of the Bible. Faithful to this first principle, and guided by superior knowledge of original languages, philology, and church history, our more recent exegetes have gradually extracted from the most important *formulas* of the sacred sources a meaning that the composers of the Symbolic Books surely could not have dreamed of, given the state of the ancillary sciences at that time. The number and influence of Protestant theologians who take the Symbolic Books to be the *non plus ultra*[37] of exegetical insight – or rather who seek to adopt them in place of the infallible church as the guardian of reason – have considerably decreased, and even the terms *orthodox* and *heterodox* are being used less and less frequently and with less and less animosity. But in so far as, on the one hand, advocates of the symbolic doctrine – or as they express themselves, of the *pure doctrine* – still arise from time to time who lack neither acuity nor knowledge of the ancillary historical sciences; and in so far as, on the other hand, the defenders of the free use of reason are in disagreement among themselves about the most significant results of their exegesis; in so far as they diverge from one another in explaining central passages; and in so far as the important meanings of the terms *faith*, *revelation*, *inspiration*, *supernatural*, etc. seem sometimes to be left intentionally indeterminate, while sometimes defined by directly opposed features – it is becoming increasingly evident that the lofty aim of positive theology cannot very well be reached through the use of the ancillary historical sciences alone, and that there must be certain *guiding ideas* that cannot be drawn from sacred sources by any grammatical, philosophical, or historical erudition, [58] or made to agree with the spirit of those sources. One must be in agreement about the thoroughgoing determination of these ideas *beforehand* if one is ever to arrive, through an appropriate use of erudition, at something settled and firmly established. But, then, are our more famous theologians even in agreement about whether something settled and firmly established is possible

[c] That this does *not* apply *to all* who carry such titles would go without saying were I not also read by people for whom nothing goes without saying.

[37] Highest point.

in the domain of their science, or indeed even desirable? And do not those who expressly cast doubt on this in their writings forget that all their works have, and can have, no other aim than to settle and firmly establish something? Do not our most famous exegetes still dispute the preliminary question of whether the pure idea of the deity is obtained from the Bible, or whether it must instead precede all exegesis as the highest criterion of the manners of representing the deity that appear in the Bible? Have not our theological moralists disputed until this very hour the idea of moral obligation and its ground – namely whether they must first be obtained from the Gospels, or whether they instead serve as the basis for the proper meaning of the Gospel teachings? And are those who are in agreement among themselves about the natural origin of the ideas of God and morality, and who include them among the most significant basic doctrines of their systems, in agreement among themselves with regard to even a single fully determinate feature of these principal ideas? And how should they be when even professional philosophers, who make the correction and establishment of those ideas into their chief occupation, are tangled up in a highly involved feud over every feature of these ideas?

If positive *jurisprudence*, taken as a whole, has fallen behind positive theology, the cause of this is in no way due to the circumstance that it has been developed by less numerous and skillful [59] hands; rather it lies in the nature of its subject matter, which depends more on the lawgiver than on the law expert. In modern times, even positive jurisprudence has gained considerably through its ancillary historical sciences. It has several more advantages to draw from them than theology does from its own ancillary sciences because jurisprudence relies more on facts than theology does and has a much richer set of historical sources. But should not the frequent, extensive, and one-sided occupation of the spirit with the immeasurable content of its memory, which is unavoidable in the use of those sources, partly contain the most natural ground of explanation for the *fact* that our lawyers, including even some of the most famous and most deserving among them, are still continuing, with all the previous advances of their science, to build positive right – not only to the extent that it is *positive* but also to the extent that it is *right* at all – on mere historical data? Should not the custom of having reason measure each of its steps by history partly contain the ground of explanation for this fact? Is this fact not fully explained when these circumstances are taken together with the exclusive high regard for historical results that is occasioned by them, and that is bound up with a disdain for philosophical results? In so far as there can be, and actually are, positive laws that in all of their *political actuality* are *morally impossible*, the moral possibility of a positive law depends in no way on its political existence. And in so far as *all rights*, with the sole exception of the right of the stronger, can be determined only by laws that are morally possible, this moral possibility must be the first *ground* of all rights and thus also of positive rights. It is the highest basic rule according to which the meaning of positive laws must be determined; and whenever a case comes up in which one of these laws does not admit of any meaning whatsoever that can be reconciled with this rule, [60] it is the most sacred duty of the law expert to point out the invalidity of such a law to the lawgiving power and to press for recognition of this fact. Now, if this highest rule of right is not firmly established in any universally accepted *basic principle* that is secured against all ambiguity; and if it is set aside by teachers of positive right as an insoluble and dispensable problem of metaphysics; indeed, if it is lost from sight even among the historical grounds of positive laws – then at that very moment this rule will be replaced by the miserable *letter* of even such laws that perpetuate the barbarity of the dark ages in which they originated. It will be replaced by those laws in whose existence the self-interest and imperiousness of the stronger oppressors had at least as much of a role as the effort of dawning reason to establish the vaguely discerned rights of humanity. Would that heaven wanted any of at least the more famous and more deserving lawyers to belong among the defenders of that *letter*! But positive jurisprudence, like positive theology, has now more than ever its orthodoxy and heterodoxy, an historical faction and a philosophical faction, one concerned with building on tradition and current possession and one with building on the moral *ought*. From time to time their conflict extends over into a number of very important subjects that at present concern nothing less than the rights of princes in general, the legitimacy of the death penalty, serfdom, slave-trade, and other similar matters. And this conflict is all the more difficult to resolve because, given the still wholly undecided line of demarcation between positive and natural right, it is sometimes carried on in one domain and sometimes in the other.

It is not easy to blame a legal scholar of the historical faction for adhering exclusively [61] to the facts when one considers that his philosophical opponents are in actual agreement only with regard to the claim that there is a highest rule of right but not at all with regard to the question of what this rule consists in. The dispute over the fundamental concept and first principle of natural right has become more intricate and more conspicuous the more zealously this philosophical component of the science of law has been developed in recent times, and it has contributed in no small way to making us accustomed to distinguishing natural right only by a kind of opposition to positive right, and to reckoning the latter as *settled* and the former as *disputed*. *Philosophers*, of course, have *several* first principles of natural right, of which only one or none can be genuine; but *philosophy* to date has yet to establish *any* of them – if one does not want to call the opinion of *one* man or *one* faction "*philosophy*" at the expense of all others. Sometimes the *ground* of natural right is confused with its *basic principle*; sometimes the ground for cognition of this principle is separated from the ground of its existence and bindingness. One writer believes that natural right is wholly independent of morality; another thinks that the two flow so much into one another that any attempt at determining a boundary between them must simply be abandoned.

The *ground* of natural right is sought by some in a *state of nature* that preceded all civil constitutions, and by others in a *society* that is present now. For some, a *state of nature* means a mere state of non-rational animality in which no other right counts but the right of the stronger, whereas for others it embodies the *original predispositions* of human nature, considered in their complete purity and unhindered [62] use. The *original predisposition* that is supposed to contain the ground of natural right is sometimes passed off as a self-interested drive, sometimes as an unselfish drive,[38] sometimes as the drive for self-preservation, sometimes as an innate social inclination, sometimes as a mere need of sensibility, and sometimes as reason's distinctive manner of acting. Through each of these different derivations a *different* first principle of natural right is obtained, each of which announces its indeterminacy and inadequacy conspicuously enough by the *different formulas* in which it is dressed up even by those who believe that they are in agreement about its essence. Perhaps only half of those working on natural right, however,

38 Translating *eigennützigen* as "self-interested" and *uneigennützigen* (literally "non-self-interested") as "unselfish." Cf. below, n. 42.

find it worth the trouble to dispute with one another over these formulas (each of which is declared by its defenders to be the only possible first principle). This feud is declared by the rest to be a mere *dispute about words*, for they believe that what matters is not so much the *expression* of the principle but its *meaning*. They believe that the variety in manners of human representation regarding one and the same object also necessitates a variety of formulas, and that natural right would obviously have far more to gain if it were supported by *several* principles instead of only *a single* principle. But this very indifference regarding the unity of the principle may very well demonstrate – even more than the dispute about it does – how far we still are from a thoroughly determined fundamental concept of natural right. Once it is discovered and purified, this concept will make impossible all variety in manners of representation – and, to the extent that philosophical language does not have synonyms, all variety of expression, too – just as certainly as it itself is necessarily a *single* concept grounded in the *common* character of humanity that is shared by all individuals. [63] Yet, how is the thoroughgoing determination of that important fundamental concept to be possible as long as we have nothing but disputed opinions to show for regarding the *relation of the sensible drive* to the *spontaneity of reason*? How is it possible as long as independent thinkers are in disagreement about the essential difference and the essential connection between *sensibility* and *reason* and, consequently, as long as those matters remain wholly undecided which alone can determine the nature of the demands of sensibility that are grounded on our need, as well as the nature of the restrictions of the demands that are grounded on the positive power of our spirit? How is it possible as long as we have no science to offer of the original constitution of our faculty of representation and desire, a science that rests firmly on a *universally accepted principle*? Hence, the shaking in the domain of *natural right* and in all the related fields of *positive right* will either continue forever, or it will accelerate the discovery and recognition of this new science. Without this science no unity among independent thinkers is conceivable concerning a first principle of natural right – or, indeed, concerning any determinate concept of *right at all*.

One may not so easily concede the indispensability of the aforementioned new science for the grounding of *morality*, for it cannot be repeated often enough with regard to morality that it rests firmly on an unshakeable ground, and that it has already been brought to a degree of evidence that yields little or nothing to mathematical evidence. It is said that

> nature would have provided very poorly for the well-being of humanity and its lofty intentions if she had left the indispensable cognition of the moral law to the speculations and quarrels of the philosophers. In fact, whereas morality occasions misunderstanding and conflict the moment one tries to fathom it by *reason*, this very same morality announces [64] its presence as well as its absence in human actions through unambiguous, agreeable and disagreeable sensations to which even the long habit of vice can hardly become sufficiently callous. People from the lower classes and youths who have scarcely moved beyond their childhood years not only know how to distinguish moral actions from immoral ones but can also specify a precise degree of morality for them – even when only the *external* circumstances of a moral event are determined and clearly presented to them. In every textbook of theoretical philosophy, more or less essential errors and contradictions crop up; but it might be difficult to cite a compendium of morality in which an immoral action is passed off as moral, or in which one of the essential features of the concept of morality is lacking. What follows from all of this is that morality could be the most reliable and most settled as well as the most important and most commonly useful among all the sciences.

– Nevertheless, the reliability of morality is so far from being universally illuminating that even to this day it is being disputed just as stubbornly as it is being defended. And it is fair that we listen to its opponents as well, who assert:

> If more agreement is found among the moralists than among the metaphysicians, this is a consequence of positive laws and all the forms in general that had to be introduced by civil society for its preservation, forms which have connected honor and shame, reward and punishment to the *manners of representation* that are indispensable for this preservation. Customs and education, as modified by these manners of representation, contain the ground of the [65] so-called moral sensations, which by means of pleasure announce agreement with the priorities of society and its positive bulwarks, and by means of displeasure announce conflict with them. These sensations occur, however, only if the external circumstances of climate, sense organs, etc. have occasioned and

> encouraged these artificial dispositions. Finally, in all cultivated nations that have moved beyond the state of nature, these sensations had to be all the more striking among the young and the lower classes because that age group and those classes are most receptive to custom and education and are least capable of modifying through independent thinking the impressions received from both. As a result of the very ambiguity in the meaning of their words, the formulas of the moralists were always capable of adopting, even in the most dissimilar systems, whatever meaning corresponded to the politically necessary manner of representation that had been introduced – a meaning which also, however, begins to be disputed as soon as an attempt is made to trace it back to the so-called *internal* grounds of morality. With every effort of thinking minds to illuminate these formulas fully, and with every attempt to subordinate all of them to a common principle, their meaning is elevated beyond the common and confused manner of representation. But to the same extent that this is happening, the incompatibility of these formulas becomes all the more conspicuous and the dispute between their defenders becomes all the more intricate – a dispute which, reduced to its simplest terms, leaves no impartial spectator to doubt that it is precisely among the moralists where *whether or not there is a moral law* is least of all settled.

In my view, the most striking thing about this dispute between the opponents and defenders of the reliability of morality is that both of them, as a result of a common misunderstanding, confuse a science with its [66] subject matter, [the science of] morality with morality,[39] and the ground of the latter with the basic principle of the former. The defenders project the existence, necessity, and sacredness of the moral law onto the science of these properties, while the opponents project the indeterminacy and wavering of the science onto the moral law itself. Both sides consider [the science of] morality[40] to be incapable of improvement – the defenders because they presume it to contain already fully developed and purified principles, the opponents because they deny it all possible principles. As a result, and to the extent that it depends on them, both hinder the advances of the science. From time immemorial, *reason* and

[39] In this sentence the terms translated as "morality" are (in order): *Moral*, *Moral*, and *Moralität*. See above, the Third Letter from the *Merkur*, p. 11, n. 59.
[40] *Moral*.

the *sun* have illuminated and nourished the sphere of human perception and activity. From its beneficent effects one came to know the illuminating and warming powers of the sun long before beginning to investigate, in a scientific manner, the way these powers operate. It would be absurd to confuse cognition from powers that do not depend on our insight into them, and which were always present and operative, with the science concerning the mode of their operation – a science that can become a genuine science only through gradual advances, and that depends in part on the current state of our other insights. But it would be just as absurd, I claim, to deny the existence of these powers on account of the fact that the cognition of their mode of operation has not yet risen to the rank of a completed science.

To claim with the Popular Philosophers that one should enjoy and make use of the benefits of the sun and reason without brooding over how we came to acquire them would be tantamount to using an allegory to conceal a no less absurd notion. The further reason advances in its effects in a cultivated nation, the greater its need becomes to act according to a distinct representation of its laws. [67] The same idea that has become distinct through an analysis of its immediate features becomes indistinct the very moment the discussion turns to the features of those features; and the determination of them gives rise to a dispute. There are sicknesses against which the human body is protected by the tender age of childhood, and that would never appear without the developed organs, nourishment, and occupations of a more mature age. And there are errors that presuppose a considerable degree of cultivation of spirit, errors that are impossible when the concept they concern is in a state of utter confusion; they crop up only slowly, during the gradual development of a concept that becomes *complete* only after many unsuccessful attempts. Yet, through the nourishment drawn from a growing abundance of half-true insights as well as through the increasingly skilled astuteness of the defenders of these insights, these errors are also bound to become more and more serious. Perhaps this applies more to the idea of morality than to any other idea. The more the people of an age think, the more pressing the need becomes for thinking this idea *correctly*, and the greater the danger becomes of thinking it, too. The idea of morality is thought incorrectly as soon as one of its essential features is passed over when thinking it or as soon as something that does not belong in its basic concept is included in it; and this idea can be protected against such incorrectness only by a fully completed development of its features, one that extends to the boundary of all that is comprehensible. As long as its last divisible components remain unanalyzed, as long as the components that are found are not fully determined and recognized as *first principles*, and as long as there is no certainty that a lack or excess of essential features is not lying hidden in the undeveloped components, the idea will not be thought either *purely* [68] or *completely*, and will more or less be a plaything of chance.

The idea of morality has made exceptional gains through the fact that our professional moralists have generally adopted the distinction between *morality* and *legality* and have sought in the *ground of its bindingness* the essential feature distinguishing the moral law from every other sensible drive. But on account of this very same fact, any mistake about this ground becomes all the more serious the more the *entire meaning of the moral law depends* on the determination of it. In all the explanations that previous philosophy has given for this ground, the *drive for pleasure* and the *law of reason* appear more or less expressly as essential features of this ground.[d] In no way do I want to claim here what I hope to be able to prove rigorously for the first time on another occasion, namely that the idea of morality in all of these explanations turns out to be incorrect because of the essentially superfluous feature of the drive for pleasure or because of the essentially incomplete feature of the law of reason. But it cannot and should not be left unmentioned here that the *mutual relation* of these two features is entirely undecided even among those philosophers who expressly declare themselves for both, and that our thinking moralists are less in agreement at present than ever before with regard to the question of whether in moral lawgiving the drive for pleasure is subordinate to reason or reason is subordinate to the drive for pleasure.

[69] Some philosophers find in the drive for pleasure the *necessity* through which the rule of reason becomes a binding law for the will. They take this drive to be the genuine lawgiver, making use of reason only for the *execution* of laws that obtained their sanction solely through this drive – laws that, no matter how beneficial the result of their observance is to the public, are able to hold interest for every individual

[d] [This is true] even in the *Stoic philosophy*, which excludes pleasure from the motives of morality only in the form of *lust*, and derives the desire for the *highest good* from a correct judgment of the understanding – just as it derives the desire for illusory goods from an incorrect judgment of the understanding, which this sect mixes up with sensibility.

will only through the pleasure that their observance affords or promises, or through the displeasure that it prevents. Other philosophers, in contrast, recognize reason to be the genuine and rightful lawgiver but deny it, in the form in which it is present in the human spirit, the spontaneous faculty for bringing about the actual *acceptance* of the laws that are given by reason.[41] For while such laws are *valid* in themselves without the sanction of the drive for pleasure, they are without the executive power that, for finite beings, can lie only in this drive.

The philosophers of the first group, who believe that they have discovered the determining ground of moral bindingness in the drive for pleasure, quarrel with each other about the manner in which this ground is present in that drive – whether it inheres in this drive originally, innately, and naturally or is derived, acquired, and artificial. Some hold the opinion that in the state of nature the drive for pleasure gives its sanction to no other law than that of instinct, and that, if this drive is to urge observance of a law that curbs instinct, it can obtain its direction only from outside, from custom and education, and from the institutions of civil society. The political state, for instance, is forced by the self-interested drives *of all* who are united within it to limit the self-interested drives of *individuals*, and, through its superiority in prudence and power, it is in a position to bring about the acceptance of these limitations [70] by connecting artificial, private advantages and disadvantages with the advancement or diminution of the common good.

Because they are divided between essentially different opinions even with regard to the specific *manner* in which moral bindingness is grounded in the natural drive for pleasure, the defenders of the *natural* origin of moral bindingness in the drive for pleasure are all the less able to make common cause against their opponents, whom they blame, not unjustly, for the theoretical annihilation of all morality. *Some* of these defenders seek the nature of the drive for pleasure in sensibility – or rather, in the need of sensibility – and confuse sensibility in general with sensibility as it is modified by the sense organs. Moreover, they classify all possible kinds of pleasure under the genus of physical pleasure. They declare morality to be refined and well-understood self-interest, and virtue to be a means for the necessary end of that drive for enjoyment

[41] Here *wirklich geltend* (actually accepted) contrasts with *an sich gültigen* (valid in themselves) in a way that parallels Reinhold's frequent distinction between *allgemeingeltend* and *allgemeingültig*.

which has been extended by reason (or to be a means for obtaining happiness, which is supposed to consist in the highest degree and longest duration of the greatest possible sum of agreeable sensations). *Other* defenders of pleasure, in contrast, believe that two wholly different drives for pleasure have to be assumed in human nature – a self-interested one, which has an individual's own well-being as its object, and an unselfish[42] one, which has the well-being of others as its object. Pleasure in the well-being of others and the unselfish interest in the common good presuppose, according to their opinion, a distinct *sense* in the mind, which, under the name of *moral sense*, must be distinguished from sensibility and adopted as the ground of moral bindingness without, however, being further explainable.

Those who recognize *reason* as the moral lawgiver are in disagreement among themselves [71] as to whether they should concede this honor to *human* or *divine* reason. Some assert that morality is the natural way for a will to act that is determined by human reason, and that a will determined by reason can will nothing but *perfection*, which is the natural *object* of reason. They are also quite in agreement that the perfection of moral actions consists in their *end*. But what is this end? If it is, again, perfection, what is to be understood by perfection in this case? Is it the agreement of all inclinations and dispositions for the greatest possible capacity for enjoyment? Is it the greatest possible development of all human powers? Is it the greatest possible well-being of humanity in general? Or is it all of these taken together? And if this is the case, which among the different grounds of motivation determines the *moral* will in the *first* instance? On this topic, the opinions of the defenders of the principle of perfection are so diverse that, upon closer examination, they have nothing but the expression *perfection* in common amongst themselves.

The *supernaturalists* hold the opinion that they have settled this disagreement, like all other disagreements concerning moral bindingness, by seeking this ground in the divine will, which is determined by infinite reason but which, on precisely this account, is inscrutable by finite reason and known to human beings only through *revelation*. But supporters of this opinion must either accept an immediate divine inspiration that initiates each human being into this incomprehensible will, or they

[42] *Uneigennützigen*.

must accept infallible interpreters for the meaning of the sacred sources; and they must allow continual miracles to secure the authentication of both against all fear of illusion and error. Moreover, they are no more [72] in agreement among themselves than any other faction is with regard to whether the human will is determined to conform to the divine will by reason, by the drive for pleasure, or by the immediate influence of the deity. Or what comes to the same thing, they are in disagreement about what the *internal* ground of moral bindingness consists in. Here I will remain silent about the idea of *free will*, which is intimately connected to the idea of morality, and which at the present time is being denied more than ever by the fatalists, doubted by the dogmatic skeptics, misconstrued by the determinists, and sought outside nature by the supernaturalists. The inadequacy of all previous discussions of this important idea has become so striking to many of our most prominent philosophical writers that they have no qualms about claiming that the question, What does freedom consist in?, and hence also the question, Can freedom be thought?, are absolutely unanswerable and therefore wholly a matter of indifference for morality.

To be precise, the *shaking* of the *scientific foundation* of *morality* that has become so striking through all of these phenomena consists in the wavering of all previous manners of representation regarding *reason*, the *drive for pleasure*, and *their relation to one another*. It clearly reveals how far we are from a finished *thoroughgoing* development of the concepts of *reason* and *sensibility*, the spontaneous power of the one and the drive grounded on need of the other, the determining and determinable in morality – a development that is possible only by means of a science of the human faculty of representation and desire that is firmly established on a *universally accepted principle*. Hence, either this shaking must continue forever to the great detriment of moral culture, or it [73] must lead to the discovery and recognition of that new science.

Now, this *sketch of the shakings* in the fields of all the sciences whose principles presuppose self-cognition of the human spirit may, of course, seem to many to be a satire of the spirit of our age. But in my eyes it contains the materials that a more adept pen than mine could work up into a most convincing eulogy of that same spirit. To be sure, philosophers have been disputing from time immemorial, and so it was that in the golden age of Greek philosophy four opposing principal systems came to the fore: the Platonic, Aristotelian, Epicurean, and Stoic.

But never before has the dispute between philosophers been extended to so many fields of science or carried on by so many excellent minds. Never before has the influence of the subjects of this dispute on the well-being and worth of humanity, or the influence of the dispute on these subjects – in a word, its practical interest – become more visible. Never before have the undecided points, whose decision was partly the aim of the dispute and partly a necessary effect of it, been laid out with such precision and traced back to such simple principles. Never before has this dispute heralded such a universal and lively exertion of the noblest powers of the human spirit. After much successful preliminary work as well as many unsuccessful attempts, after many important and actually resolved problems, and after many useless, insipid, and unanswerable questions of dispute – the immense and decisive question concerning the *one thing needed* now resounds unanimously across all scientific fields that must obtain their principles from the nature of the human spirit. *Metaphysics* demands a universally accepted principle for all philosophizing in general, *history* a highest viewpoint for its form, *aesthetics* a highest rule [74] of taste, *religion* a pure idea of the deity that is traceable back to universally accepted principles, *natural right* a first basic principle, and *morality* an ultimate, basic law. That the *doctrinal structures* of all of these sciences, which rest firmly on unshakeable grounds *with regard to their subject matter*, have progressed up to an arch – indeed, so far up that one sees the need for the missing *keystones*[43] – is a merit of our age that can be surpassed only by the merit of having discovered, hewn, and set those keystones themselves. Likewise, once these stones are brought to the right place and position, there will be time for all the beams, braces, and the entire *frame* – which by its very wavering announces clearly enough that it is but a frame – to be cleared away not only without damage to but also for the betterment of the building. With one final and most violent shaking, the one-sided *opinions*[44] of the philosophers on subjects about which humanity is destined not to be always merely *having opinions*[45] will crash down in order to make room for *firmly standing basic principles*.

[43] Cf. Kant, Preface, *Critique of Practical Reason* (5:3). [44] *Meinungen.* [45] *Zu meinen.*

D[46]

Selections from the Third Letter, "The shaking in the domain of the philosophy of religion heralds a reformation of this philosophy: my judgment regarding the Kantian philosophy in general"

And now, dear friend, let us return to *your* portrait and see if it does not perhaps constitute a complete whole once it is taken together with *mine*. If the phenomena that you [75] have arranged together actually share a common ground, then this ground is none other than the old and still persistent misunderstanding – which has become more visible now than ever before – regarding the *limits of the faculty of reason with respect to the affairs of religion*. The indeterminateness and incompleteness of our scientific concepts of *reason* and of *its relation* to the *other* equally misunderstood *faculties of the human spirit* is thus no less the genuine cause here, too, of the wavering of all accepted basic principles than it is in the other scientific fields that I have elucidated. This causal role has come to our attention much more in the shaking of religious manners of representation than in the shaking of all others and, in fact, has struck our attention in a fully immediate way. Here the disputed points have already been reduced to such simple terms that a number of the disputing factions are latching directly onto reason itself, which they elevate or degrade depending on whether or not they believe that they have cause to be satisfied with its actual or alleged decisions. There are, of course, those who feel dissatisfied, who press against reason with a certain passionate vehemence and storm it for more satisfying answers; and after battling with it for a time in vain, they either take up sides with the faction against reason or escape beyond the confines of the battlefield as indifferent spectators. There are those who feel satisfied, who precisely on account of their satisfaction are content with previous answers that repeat reason's old proofs with various new expressions and turns of phrase; and they get caught up amongst themselves in what is truly a dispute about words concerning those expressions – a dispute in which they commonly forget the objections of the dissatisfied ones to the matter at hand,

[46] These selections from the 1790 edition (pp. 74–7, 84–7, and 90–7) are revised and heavily expanded versions of pp. 105–7, 116–18, and 122–3 of the First Letter from the *Merkur*.

provided they do not take themselves [76] to have defeated those objections, by the aforesaid new expressions, as errors refuted long ago.

But the truly independent thinkers on both sides, on whom the fate of the whole dispute depends in the end, in no way consider the dispute to be settled. And their persistent effort – which is more lively today than ever before – to justify their satisfaction or dissatisfaction with the previous decisions of reason through *new* grounds is keeping the dispute alive. Moreover, it is steering this dispute in a fortunate direction, one that is making ever more indispensable a new solution to the old problem concerning the faculty of reason and, as a result of the preliminary establishment of its conditions, is bringing this solution ever nearer.

The persisting dispute over each of its questions is the most convincing proof that the answers to every question in so-called *natural theology* that reason has given – or more precisely, the answers that have been given in the name of reason – lack that evidence, which, especially in such important matters, ought to be expressed in terms of universal validity. The most striking example of such a question is that which concerns *the existence of the deity*. Let us stay with this example.

We shall suppose once and for all that it was reason which, from the first stages of its development, unceasingly raised this question. I know that believers and nonbelievers reject this supposition. Believers claim that reason could never arrive at this question on its own, and nonbelievers claim that reason declares this question to be superfluous. But I know that you, my friend, are neither a believer nor a nonbeliever of this sort, and that you are in agreement with me that reason not only can raise this question but also must raise it. – Now given this supposition, it had to become impossible for reason in [77] its attempts to answer this immense question to pass by the science that contains its most distinctive concepts, principles, and basic principles[47] – in a word, [the science of] *metaphysics*, which today is so denounced. Moreover, this science owes its origin as well as its gradual cultivation chiefly to the question of God's existence. In fact, the whole subject matter of this question can be thought in no other way than with concepts that become more metaphysical the more they are purified from the foreign admixtures of fantasy and the sediment of common prejudices, and the more firmly one's eyes are fixed upon them in continual examination. To be sure, one still adduces even in our

47 *Begriffe, Prinzipien und Grundsätze.*

day so-called historical, physical, and moral proofs for God's existence; but the necessary relation of such proofs to the metaphysical concept of an *unconditioned necessary existence* is no longer a secret to our independent thinkers and has not been for a long time. And many among them have shown with the most fortunate astuteness that the metaphysical notions lying at the basis of *natural* theology could indeed be confirmed by natural and even supernatural *revelation*, but not replaced by or derived from it.

. . . [84] If in the investigation of this domain one does not want to lose oneself outside it in the infinite space in which fantasy plays, then its limits, before all else, must be precisely and definitely specified. That is to say, for the following questions an answer must be found that rests firmly on a universally accepted principle: What is *cognizable* in general? What is to be understood by the *faculty of cognition*? And in what in general does the distinctive occupation of *reason* in cognition consist?

I think, dear friend, I see you shaking your head over these problems. Not, for example, because you remain unconvinced that their solution is the *only possible* path that could at all lead to our goal. "But (I hear you saying) these questions still remain problems after everything that has been accomplished in speculative philosophy to date by the whole lot of men, great and small, and precisely this little fact provides a strong presumption that they will also remain problems forever." – Admittedly, in the foregoing I was able to indicate only in a very cursory manner the course that the human spirit had to take in order to arrive at these problems; nonetheless, it seems to me that your objection can be answered from what has already been said. All the more essential fates that our speculative philosophy has experienced until now had [85] to be *undergone* before one could think of even *posing* those problems – let alone solving them – in their distinctive meaning, and thus in that meaning that is determined by the aim of their solution. It probably never could have occurred to all those philosophers who believed that they had *already found* the grounds for cognition of the basic truths of religion and morality – as well as the first principles of natural right and morality – to ask themselves in earnest *whether* and *how* it would even be *possible* for reason to lay down universally valid principles and grounds of cognition. This is so because they believed that their reason was in *actual possession* of such principles and grounds of cognition. And had these questions been posed to them by others, they would have presented reason's alleged possessions in lieu of any answer. The *atheists* and *supernaturalists*, who likewise *forestalled* those questions by means of decisive answers, although of a wholly other kind, would have proceeded in the very same manner. And now I ask you, dear friend, not indeed to forget that the philosophical world has from time immemorial consisted mainly of *dogmatists*, such that for every skeptic one could perhaps count a hundred dogmatists.

This very wide and heavily trodden path up to the posing and solving of the problems occasioned by critical doubt was in any case unavoidable, and it was even indispensable as an early preparation for their solution. Without the zeal of the dogmatists, which was sustained and enlivened by a sweet imagining of found truths, those numerous and in part marvelous preliminary exercises of the philosophical spirit would not have been achieved to which reason owes that degree of development which more profound undertakings presuppose. [86] During this protracted period the merit of *skepticism* consisted in little else than forcing the dogmatists partly to sharpen their old proofs and partly to think up new ones, setting bounds to their self-complacency, and keeping their zeal alive. But it was never capable of tearing them away from their supposed cognitions of the supersensible. It had nothing better to give them in return. And to the question, *What is cognizable?*, it would have had no other answer than, *Nothing*! – or at most, *I do not know*! The dogmatists thus proceeded unhindered on their paths and had to proceed *far enough* for them and their spectators to see that these paths were leading them further away from their goal the further they advanced along them. Moreover, they had to proceed on these paths far enough for the skeptics to be convinced by the appearance of what looked like a *third* path that had never been trodden before and that was secured against all their previous objections. *Before* this point in time it would have been neither advisable nor possible to hold the dogmatists up in their advances. Nothing is more understandable than why this moment did not come sooner. The history of peoples and epochs that have achieved something noteworthy in the sciences shows us clearly enough the causes by which the advances of philosophy were often interrupted or rendered difficult. After the revival of the sciences among us, the dogmatists needed a fairly long time before they could appear in two main factions, the *orthodox* and *heterodox*, that would more or less keep one another in balance – before the *latter* were allowed to take care of their natural necessities in a sufficiently free and open manner and before the *former* felt themselves forced to call on reason for help. Moreover, a fairly long time was needed before the difficulty of a verdict finally became so enormous and striking over the course of the continuing battle that the restrained contingent of even the [87] professional theologians and philosophers arrived at the thought that the whole feud could not come to an end at all, or at least in no way by means of the weapons used heretofore. But the important interest that humanity takes in the still undecided main question,[48] which concerns nothing less than the scientific foundations of religion, is ever persistent. Hence, however much the views that declare the dispute between the naturalists and supernaturalists to be necessarily interminable – and thus also in vain – serve to accommodate the *empiricists*, there remains decisive support for the opposite conviction "that this dispute depends on a misunderstanding with which it must some day terminate on its own."

... [90] Since each side must now justify before its opponent its familiarity with reason, each disputant feels compelled to acquire proofs for grounds that will also be illuminating for his opponents – proofs that until now have satisfied only himself and his faction. Each disputant must therefore go beyond the principles that he previously held to be basic, inquire into features of reason that he has not yet found, and seek to ground in a universally valid way – that is, in a way that is valid for himself and his opponents – his cognition of the faculty and entitlements of reason. Hence, none of the disputing factions can be any more content with its own previous cognition of reason than it is with its opponents' cognition of reason. None can rest satisfied with its old investigations, and thus the need for a new investigation into the faculty of representation must ultimately become universally accepted by the thinking minds of both factions, just as now each faction is already convinced that reason has been misconstrued (by its opponents).

The problem regarding *what reason is capable of* is thus prepared, set as a task, and necessitated by the prevailing circumstances of our day. It would indeed be no small merit of our century to have [settled] the old and unholy misunderstanding of reason, reason's misunderstanding of itself. However unavoidable this misunderstanding was for the human spirit on the long and difficult path that it had to traverse prior to the

[48] *Hauptfrage*, used here to refer to the question of God's existence, which Reinhold treats as one of the two "main questions" of the metaphysics of philosophy of religion.

scientific cognition of its faculty, it nevertheless [91] belongs among the worst ills from which humanity has ever suffered. For centuries it has bred all kinds of misfortune in the world. It has cost cultivated nations the bloody and unbloody feuds between orthodoxy and heterodoxy, made inevitable nonbelief and superstition, squandered the energies of many excellent minds with useless hair-splitting and squabbling, and seemed as if it would have to continue forever with all of these sad consequences. – It would then indeed be no small merit, I say, to have drawn out *this* misunderstanding from the obscurity of confused concepts and, as a result, to have arrived at a problem whose solution offers us hope for nothing less than universally valid first principles for our duties and rights in this life and a universally valid ground for our expectation of a future life. Such a solution promises the end of all philosophical and theological heresies and, in the domain of speculative philosophy, an everlasting peace of which not even *Saint-Pierre*[49] had dreamed. But what if the solution of this immense problem were reserved for our century, which is nearing its end, and the majority of Germany's sound minds that occupy themselves with philosophy were to come to an agreement concerning universally valid principles before this century has entirely run out? Moreover, what if these minds, which from now on would cease working unknowingly and unwillingly against one another, were to begin voluntarily with joined forces to make universally acceptable that which they had found to be universally valid? In that case a more shining crown could hardly be placed on the merits of our century, and Germany could not open the business of its sublime vocation as the *future school of Europe* with a better-grounded and more appropriate beginning.

I know, dear friend, that my hopes [92] must seem enthusiastic[50] to you. For until now I have been unable to show you much more than the need, which is more pressing today than ever before, for the *object* of those hopes. What will you think, then, of the composure[51] of my philosophy if I tell you that the *ground* from which I expect the fulfillment of my hopes is available in a *single* book? Of course, it is a book that, years after its existence was scarcely noticed, has for several years now

[49] See above, the First Letter from the *Merkur*, p. 123, n. 22.

[50] *Schwärmerisch*, a term also connoting fantasy, or a belief in the fantastic.

[51] *Kaltblütigkeit*, literally "cold-bloodedness," used here in the sense of restraint to contrast with enthusiasm.

become a sensation incomparable to any other. It has set our philosophical public into wholly extraordinary activity and has won for its author an admiration such that attempts to disparage it are revenged with indignation and scorn even by its opponents. Yet, according to the admissions of the author himself and of those whom he recognizes as his genuine students, this same book has *not been understood* by most of its previous reviewers.[e] The *majority* of our famous philosophical writers has declared itself to be *against* it, and some of them are engaged right now in trying to show, in journals and series established primarily for this purpose, that in respect of what they find *true* in the book, its content is *old*, and in respect of what they acknowledge as *new* in it, its content is in part indemonstrable and in part inconsistent. The *gospel of pure reason* is foolishness to the heterodox and an offence to the orthodox;[52] and in no book, with the single exception of the *Apocalypse*, perhaps, has one found such various and quite contradictory [93] things. The Critique of Reason has been proclaimed by *dogmatists* to be an attempt of a *skeptic* who undermines the certainty of all knowledge, by *skeptics* to be an arrogant presumption to erect a new universal dogmatism that rules atop the ruins of previous systems, and by *supernaturalists* to be a subtly raised artifice for supplanting the *historical* foundations of religion and for grounding naturalism without polemics. It is proclaimed by *naturalists* to be a new support propping up a sinking faith-philosophy, by *materialists* to be an idealist refutation of the reality of matter, and by *spiritualists* to be an irresponsible restriction of everything actual to a corporeal world that has been disguised by the term "domain of experience." It is proclaimed by *eclectics* to be the founding of a new *sect* the likes of whose universal smugness and intolerance have never before been seen, a sect that threatens to press the enslaving yoke of a system upon the neck of a German philosophy that has only recently been freed. And, finally, the Critique of Reason is proclaimed by *Popular Philosophers* sometimes to be the *laughable* enterprise – in the midst of our enlightened age of good taste – of driving *common sense* out of the philosophical world through

[e] On this topic, I refer my readers to the treatise, "On the Previous Fate of the Kantian Philosophy," which is to be found added as a *Preface* to [my] *Essay on a New Theory of the Human Faculty of Representation* [*Versuch einer neuen Theorie des menschlichen Vorstellungsvermögens*], but which has also been printed separately by [the same publisher,] *Mauke in Jena* [1789].

[52] Cf. 1 Corinthians 1: 23.

scholastic terminology and hair-splitting, and sometimes to be the *irksome* stumbling block that makes inaccessible the way to folk philosophy that has recently been paved by so many easily understandable writers, a stumbling block by which the understanding of hopeful youths is already being thwarted and the philosophical reputation of famous men destroyed. Admittedly, I can answer these accusations here with nothing else than the assurance, significant only in the eyes of my friend, that in the Critique of Reason I have found *the very opposite* of *every* objection that has come to my attention. [94] I discovered this after taking the leisure time to read through the work *five times*, entirely free from all preoccupations and worries, and with as much attentiveness as I could muster. Moreover, I brought with me to my first readings all the prejudices unfavorable for the work that one can presuppose in a human being who, after a ten-year occupation with speculative philosophy, had finally traded all the dogmatic systems that one after another had been adopted by him for nothing less than a dogmatic skepticism. The varied and *contradictory reports* about the actual nature and value of the Kantian philosophy that its opponents are allowing to reach the public are precisely what absolve me, before you and every fair thinking person, from the hateful reproach of "wanting to be more clever than the majority of my philosophical contemporaries." Nevertheless, on account of my judgment of this *new philosophy*, I would be forfeiting all good opinion of my power of judgment and discretion among that majority of the public if my judgment were to be publicly known. But even with this and every other danger, I would have no qualms about confessing loudly and publicly what I swear to you here: that I consider the Critique of Reason[53] to be the greatest among all the masterworks of philosophical spirit known to me, that through it I have been put in a position to answer *all* of my philosophical doubts in a way that fully satisfies my mind and heart, and that according to my most lively conviction it has furnished *all* the data for the solution of the *immense problem* that has been brought forward and thrown open as a result of the shaking in the fields of the sciences that I have depicted. The *fully new* and *wholly complete* development of the *faculty of cognition* that [95] is contained in it *unifies* the acclaimed but contradictory viewpoints from which *Locke* and *Leibniz*

[53] This is perhaps the most striking example of Reinhold's unusual procedure of not giving the full title, even when he is very clearly referring to Kant's *Critique of Pure Reason*.

investigated the human spirit, and it fulfills – indeed surpasses – even the strict demands that *David Hume* has made on philosophy in respect to the certainty of its principles. All of its major components can be traced back to a *universally accepted ground*[f] – which needs only to be vested in a determinate expression and laid out in connection with its consequences in order to become a *universally accepted principle*. As such they would stand firm in a very simple and readily understandable system that could be surveyed in a single glance. On this view not only could a new universally valid *metaphysics* – that is, a genuine science consisting partly of universal and necessary predicates of objects that can be conceived and cognized, and partly of the necessary features of objects that cannot be conceived but can only be thought through reason – be derived with certainty and ease and in a sense that, while previously misunderstood, would satisfy the legitimate demands of all factions; but on this view one could also derive the highest viewpoint of all history, the most fundamental rule of taste, the principle of all philosophy of religion, the first principle of natural right, and the fundamental law of morality. And, consequently, at precisely that point in time when the need for a complete reformation of philosophy had risen to its most extreme on account of a universal shaking in [96] all the fields of the philosophical sciences, we would also have obtained the only possible and fully sufficient means for such a reformation; and we might look forward with joyful expectation to one of the most universal, remarkable, and beneficent revolutions that has ever occurred in the human spirit.

I hope to convince you of the well-groundedness of this expectation by gradually laying out for you in my following letters the most significant *results* that the Kantian philosophy puts forward concerning the *principal theme* of all philosophy, namely *our duties and rights in this life and the ground for our hope in a future life*. Moreover, by making you familiar in advance with the *consequences* of the critical system, I invite and prepare

[f] I have *attempted* to achieve this in my *new theory of the faculty of representation*. [This is a play on the title of Reinhold's 1789 book, which can also be translated as *An Attempt at a New Theory of the Human Faculty of Representation*. See above, n. e.] If this attempt is not wholly unsuccessful, it lays out in a new way the entire Critical *Elementary-Philosophy*, *independently* of the grounds on which it *firmly rests* in the *Critique of Pure Reason*. And because it leads to the very same results by a wholly different path, it serves as a confirmation of the Kantian discoveries in a way similar to *proofs by calculation*. [Cf. Reinhold's earlier note on "grounds" and "results" at the beginning of the Fourth Letter from the *Merkur*, p. 117, n. m. "Elementary-Philosophy" is the name Reinhold chose for his own first system, but it is not a term or notion that Kant ever endorsed.]

you for the study of its *grounds*. Hence, I shall report the results themselves, independently of the premises for them that are developed in the Critique of Reason, by tying them instead to convictions that are already present and by seeking to make visible their connection to the most essential scientific and moral needs of our age, their influence on the settling of old and new disputes of philosophers, and their agreement with what the most profound philosophical minds of all time have thought with regard to the most remarkable problems of philosophy. In any case, I shall be dealing only with the *external* grounds of these results, and I request, therefore, that you hold back your judgment concerning the *internal* grounds until you have found the leisure time to draw them out from the source itself. The unphilosophical and philosophical prejudices that stand opposed to the results of the new philosophy – and which I know only too well from my own experience – are all the more difficult to refute by the internal grounds anyway [97], for they partly make the will disinclined, and partly the understanding less disposed, to become eagerly and successfully involved in the by all means difficult study of the Critical system itself. Because our exchange of letters has been occasioned by your misgivings about the present state of religious affairs, allow me to begin my next letter with that result which, in this regard, must interest you above all others.

E[54]

Selection from the Fourth Letter, "The result of the Kantian philosophy on the question of God's existence, compared with the general as well as particular results of previous philosophy regarding this subject"

[101] Because the supporters of *dogmatic* theism have on their side the majority of public teachers of philosophy, or as they express themselves, the *professional philosophers*, they are all [102] the more inclined to hold their faction to be the only genuine philosophical public and to look upon dogmatic skeptics, atheists, and supernaturalists as nothing but long-conquered and disarmed opponents – or rather, as *non-philosophers*

[54] This selection from the 1790 edition (pp. 101–17) is an entirely new addition inserted at p. 132 of the Second Letter from the *Merkur*, except for the last three paragraphs of the selection (pp. 116–17), which are a heavily revised version of pp. 132–4 of the original Second Letter.

banished forever from the domain of philosophy. But you, dear friend, are not known to me as a typical dogmatic theist. For you, the dogmatic skeptic *Hume*, the supernaturalist *Pascal*,[55] and the atheist *Spinoza* are philosophers no less than the dogmatic theist *Leibniz* is. Thus, when I ask you about the result of *previous philosophy* regarding God's existence, I know that you will not refer me to the dogmatic-theist answer any more than you will refer me to the atheist answer, regardless of the fact that you have been convinced until now by the correctness of the former. Rather, you will distinguish the *particular* results of philosophical factions from the *general* results of *philosophy itself* and concede to me that the representatives of *philosophizing reason* (which may no more be confused with the reason of dogmatic theists than common sense may be confused with the manners of representation of individual nations and classes of human beings) *have decided nothing positive* with regard to the question of God's existence. This, of course, has already been repeated often and loudly enough by the supernaturalists (ever since they became used to giving up their unfairly contested right of citizenship in the philosophical world and ultimately even to refusing for themselves the title of philosopher as a term of insult). – This is the usual text of the modern panegyrics that are held for common sense at the expense of philosophizing reason. But this observation has a wholly different meaning for me than the one it must have in the eyes of the enemies of philosophy. [103] They overlook an essential distinction here, which imparts a wholly different meaning to the question of God's existence depending on whether it is the subject of common sense or of philosophizing reason. With respect to common sense the question is, Is there a ground (a cause) of the world that is separate from the world? But with respect to philosophizing reason the question is, Is there a *ground of cognition* for this cause – that is, a ground for conviction in its existence that can be understood by every thinking mind and that must be found to be true by every mind that understands it? A deliverance of common sense is not a judgment of rational, analytical, demonstrative reason but rather the expression of presuppositions that are wrested through irresistibly felt needs and represented by clear but indistinct concepts. It is a taking-to-be-true that is an effect of motivations grounded in the original predispositions of human nature – motivations that never cease operating but always go unrecognized.

[55] Blaise Pascal (1623–62).

Ultimately, a deliverance of common sense is a belief that is based on grounds that are undeveloped and thus also partly misunderstood. Because philosophizing reason, in contrast, properly deals with *only* the *grounds* of each conviction, it cannot be in accord with itself about any conviction until it succeeds in having *fully* developed those grounds, completed an analysis of them that extends to the boundary of all that is comprehensible, and traced back, in an illuminating way, each relevant feature to a principle universally accepted among philosophers. Because philosophizing reason has not fulfilled these conditions in any of its previous answers to the question of God's existence, it is understandable enough why it has been divided over this question, just as common sense has been in accord with itself over it.

[104] The question, Is there a ground for cognition of God's existence?, has until now been answered *affirmatively* by one main faction of the philosophical public and *negatively* by another. It cannot be denied that the main faction responding negatively is caught up in an internal struggle with itself, for it is divided into two separate factions, the *atheist* faction and the *dogmatic-skeptic* faction. The latter rejects any ground for cognition of God's existence because it declares the whole question to be absolutely unanswerable, and the former rejects any such ground because it believes that it is able to demonstrate God's non-existence. One faction considers the concept of a cause of the world that is separate from the world to be *groundless*, while the other considers it to be *contradictory*. But philosophy of religion can in no way draw from this dispute between its opponents the advantage that one is at first inclined to expect from it, because the *main affirmative faction* is no less divided into two separate and mutually opposed factions – namely the *dogmatic-theist* (naturalist) faction and the *supernaturalist* faction. The dogmatic theist claims to have found a ground for cognition of God's existence *within* the domain of reason, and the supernaturalist *outside* that domain. The former calls this ground a *proof from reason*, and the latter *revelation*, and while the former disputes the *faith* of the latter, the latter disputes the *knowledge* of the former. Each of these *four* factions has the other *three* against it because each belongs to *two* opposed main factions, and consequently each faction campaigns sometimes *for* the allies of its opponent and sometimes *against* its own allies. On the one hand, the dogmatic theist makes common cause with the supernaturalist in *affirming* a ground for cognition of God's existence, and the dogmatic skeptic makes common cause with the atheist in *denying* such a

ground; on the other [105] hand, the claim "that the question concerning the existence of God can and must be decided by reason" binds the dogmatic theist with the atheist against the dogmatic skeptic and the supernaturalist, who are bound to one another by the opposite claim.

I have easily been able to foresee that the task of placing *all* the results of previous philosophy concerning God's existence under these *four main points of view* and arranging *all* of previous philosophy – with the single exception of the *Kantian* or Critical philosophy – under *four factions* with respect to this subject could entangle me in varied and stubborn opposition. For I have a rather precise familiarity with the manner of representation belonging to the best known of my philosophical contemporaries in our fatherland. Scarcely had I publicized the main points to which, according to my conviction, one can trace back the peculiar dispute that remains interminable without the mediation of the Critical philosophy – the main points by which I compared the result of previous philosophy to the result of the Kantian philosophy regarding God's existence[g] – when I was ridiculed from podiums and in critiques and anti-critiques (in the manner of our folk philosophy). Moreover, I was opposed in several treatises without being able to forestall – by the determinate and clear discussion that I offered of these main points in the First Book of my[56] *Essay on a New Theory of the Faculty of Representation* – the misunderstandings on which those objections were based. Because several of the objections that have been brought to my attention actually come from astute men whom I esteem, and because my *historical-philosophical result* contrasts quite sharply with our previous manners of representation, it might not [106] be entirely superfluous – even with respect to you yourself, my astute friend – to prepare that result by way of a few preliminary remarks before I develop it further.

I know that there are many thinking minds who do not adhere to any definite answer regarding the question of God's existence because they have never in earnest set this question before themselves. To be sure, the causes of this neglect can be thought to be many and various, but to my knowledge there is not one that a man might boast about or on account of which he might claim the title of philosopher. Such an *indifferentist* may

[g] In the *Allgemeine Literaturzeitung*, 1788, no. 231. [Reinhold's essay there, "Neue Entdeck" ("New Discovery"), corresponds to pp. 76–82 of his *Essay on a New Theory of the Human Faculty of Representation*.]

[56] Omitting italics in the translation of *dem ersten Buch meines*.

perhaps be permitted this title in other respects, but we can in no way be concerned with his opinion if the question is about what philosophizing reason has *decided* regarding God's existence by the vote of previous philosophy. And neither the actual existence nor the large sum of indifferentists who do not belong to any of the four factions can be cited against my classification of the philosophical public.

I know that the meaning of the specific basic claim with which I have attempted to express the shared opinion of the supporters of each faction takes on very different modifications in very different minds, and that, for many who believe that they possess a decisive answer to the question of God's existence, it must be extremely difficult to determine, according to this answer, the faction to which they belong. And I know that even many professional philosophers would run into difficulty if they had to offer a *determinate* account of what they have thought of until now as atheism, dogmatic skepticism, theism, and supernaturalism. At the very least, the opinions of the best-known philosophers regarding the meaning [107] of these headings are extremely varied. The indeterminacy of all previously adopted principles[57] not only leaves a space for the free play[58] of fantasy but even requires every thinking mind to fill in, in whatever way it best can, the gap that reason has left in the meaning of any so-called basic principle.[59] Thus, many who *leave open* the question of God's existence out of convenience, or out of annoyance at unsuccessful attempts, consider themselves with full conviction to be *dogmatic skeptics*.[60] Far from being convinced by the unanswerability of this question on genuinely skeptical grounds, they believe that they have all the more right to the title of skeptic precisely because they have succeeded (admittedly easily enough) in *doubting* even the basic claim of dogmatic skepticism itself. Similarly, many who along with *Mendelssohn* demonstrate God's existence while otherwise adhering in word and heart to the doctrinal concepts belonging to the orthodox theology of the Lutheran, Reformed, or Catholic Church will consider themselves insulted by the title *dogmatic theist* – simply because under this title they are used to thinking of a *naturalist* who not only owes to reason his conviction in God's existence but also indiscriminately denies *all revelation*.

57 *Prinzipien*. 58 *Freier Spielraum*. 59 *Grundsatz*.

60 That is, philosophers who are thoroughgoing skeptics about philosophical positions as such, but not necessarily on the basis of traditional skeptical arguments. Cf. below, n. 62.

I know that many, because they profess certain *coalition systems* that have emerged from the manners of representation belonging to more than one faction, believe that they have reason to protest against every one of the four factions. The aforementioned indeterminateness in the principles and basic claims of the four factions makes it understandable enough how it happens that, despite all the contradictions in which they stand to one another as a result of their essential features, these principles and basic claims still quite frequently [108] get along in one and the same mind. There are writers who with true conviction defend atheism as philosophers and supernaturalism as theologians, and who would know of the non-existence of God through reason if they did not believe in the existence of the God of revelation. Other writers, through a much more limited exertion of their power of thinking, have succeeded in making their naturalism – which they believe they have to profess as professional philosophers – so malleable, or as they describe it, so *moderate*, that it not only gets along very amicably with supernaturalism but also offers supernaturalism its *right* hand on public occasions. And this is an honor that supernaturalism, which has here and there become moderate as a result of moderate theologians, knows in turn to reciprocate when the opportunity arises. What all has the inconsistency of human beings not combined! What, if anything, cannot be assimilated into the representation of an object that can be *correctly* thought of only through entirely *pure* ideas of reason – what cannot be assimilated into the concept of the deity – as long as fantasy, while thinking it, is not reined in by any *universally accepted* rules, and as long as reason, in its activities, goes to work not so much according to the fundamental law of its universal form as according to the demands of individual needs and to the viewpoints that custom, education, passion, and the like have established! Certainly there are claims that, having once been based on a misunderstanding, are defined by reason to be points of agreement unifying two factions into one main faction, and in my classification I myself have cited these claims. But, in addition to these points of agreement, one should also not forget the points of disagreement that are inseparable from them, which can be overlooked simply because of a stubborn, one-sided attention to the other points. [109] For every *one* dogmatic theist who misperceives the sharp – but certainly not on that account universally visible – boundary that separates him from the supernaturalist, there are perhaps *ten* supporters of this faction who look upon supernaturalism as their worst enemy and would much sooner make common cause with atheism than with it. For every *one* supernaturalist who calls upon atheism for help against dogmatic theism, there are surely a *hundred* who combat atheism with dogmatic theism, and who forget their antipathy for the latter as long as they believe they can use its weapons. And this will go on until they eventually abandon it for, say, dogmatic skepticism and, after the latter has rendered its service too, take their doctrinal structure to be firmly grounded forever atop the ruins of this skepticism.

I know that several of those whom I have included among the dogmatic theists believe that they have safeguarded themselves against being put under this heading by refusing the title of demonstration or even of apodictic proof for their ground of conviction in God's existence. To be sure, the usual, extremely unsettled concepts of *demonstration*, *proof*, *certainty*, etc. are of no small help to them in this apology. But, however much they may call their conviction merely probable or a settled certainty, as soon as its ground is supposed to be *objective* – that is, to lie outside the form of the mere faculty of representation in *things in themselves*, which are taken to be cognized – the derivation of their conviction from such a ground is a *dogmatic proof*, and its advocate belongs among those who hold God's existence to be *cognizable* (as probable or settled) through the mere use of reason.

I know that the concept of *atheism*, which has been ambiguous since time immemorial, has become even more indeterminate as a result of several recent attempts [110] to elucidate *Spinozism* and to save *Spinoza* from the reproach of atheism.[61] Through a rather common confusion of *ground* with *cause*, the name *God* has been carried over from a ground that is *separate* from the world (a cause) to a ground of appearances that is present in the world itself (a substance). And it is even believed that the distinction between *God* and *world* demanded by ordinary usage is sufficiently accounted for by letting the *first* term designate and comprise the unchanging, necessary, and spontaneous, and the *second* the changing, contingent, and passive. Whether according to this presupposition *Spinoza* must be called a *theist* or *deist* – or neither a theist, deist, nor atheist – is something about which his vindicators are not entirely in agreement among themselves. But they commonly pass over this

[61] See especially Johann Gottfried Herder (1744–1803), *God: Some Conversations* (Gotha, 1789), trs. F. Burkhardt (Indianapolis, Bobbs-Merrill, 1940).

difficulty *by* assuming an indifference about the title that ought to belong to *Spinoza*, an indifference that is just as resolute as their passion regarding the title that ought not belong to *Spinoza*. Because, according to my conviction, the word *God* has been defined by ordinary usage – both common and philosophical – as not just one among other grounds of appearances but rather as the *cause of the world* in the strictest sense of the expression, I count every philosophy that denies such a cause as belonging to the *atheist* faction. And I know that I have on my side all the friends of philosophy who are convinced with me that no force of genius can give someone the power and right to do violence to ordinary usage, and that confusion in language is the surest harbinger of the approaching death of philosophy.

Finally, I know that the so-called *eclecticism* of our *Popular Philosophy* instills in its followers [111] a terrible panic at the terms *faction*, *sect*, *system*, and the like, and that an eclectic of this kind would rather renounce the title of philosopher than accept it under the condition that he acknowledge in advance his place among the four factions. Everyone appeals to his own individual philosophy, which is certainly a distinctive aggregate of reminiscences from what often is fairly wide reading – a single whole patched together, in its unique way, from variously garbled fragments of the most diverse doctrinal structures. But just as every individual has its species, and every species its genus, so I believe I am in no way detracting from the individuality of our Popular Philosophers when I designate as *four* answers the *two possible* answers – which must come out either *affirmative* or negative – that they can give to the *two* main questions concerning God's existence: Is there a *ground of cognition* for God's existence?, and, Is *reason* capable of satisfactorily answering the question of God's existence? Moreover, it is in no way to detract from their individuality when I designate as *factions* the advocates of each of the different answers or impose on these factions the titles that ordinary usage has determined for them in respect to those answers.

Even an independent thinker of the highest rank *must* embrace one of these factions – or rather, he belongs to one of them with a necessity from which only the Critical philosophy can save him. But with the title that he cannot avoid of dogmatic theist, atheist, dogmatic skeptic, or supernaturalist, he is in no way declared a parrot of an alien opinion or even a mere follower of a system of one or another of his contemporaries or predecessors. The distinctiveness of his philosophy remains for him just as completely uncontested [112] as does the individuality of his person by the titles *human being*, *European*, *German*, *philosopher*, etc., which he shares without reluctance with so many other persons. His reason could not be called *reason* if it were not something common to every human faculty of representation – that is, if it did not have a form that according to its essence must be exactly the same in all individuals. However excellently and distinctively it may distinguish itself by the degree of its power and by the difference in materials upon which it works – materials that may be presented to it by more finely tuned sense organs and a more lively power of imagination – it is nevertheless bound even in its most distinctive activities by laws that leave a stamp on these activities, a stamp that allows them to be placed in *one* class with the activities of reason of others and that necessarily divides them into species and genera.

Therefore do not, dear friend, let yourself be thrown into confusion about my *four factions* on account of the past and future protests of the opponents of the Kantian philosophy. These opponents either still do not possess a definite answer to the question of God's existence, or this answer must be grounded on the old foundations of either dogmatic skepticism, atheism, dogmatic theism, or supernaturalism. And this holds true no matter how carefully they distinguish their obtained answer from every previously adopted answer, no matter how unsystematic the form they give to its grounds, and no matter how unrecognizable, even in their own eyes, they have made its metaphysical outlines through the art of wit and the magic of fantasy. For either they have found the immense question answerable through *objective*[h] [113] *grounds of reason*, or they have not. In the first case, either they believe that they *cognize* the existence of a ground of the world separate from the world, or they believe that they *cognize* that there is no such ground, and then they are either *theists* or *atheists*. In the second case, either they adopt grounds for God's existence that lie outside the domain of the human faculty of

[h] I call "*objective*" those grounds for the existence of God which were previously believed to have been found in the nature of *represented objects* that were taken to be *things in themselves*. In contrast, I call "*subjective*" those grounds which the Kantian philosophy discovered for this basic truth of religion in the *form* of the mere (theoretical and practical) faculty of *pure reason* – grounds that consequently are found only through the analysis of the faculty of representation, and that abstract from all supposed cognition of *things in themselves*, upon which so far all dogmatic philosophy has been built.

cognition, or they adopt no such grounds, and consequently are either *supernaturalists* or *dogmatic skeptics*.[62]

I have the feeling that the necessity of belonging to *one* of these *four* factions must leave a thinking mind that does not yet possess a determinate answer to the question of God's existence in a quandary that deprives him of all desire to seek out this answer in *previous* philosophy – if we pass over the *Kantian* philosophy. Whichever of the four previous answers he may one day declare himself for, he knows in advance that he has not just the majority of the philosophical public *against* him but *three-fourths* of the esteemed counsel of independent thinkers, and that he has to *defend* a basic claim that is rejected by a very striking and fully settled majority of equally important votes. Even if this majority of votes is no proof against the basic claim that he has voted for, it is still a most unsettling external ground against that claim. It is a ground that he must count as valid until he is convinced, by a [114] completed investigation in which he has examined the grounds of every faction, that *philosophizing reason* has expressed itself only through *one-fourth* of its representatives – that is, through precisely that fourth whose grounds had the luck of winning the approval of *his* individual reason above all others, and which he would have to hold outright as the complete and only true *philosophical* public to the exclusion of all the rest. Until then he must accept with me that *philosophizing reason* has either not expressed itself at all, or it has expressed itself through the majority of its representatives, through three factions against one, with regard to the question of God's existence – that is, with regard to the following basic claims:

1 *For dogmatic skepticism*: "that the question of God's existence *cannot* be answered at all."
2 *For supernaturalism*: "that it can be answered only through *revelation*."
3 *For atheism*: "that it must be answered *negatively* on *objective* grounds of reason."
4 *For dogmatic theism*: "that it must be answered *affirmatively* on *objective* grounds of reason."

[62] What Reinhold appears to mean by this term is not a general skepticism that is itself based on traditional dogmatic arguments but rather a skepticism that is aimed specifically at *dogmatic* claims that there is a well-grounded answer for questions concerning matters such as God's existence.

Each of these claims is adopted by only *one* faction and rejected by *three*. Thus, through its four factions, philosophizing reason has either decided nothing at all about the question of God's existence, or it has decided *that the four previous answers are wrong*. But in the latter case it has decided, through those same factions, about the *truth* of the contradicting counterclaims of these answers. And, hence, through the negative decisions of three factions against one, the following propositions stand firmly as the result of previous philosophy in general [115]:

1 The question of God's existence can be satisfactorily answered.
2 The question of God's existence cannot be answered through revelation.[i]
3 The question of God's existence cannot be answered negatively on any objective grounds.
4 The question of God's existence cannot be answered affirmatively on any objective grounds.

How would you respond, dear friend, to the fact that exactly these *four propositions*, about whose truth *three* factions must be in agreement against *one* precisely because they are in agreement about the falsity of the [original] claims that contradict them – propositions that can be looked upon in this respect as deliverances of philosophizing reason through the majority vote of its independent thinkers – are derived by the Kantian philosophy from one single principle? How would you respond to the fact that they are the *positive* results that the Critique of Reason has brought out by a wholly different path – namely through the analysis of the mere faculty of cognition – and that they express the conditions that the new philosophy establishes as the only secure ground of conviction in God's existence?

After developing the thoroughly determined idea of the deity from the *form* of theoretical reason and tracing back its essential features to universally accepted principles, the new theory of pure reason puts forward in the form of practical (operative in morality) reason a ground [116] that requires the acceptance of the existence of the object – incomprehensible in itself – that corresponds to that idea. In this way it answers the question of God's existence, *first*, in a manner satisfactory to all who

[i] Even the majority of today's most zealous admirers and advocates of *revelation* teach that God's existence can in no way belong among the revealed articles of faith.

have studied and understood this theory; *second*, from mere natural grounds of reason; *third*, affirmatively; and, *fourth*, from merely subjective grounds that are present in the form of reason, independently of all allegedly cognizable *things in themselves*. And, consequently, it fulfills what philosophizing reason, through the majority vote of its representatives, had demanded for this answer but had lacked in all previous answers.

I know, dear friend, that the *ground of moral faith* that the Kantian philosophy puts forward as the only philosophically demonstrable ground of conviction in God's existence must still seem puzzling to you. I must, at least for a time, however, refrain from making you familiar with the inner constitution of this ground of conviction and with its proofs because doing this without prior and, in fact, very precise familiarity with the *whole Critical system* is impossible. But you know (and I bid you not to forget this) that I am dealing only with *external* grounds for now, and in light of this fact you can leave, for the time being, the correctness of the *internal* grounds aside.

The new *philosophical* answer to the question of God's existence that is to meet the needs of our age, satisfy the legitimate demands of previous factions, and decline their presumptions can in no way contain *new*, never-suspected grounds that have never before been operative. Rather it must make visible, in their genuine constitution, the ever-present and continuously operating motivations for conviction in God's existence despite all the misconceptions about them, [117] and it must express them through *basic principles* that are secured against previous as well as future misunderstandings by a determination of their features that is traced back to universally accepted principles. This answer must completely overthrow the *four* wavering main systems – but only in order to erect a *new* system from the usable materials that are contained in each of them, a system that will not only not lose anything but rather will gain more and more internal stability as well as external usefulness with every future advance of the human spirit. It must separate the distinctive truth that each faction has seen from its point of view from the falsity that was unavoidable in the answers of each because of the onesidedness of that viewpoint; it must take up the truth in each ground of conviction and exclude what is false. And in making visible the common misunderstanding that hid from the disputants the points of agreement and disagreement in previous opinions, it will forever put an end to the old dispute that for so long was regarded as necessarily endless. Finally, this answer must be illuminating to the most astute and experienced thinkers in its *grounds* and to the most elementary common sense in its *result*.

In as illuminating a way as can be done without developing its *internal grounds*, I hope to show you in my following letter that the new answer put forward by the Kantian philosophy perfectly fulfills all of these conditions. Some relevant preliminary remarks will conclude the present letter.

F[63]

Selection from the Eighth Letter, "The result of the Critique of Reason concerning the future life"

As I mentioned in my last letter, the Critique of Reason has discovered and forever established the highest basic principle[64] of all philosophy of religion in the nature of practical reason, which makes necessary both the *expectation of a future life* and belief in the existence of *a highest principle*[65] *of moral and natural laws*. So far I have attempted to show that, *in so far as* the sole secure ground of conviction in God's existence is determined by that highest basic principle,[66] the eventual, universal recognition of it in the philosophical world must ultimately be brought about through the natural and gradual course of [173] development of the human spirit. I have also attempted to show that the universal grounding of religion on morality in the *philosophical world* and the reunification of both in the *Christian world* depend on this recognition. All of this must be able to be shown through the very same principle[67] of pure philosophy of religion *in so far as* the sole secure ground of conviction in a *future life* obtains its true meaning and evidence through it as well. The two articles of faith of practical reason are so intimately bound together in their nature, source, and fate that almost everything that is true of the one in these respects also applies to the other. The purpose of my present letter is to make this application easier for you by means of a few suggestions – an application which with regard to the main issue I leave to your own astuteness.

[63] This selection from the 1790 edition (pp. 172–8) contains heavy revisions of pp. 167–72 of the Fifth Letter from the *Merkur*, with a few elaborations, including an added footnote on p. 173.
[64] *Höchsten Grundsatz.*
[65] *Höchsten Prinzips.* [66] *Höchsten Grundsatz.* [67] *Prinzip.*

I divide the interest that the thought of an unbounded continuation of our existence must hold for us into a *sensible* and a *moral* interest. They behave in opposition to one another like *instinct* and *reason* – or to speak more precisely, like the *sensible drive*, which is grounded on mere need and is dependent on the nature of receptivity and the objects of its satisfaction, and the *spontaneity* of spirit, which guides itself solely by its own laws. The sensible drive, which always has only the state of the sensing subject – to the extent that it is *sensing*[j] – for its object, is determined by the *understanding* by means of the concept of [174] subsistence as a striving for the *persistence* of that state, and is determined by *reason* as a striving for an *unbounded* persistence. However much the sensible drive for life may be intertwined with the form of our faculty of desire, at least this much is still certain: that it is present and that it can set no boundaries for itself in the healthy state of the flesh and the soul. Surely you are in no need of proof, dear friend, that the interest that the continuation of our existence has for us on account of *this* drive cannot yield any ground of conviction whatsoever in the actuality of this continuation. The *moral* interest, in contrast, which was first resolved into its pure elements by the Critique of Reason, has a wholly other source. This interest is grounded on either the merely felt or distinctly developed necessity – which reason encounters in the original constitution of its nature – for assuming on behalf of the moral lawgiving of reason a world in which morality and happiness stand in most perfect harmony. In such a world, the object of the two unified necessary drives of human nature – the highest *happiness* that is determined by the most perfect *morality*, or the *highest good* of the human spirit – is attainable through an endless progression and approximation. If the ground of this interest is not to be found in the form of reason, if it is otherwise than what I can only presuppose and not prove here, then we would be dealing here with the satisfaction of a drive that has no more necessity than our existence itself, with which it would at the same time have to cease. That is, it would have fully achieved its entire aim [175] by continuing to contribute to our self-preservation for as long as we ourselves exist. But we are

[j] For this reason also the modifications that *outer* sensations receive through the five senses in *this* life are very difficult to separate from the idea of a *future* life. If it were not impossible for the common man, because of the dominance of his fantasy over his power of thinking, to think of a future life as a state in which nothing is felt, tasted, smelled, heard, or seen, then all sensible interest in this life would disappear for him as a result of such a representation.

dealing here with the interest of the *moral law* itself, which is wholly independent of our needs and sensible drives and stands in no other relation with them than that of restricting the former and subduing the latter; it is an interest that demands unconditional respect from us, and that we must recognize no matter how much our inclination is to rise up against it. And it is this interest that makes absolutely necessary the expectation of a future life irrespective of any advantage it may have for us. It is the absolute necessity of the (properly understood) moral law that requires us to infer the actuality of the continuation of our existence, an actuality that is inseparable from this necessity. We infer this existence not because the actuality of this law, which follows from its absolute necessity, would otherwise be indemonstrable, but because in one and the same consciousness the conviction in the actual continuation of our existence is inseparable from the conviction in the actuality of the moral law – provided that the distinct representation of this inseparability is not hindered by metaphysical prejudices regarding the nature of the soul or by an incorrect concept of the moral law.

Both types of interest in a future life are grounded in the original constitution of the human faculty of representation and desire, and for that very reason both interests are also equally necessary. Nevertheless, precisely as a consequence of the nature of that constitution, the moral interest could not possibly proceed in the course of its gradual development at the same pace as the sensible interest. Before the former could be even vaguely discerned, *moral feeling*, through which practical reason announces its activity, first had to be awakened. Before it could be traced back to determinate [176] and distinct concepts, the scientific cultivation of morality had to advance rather far. Before it could be derived from its first source, from the form of practical reason, the *Critique of Pure Reason* had to discover this form through a completed analysis of the faculty of cognition. Finally, before it can be universally understood and accepted *in this derivation of it* by even the best minds, the Critical philosophy will have to be treated by several independently thinking minds and presented more simply and comprehensibly. Entrenched metaphysical and hyperphysical prejudices will have to be rooted out. In a word, a reformation of philosophy will have to lead the way, a reformation of which the majority of professional philosophers are still unable to dream.

Similarly, the moral interest in a future life could not reach the consciousness of the human spirit in any representation, however obscure, before *reason's idea of the deity* had become visible in the dawning of moral feeling, which presupposes some antecedent degree of cultivation that is possible only in social life. The bound powers of spirit of the crude child of nature, who had not yet become a citizen, were exhausted in the satisfaction of sensory needs and, in general, with the sensations of all that was *visible* and *present*; and only in the bosom of society were moments of leisure reserved for these powers to elevate themselves gradually to that which is *invisible* and *in the future*. Only through civic relations could a succession of experiences be introduced out of which the concepts of right and wrong, of good and evil actions, of reward and punishment, and finally of an *invisible bestower of both* could gradually develop. [177] The *events* by which these concepts were explained, confirmed, or rendered more genuinely *perceptible* – the *blessing* that *followed on the heels* of the righteous and the *curse* that *followed on the heels* of the wicked – announced, at first, nothing but *temporal* rewards and punishments from the invisible judge. Hence, *for a time* just about everything that one hoped and feared in regard to the deity was restricted to the *present life*. And it becomes easily understandable why one finds in the remnants of the most ancient history such exceptionally old and frequent traces of moral faith in the deity rather than of the moral expectation of a future life. Perhaps in this regard those [scholars] might not be all that mistaken who have sought to find, even in the most ancient religious history of the *Hebrews*, irrefutable proofs that faith in the deity is much older than belief in the immortality of the soul.

The expectation of reward and punishment presupposes conviction in the existence of a judge, and, before they had contrived for themselves the late-emerging metaphysical concept [of immortality], future rewards and punishments were the first and only possible features in terms of which human beings could think of their survival after death. Conviction in a distinction between the nature of the soul and that of the body was certainly not what *first* awakened, furthered, or raised to certainty the thought of life after death, of a being without a body – a thought that even today has to struggle with so many difficulties. Even the sensible interest in the continuation of existence after death needed for its own awakening and development the earlier, or at least contemporaneous, concept of future rewards and punishments. For if the drive for life were to open up prospects beyond the grave, something had to exist [178] to which this drive could securely fasten itself after the arena of the visible world – which death supposedly closed it off from forever – had nothing more to offer. The faith in God's existence that emerged earlier opened up an *invisible world* to the human spirit. And the more the conviction concerning a superhuman recompenser of good and evil was disseminated and implanted by priests and lawgivers, or by religious and political institutions, on the one hand; and the more frequently and widely the observation imposed itself that not all those clearly marked as righteous and wicked *had received their just retribution here below* [on the other]; the more unavoidable, interesting, and illuminating the thought had to become of representing an *invisible* recompenser as also existing *in the future*. This thought allowed death to be represented as a passage into another world, one in which human beings who had strove *after God* here below could expect a blessed existence *with God* (in heaven), while those who had led a *godless* life here below could expect an agonizing existence (in hell) far removed from the seat of the deity.

G[68]

Selection from the Ninth Letter, "Elucidation of the metaphysical ground for cognition of the immortality of the soul with regard to its origin as well as its consequences"

[192] I confess to you that even the idea of an *unextended substance of a representing being* – which, however misunderstood, lies both at the basis of the *metaphysical ground for cognition* of a future life and at the basis of all *rational psychology* to date – is grounded in the nature of theoretical reason itself and arises from its original constitution. Hence, I shall employ the term *psychological idea of reason* to refer to this idea as well.

For this same reason, I could also never think of rejecting every use of this thoroughly rational idea, and least of all that use which is made of it in defending the basic religious truth of a future life against its *materialist* opponents. Since these opponents take to the field with nothing but entirely metaphysical weapons,[k] the use of this kind of weapon *for*

[68] This selection from the 1790 edition (pp. 192–203) is a heavily revised and much-expanded version of pp. 71–9 of the Sixth Letter from the *Merkur*.

[k] The dress and trappings do not change anything with regard to the matter itself: the *blade* is metaphysical every time, or the weapon, like the sword of some short rifles, has no blade at all.

resistance will remain not only legitimate but even necessary as long as the feud lasts – or what comes to the same thing, as long as, on account of its previous weaknesses, philosophy of religion will incite attack.

The psychological idea of reason would [193] not at all deserve this name if it did not admit of a meaning in which it is absolutely irrefutable. Yet when taken in this meaning, by which *materialism* is certainly refuted, reason signals by the necessary representation of an unextended, representing substance nothing more than "that it is impossible to represent the representing subject as something that fills up space – something representable solely through *outer* sense."[69] Therefore the materialist is in no way justified in attributing any predicate attributable only to a substance that is representable in space – e.g., *destructibility* – to a substance that defies all representability in space.

The *spiritualist*, who turns a mere idea into a complete *cognition*, holds the feature of being *unextended* to be a property that belongs to the substance of the soul *in itself*, independently of its representability, which is grounded in the nature of our faculty of representation. In so far as he in no way derives the denial of extension of the representing subject from an impossibility, grounded in the nature of the mind, of representing this subject in space, he concedes to the materialist that non-representability[70] in space is no ground for denying extension to the soul. Hence, both opponents are treating the soul as a *thing in itself*, and their dispute about its nature (because one knows exactly as much about it as the other, and consequently neither can be superior to the other) must persist forever. The advocate of the *moral ground of cognition*, in contrast, adheres strictly to the modest[71] meaning of the psychological idea of reason. Satisfied that he can prove to materialists that no predicate presupposing *extension* can be attributed to the representing subject without misconstruing essential [194] laws of the faculty of cognition, he in no way believes thereby that he knows the substance of the soul in itself better than the materialist, or that he can prove along with the spiritualist that this substance is simple *in itself*. He finds in *practical* reason a sufficient ground for believing in the immortality of the soul,

[69] Cf. Kant, *Critique of Pure Reason* (A 379, B 420), and *Prolegomena* (4:334, 351).

[70] That is, he concedes that even if a subject cannot *represent* itself as such in space, this need not reveal what the subject's nature *in itself* is like as a soul, and hence does not reveal whether or not that nature has extension.

[71] Reading *besche denen* as *bescheidenen*.

whose nature is incomprehensible to him. In order to bring about this conviction, practical reason requires from theoretical reason nothing more than proof that the destructibility of the soul cannot be proven, and that the soul, to the extent that it is representable, must be distinguished from all bodies to the extent that they are representable. The psychological idea of reason is, to be sure, an indispensable ground for the advocate of the moral ground of conviction, but it is also usable only as a *bulwark*.[72]

The contrary use – or rather misuse – of that idea, which is still quite common today, and which turns that idea from a *bulwark* into a *foundation*, is alone what I understand by the metaphysical ground for cognition of immortality. Because previous philosophy (as I sought to show in my earlier letters by indicating the various misunderstandings and disputes that until now have hindered the fulfillment of its noble vocation) has been lacking in thoroughly determined and fully developed concepts of *reason*, *understanding*, and *sensibility* and of the relationship of these different faculties to one another; because the *essential* distinction between the representations of reason (*ideas*), the representations of the understanding (*concepts*), and the representations of sensibility (*sensations*, in so far as they are related to the representing, and *intuitions*, in so far as they are related to the represented) was wholly misconstrued; because intuiting was confused with thinking, and the thinking that is distinctive of the understanding was confused with the thinking that belongs solely to reason [195]; and because it was not known that sensibility alone is capable of intuiting, that understanding is capable of thinking only that which is intuited, and that reason, in contrast, is capable of thinking only the non-intuitable and thus the supersensible – *cognition* was wholly misconstrued as well. According to the Critique of Reason, cognition (with respect to objects that are not merely forms of representations) can be ascribed to the understanding and sensibility only when these are taken together; it is thinking and intuiting at the same time. But at every turn, cognition was conflated with *necessary thinking* by reason, with representing the supersensible, with thinking the incomprehensible. The *deity* and the *substance* of the soul, which defy all sensible representation – that is, they are not representable through any intuition and thus are incomprehensible to the understanding and, in both respects, are completely uncognizable – were wrongly placed in the domain of *cognizable* things as a result of that old misunderstanding, common to all

[72] See above, Sixth Letter from the *Merkur*, p. 73.

spiritualists, which assigned to sensibility no other role in cognition than that of *confusing* cognition, while allowing the understanding to *intuit* things as they are *in themselves*. Even those who called the nature of the soul *incomprehensible* (without having a determinate concept of the meaning of this word, of course) declared at least its simplicity and substantiality to be *cognizable* because they held the undeniable necessity of *thinking* these features to be an actual intuition of the soul in itself. They believed that in such thinking they had cognized actual properties belonging to the representing being independently of its mere form of representation. That the representing subject *had to be thought* as an unextended substance was to them the same as actually *being cognized* under these features, which they believed were taken not *subjectively* from the mere form of the faculty of representation [196] but rather *objectively* from the soul as a *thing in itself*. And in this way the necessity of the psychological idea, which was misunderstood in regard to its proper origin, became a ground for cognition of so-called *spirituality*, whose defenders fancy to have comprehended precisely what is incomprehensible about the soul, substantiality and simplicity, while typically leaving aside as incomprehensible that which is comprehensible about the soul – the faculty of representation and cognition.

Locke had already noted rather clearly that while the soul is capable of intuiting nothing but the *body* through *outer sense* and nothing but its own *representations* through *inner sense*, it is incapable of intuiting itself as distinct from its representations – much like the eye, which in every act of seeing must be that which sees and can never be that which is seen. *Kant*, in contrast, raised this important observation to the full certainty of a scientific theorem by finding its proof in the nature of *sensibility*, which was wholly misconstrued by Locke. According to Kant's theory, *pure space* is the *form of outer intuition*, grounded in the constitution of outer sense, and *pure time* is the form of *inner intuition*, grounded in the constitution of inner sense; furthermore, an object is intuitable only in so far as it is representable through the form of intuition. And thus every object of outer sense, however it may be constituted in itself, must be represented as something filling up space, as *extended*, and everything intuitable by inner sense must be *represented* as something filling up pure time, as *alteration*. From this it follows that:

First, no substance is intuitable – or cognizable, in so far as intuitability is a condition of cognizability [197] – except as representable in space and thus extended. For that which is intuitable not in space but merely in time is representable as mere *alteration* in us and, consequently, is in no way representable as subsistence. Subsisting that is intuitable, and consequently cognizable, can only be a persisting in space.

Second, whatever is intuitable through inner sense, and to that extent cognizable, is only a representation – and, in so far as it affects inner sense, it is only an alteration in us and is a sensation.

Third, the representing subject is not at all cognizable as a substance because it cannot be intuited – not through outer sense, as goes without saying, and not through inner sense, because inner sense is capable of representing only alterations and not subsistence.

Fourth, the representing subject can in no way be represented as *extended* because then it would have to be represented as something filling up space and thus as represented through outer sense – and, consequently, as something different from itself.

Fifth, the representing subject can be represented as a substance not through the *understanding*, which thinks only the intuitable, but rather solely through *reason*, in self-consciousness. And, consequently, it must already be represented as having the property of being an object of mere reason, as independent of time, as not determinable in time, and thus as *unalterable*; but, unlike that which persists in space, the representing subject is not *cognizable* through the feature of being unalterable.

Sixth, *simplicity* belongs to the representing subject only in so far as it is representable, not through outer sense or through the understanding, but solely through reason. Similarly, unalterability belongs to the representing subject only in so far as it is representable, not through inner sense, but solely [198] through reason. Reason does not have the capacity to represent any predicates but those that are grounded in the necessary laws of its thinking and that are thus eternal.

Seventh, the representing subject also cannot be *cognized* as a so-called *thinking power*, in so far as "*power*" is understood as a *substance* that is a cause; and, consequently, nothing is cognizable with regard to this power but the mere *faculty*[73] of the forms of reason, understanding, and sensibility – forms that are determined by the nature of the faculty prior to all representation.

[73] Here again the term *Vermögen* also suggests a *mere* capacity, which contrasts with the actuality of an effective power. Cf. below, n. 77 and n. 80.

Now if these results are correct, then the old disputes between the materialists and the spiritualists are thereby forever settled, without any need to call on supernaturalism or dogmatic skepticism to intervene. It becomes comprehensible all at once how the *materialist*, who had in view the *necessary extension* of a substance that is representable through the understanding and sensibility – and how the *spiritualist*, who had in view the *simplicity* and *unalterability* of a substance that is representable through mere reason – arrived at their convictions concerning the nature of the soul: namely through a common misconstrual of the faculties of the mind. They differ from one another only in so far as each *projected* a different feature, determined by a different faculty, of *things in so far as they are representable onto things in themselves*. But it is equally illuminating that by removing this misunderstanding – as soon as the principles by which it is removed have become universally accepted – all materialism and spiritualism will have put an end to themselves forever, and the untenable *metaphysical ground for cognition* of a future life, which until now was feasible for only a fourth of the philosophical world anyway, [199] will have to make way for the *moral ground*.

If after *repeated* readings, dear friend, you should find my elucidation thus far not to be entirely satisfactory – an elucidation in which, to be sure, I had to distance myself rather far from the usual manners of representation, indeed even from yours, and for which I should have requested twice as much of your attention – I suggest to you the following shorter route.[74] Hold yourself to a strict account of the representation that you have made for yourself until now of the *substance* of the soul. Because I know how much you are able to keep a tight rein on your fantasy, I can easily predict the result of this investigation. This substance is for you an unknown and incomprehensible *something*, of which you know nothing more than that it is the subject of your representations. You think of this subject as *simple* because you must distinguish it from all bodies – and as a substance because you must distinguish it from all its representations, all alterations in it. Once you have considered these distinctions – which must indeed be considered if you do not want to confuse substance with mere accidents – what feature remains left over for you by which you could count this substance among the ranks of the *cognizable*? The feature of being a *subject*? But a subject, to the extent that

[74] Cf. above, the Sixth Letter from the *Merkur*, p. 77.

it is not determined by any predicate, signifies nothing but a logical thing to which a predicate must be referred. – The feature of being *unextended*? – But through a mere lack of extension – a negative predicate – the remaining, merely *logical* subject cannot be elevated to a *real*[75] subject. Must then this feature be the mere *power of thinking*? – But if this feature does not signify the *mere faculty* for thinking, then "*power*" must mean "*substance that* [200] *is the cause of representation*," and then the missing feature of *real*[76]*substantiality* is simply presupposed again. However, if you understand by "power" "the mere *faculty* for thinking," then the *substance* to which this faculty belongs remains unknown to you despite all the cognition that is possible regarding this faculty. But is the representing subject actually the *cause* of its representations anyway? And to what extent? Is its faculty mere spontaneity, or must it also consist in a receptivity to which material has to be given for the representations of external objects by means of an impression from the outside? And in this case is not at least *outer* representation the product of *two* different powers – that of the subject in us and that of the object outside us – whereby the one is *constrained* in its operating by the influence of the other? Is it not the case that even the higher degree of activity that expresses itself in judgment (to the extent that it is not something *mediated* – that is, not an inference of reason – but rather an immediate, intuitive judgment) is bound to the form of intuition that is grounded in the original constitution of receptivity? And is it not then the case that in part even the representations of the *understanding* do not at all depend on a positive power alone but rather on a mere passively operating faculty? What else, then, remains here for the concept of power but the *spontaneity* of reason, which, to be sure, is not *constrained* by any impression or *bound* to any passive faculty – and is to that extent free, operating as a genuine *power* – but which at the same time cannot do without sensibility with respect to the materials that the understanding must present to it? If you do not therefore want to confuse the three specific operative faculties of the mind – through which, taken by themselves, no representation can arise – with the power of representing, *the complete cause* of [201] representations, then you can think of this power only as the result of the cooperation of the representing subject and external things. If you then separate the role that the representing subject has in regard to this

[75] Reading *rellen* as *reellen*. [76] *Reellen*.

power, you will obtain the mere *faculty of representation*, the theory of what the representing subject is *capable of*[77] in representing. Such a theory is not a science of the representing *power* and even less a science of the *substance* to which the mere faculty of representation belongs.

And now let us see with regard to the *basic religious truth of a future life* what necessarily follows from the features of substance, the simple, and the power of thinking, which make up the idea of a *spirit* and constitute the entire subject matter of *rational psychology*. According to what I have just said about the psychological idea of reason, I can hope that my claim will appear less strange to you when I say that what follows is none other than *indifference* or *fanaticism*, depending on whether one thinks of that idea in its natural *emptiness* and *lack of content* or fills it in through *non-natural intuitions* with the help of the power of the imagination.

To the extent that a restrained, speculative mind is in harmony with itself, thinks more consistently according to its principles, and knows how to protect its concepts against all heterogeneous additions, it will also keep *pure* its idea of reason regarding the nature of a spirit – that is, it will keep this idea of reason free from all illusions of the imagination just as it has found it empty of all intuitions of sensibility. But to that same extent, this idea whose object is incomprehensible to the speculative thinker, this substance that eludes the glance of his spirit the more he strains all of his optic nerves [202] to spy it out, this spirit that can only be thought of – this mere thing of thought – must also hold less interest for him. He must essentially distinguish this *something* in him that thinks and senses from all of his thoughts and sensations – that is, from everything actual that he cognizes regarding this something. And he must essentially distinguish it from all bodies, even from the sense organs that modify his outer sensations – that is, from everything actual that he cognizes outside this something. He thinks of this something as *simple* because he does not think of it as extended, as *substance* because he cannot represent it as an accident, and as *representing* because he must refer all of his representations to it. He thinks of it as inconceivable because it cannot be conceived as that which conceives, because it is presupposed in every representation, and because, even when it thinks itself by means of the predicate "*representing*," this something, as *subject*, can never itself be object. In a

[77] *Vermag*, a verb form of the term *Vermögen*, also translated as "faculty," as in "faculty of representation."

word, this representing, simple, and substantial something $= x$ can have as little of an effect on him as he can have on it. It intervenes in none of his representations, inclinations, and actions and is an object neither of his hate nor of his love precisely because for him it is [a something] $= x$.[78] To the degree that his *I* must be important to him – in so far as it constitutes *one* person together with his sense organs and is represented in a *single* idea (the richest and clearest yet also the most indistinct of all) with the state of the faculty of representation and desire, which expresses itself through the representations and inclinations referred to this I – to that same degree the supersensible *half* of his person must be unimportant to him. For, in order to come to know the I as substance, not only must he separate this latter half from the other half that he cognizes through outer sense, but he must also distinguish it even from everything that *inner* sense presents to him – from all representations – and even from the faculty of representation. [203] And this I rewards him for the trouble of all these abstractions with the disclosure *that it is a subject.*

H[79]

Selection from the Eleventh Letter, "The key to the rational psychology of the Greeks"

[245] Previously, sensibility was declared sometimes to be the faculty for becoming affected by means of the organs and sometimes to be the restriction of the representing power by the sense organs associated with it. In both cases it was through the feature of the sense organs that the subject to which sensibility belongs – the subject that was the mere body for the materialist but body and soul taken together for the spiritualist – was included under the concept of sensibility. In both cases it was assumed to be settled that sensibility could not be thought apart from the sense organs. Hence, sensibility was elevated by the materialist, who had in view its indispensability to the faculty of representation, to the basic faculty of the representing subject. But the subject itself was degraded to mere sense organs. By the spiritualist, in contrast, who had in view the

[78] Cf. Kant, *Critique of Pure Reason* (A 346/B 404): "Through this I or he or it (the thing) which thinks, nothing further is represented than a transcendental subject of the thoughts $= X$."

[79] This selection of the 1790 edition (pp. 245–51) is a heavily revised and much-expanded version of pp. 264–6 of the Eighth Letter from the *Merkur*.

distinction arising in self-consciousness between the *I* and the sense organs that were represented through outer sense, sensibility was excluded from the proper faculty of representation and degraded to an obstacle of proper cognition – to a shackle of the representing power. But this power was elevated to a simple, incorporeal substance. Since the feature of the sense organs was at that time indispensable to the concept of sensibility, [246] it remained, as before, impossible for philosophers to be in agreement with one another about this concept. They were forever bound to misunderstand one another, as they previously had, with regard to the term *sensibility*.

But the feature of the sense organs was taken up under the concept of sensibility only as a result of confusing the *power* of representing with the faculty of representation. Under [the term] *power*, one thought of the *substance* that possesses this faculty. Thus, whenever sensibility was understood as a property of the *power* of representing, the sense organs of course would at once impose themselves either as the representing substance itself or as a substance bound up with the representing substance, as a *subject* of sensibility. And this latter substance would be turned either into a mere excitability of the sense organs (in materialism) or into an incapacity[80] of the representing power (in spiritualism).

But if thinking minds are ever to understand one another with regard to the meaning of the term *faculty of representation*, its concept must remain exactly the same whether the representing *substance* is taken to be a spirit, a body, or both at once. And just as the concept of the *pure faculty of representation* completely abstracts from the subject of this faculty, the concept of *pure sensibility* also necessarily excludes the concept of substance and cannot contain any other feature than that through which sensibility is characterized as a component of the *mere* faculty of representation. If the concept of pure sensibility is not to presuppose as settled anything that is still very much in question in the philosophical world, absolutely nothing can appear in it that concerns the relation of the representing subject to the sense organs. And if this concept is not to confuse the question, What does sensibility *consist in*?, with the question, Where [247] does it *arise from*?, it cannot mention the disputed components of the subject of sensibility whatsoever.

[80] *Unvermögen*.

At this point, dear friend, I hear you interrupting me, "But is not the philosophical world – are not materialists and spiritualists in agreement that the *excitability of the sense organs* belongs to sensibility?" Yes! And I am in agreement with you, too – and as I may surely assume, so is *Kant*. But the philosophical world is all the more in disagreement about the question of *how* this excitability belongs to sensibility. Does it constitute sensibility by itself or only in connection with the power of representing? In no way does everyone agree that sensibility *is* the excitability of the sense organs, because otherwise one would have to be in agreement about the disputed questions of *how* excitability belongs to sensibility and *how* the sense organs are connected to the soul.

Not everything that belongs to sensibility belongs in its basic concept, which must contain only its essential features – that is, those features without which it cannot be thought at all. But now sensibility (even when *in a particular subject* this faculty is possible only through sense organs) can very well be thought apart from the excitability of the sense organs. For, as a faculty of the *mere mind*,[81] sensibility must necessarily be distinguished from the excitability of the sense organs. And while philosophers are still not in agreement as to whether the excitability of the sense organs belongs to the *power* of representing, everyone must agree that there is a component of the human faculty of representation called sensibility.

The basic concept of sensibility that the Critique of Reason puts forward designates sensibility as a component of the mere faculty of representation. It is thus designated in a sense that no faction contests [248], a sense about which they must all come to an agreement if they are not to attach contrary meanings to the term *sensibility* (now as before) without knowing it and to misunderstand one another without discerning the point of their misunderstanding.

The rights of *ordinary usage*, which until now has had the term *sensibility* denote a faculty of the mind to which the excitability of the organs belongs, can be combined very naturally with the demands of *philosophical reason*, which seeks to use this term in a particular, newly defined sense, solely for a faculty of the mere mind. One can refer to it in its first meaning as *empirical* sensibility but in its second meaning, with *Kant*, as *pure* sensibility. Pure sensibility has the faculty of representation,

[81] *Des bloßen Gemütes.*

of which it is a component, as its *logical* subject. The substance to which it and the faculty of representation belong may be a mere body or a spirit that is bound to a body. As a mere faculty, *pure* sensibility is *a priori* – that is, present in the faculty of representation prior to all affection – in so far as it itself is partly the *faculty* for being affected. In contrast, *empirical* sensibility signifies only one part of this faculty – namely, *outer sense* – and does so only in so far as it is modified by something – namely by the organic body – that is itself an *object* of outer sense and that thus presupposes this sense in the mind.

Pure sensibility is the faculty of the mind for arriving at representations through the manner in which it is *affected* in its receptivity, and it distinguishes itself essentially from the *understanding*, or the faculty for arriving at representations through the manner in which the operation of the mind *acts*. [249] Pure sensibility includes *outer* and *inner sense*, or the faculties for arriving at representations by being affected from *outside* and from *inside*.

With this explanation and division of sensibility, the conflation of essentially different faculties is removed at one stroke. *Sensibility* in general was confused with *outer sense*, and outer sense with its empirical modifications by the organs, while at times *inner sense* was projected onto the *understanding* and at times declared to be *consciousness* itself.

Every representation that *arises* through the manner in which receptivity is affected (and only *this* kind of representation) is called *sensible*. Such representation is called *sensation* in so far as it refers to the *representing*, and it is called *intuition* in so far as it refers to the *represented*.

The manner in which receptivity is affected partly depends on the original constitution of receptivity, the possibility for being affected that is determined *a priori* by its constitution – the original form of receptivity that belongs to the mere mind. But it also partly depends on the constitution of the affecting objects. Only the former belongs among the features of *pure* sensibility.

Kant has demonstrated that the form of receptivity of outer sense consists in *pure space* while the receptivity of inner sense consists in *pure time*. I confess to you that it is impossible for me to make *his* grounds understandable for you *here*, no matter how much they are convincing to me. Even with respect to *my own* grounds, regardless of how comprehensible they seem to *me*, I can offer you only a couple of suggestions. If you assume the *receptivity* of the faculty of representation to consist in the *determinate receptivity of the* [250] *manifold* that constitutes the matter in every representation, while you assume spontaneity to consist in the faculty for bringing the received manifold to a *unity* by *combining* it (as this is recognized to be the case with the understanding and reason), then it must be illuminating to you that outer sense would have to be distinguished from inner sense by a difference in its specific manner of receiving the manifold. Outer sense, the faculty for being affected by something *different from the mind*, can thus only be a receptivity for a *mere manifold in its manifoldness* – for an uncombined manifold with all of its parts *disconnected*[82] – because the combination of the manifold *in* the mind can take place only through *spontaneity*. In contrast, the disconnected manifold given to outer sense can be taken up in *inner* sense only by being grasped by spontaneity and consequently brought to a unity through the *combination* of its parts. In so far as the disconnected, juxtaposed[83] manifold given to outer sense must, then, be given to inner sense through the spontaneity that grasps *each* of its parts by combining them, it must also be given *in succession*.[84] If you now represent the form of the manifold in general, which consists in being merely *disconnected*, *juxtaposed*, and *in succession*,[85] then you have represented to yourself *pure space* and *pure time*, which I ask you to distinguish precisely from both *empty* and *filled* space and time.

In accordance with this result, everything cognizable, in so far as it is supposed to be *intuited*, must take on the form of intuition in the mind and cannot, therefore, be cognized as a *thing in itself* but only as an *appearance*: [251] as an appearance of outer sense, as something filling up space; as an appearance of inner sense, as something filling up time; as a body outside us; and as an alteration in us. In cognizing, the understanding relates itself to sensibility, which presents to it the matter provided by sensation under the forms of intuition, and sensibility relates itself to the understanding, which raises the intuitions of sensibility to concepts in so far as it combines them according to the laws of its nature.

[82] *Ausser einander.* [83] *Ausser einander, nebeneinander.* [84] *Nacheinander.*
[85] *Aussereinander-, Nebeneinander- und Nacheinandersein.*

I[86]

Twelfth Letter, "Suggestions regarding the influence of the undeveloped and misunderstood basic truths of religion on civic and moral culture"

You agree with me, dear friend, that *moral predispositions*, taken together with the physical needs of human nature, have given civil society its existence as well as its form. Throughout its modifications in various ages and among various peoples, this form has always disclosed the degree of development of moral predispositions and the degree of ennoblement of physical needs. You also do not require any further proof that, with regard to their development and higher cultivation, moral predispositions needed precisely those imperfect *arrangements* and misunderstood *events* of civic life that, with respect to the *good* in the one [264] and the *true* in the other, were brought about by the unrecognized influence of those predispositions. Moreover, you require no further proof that the first traces of morality and religion had to express themselves in political laws and supernatural facts, or that the *positive*[87] character of lawgiving and religious systems, even in its capacity as a source for the cognition of human rights and duties, and as a ground for hope in a future life, was just as indispensable as it was unavoidable.

To the extent that *truth* is a consequence of the use of our faculty of representation, it depends on the *point of view* from which objects are either perceived or investigated; and this point of view is always determined by some kind of *interest*. A newborn child fastens its look on the place from which the most light shines forth, and a thinker grasps the object of his reflections from the perspective from which he can most completely survey it, given the disposition of his spirit, which depends on his inclinations and prior cognitions. Unbalanced inclinations and incorrect prior cognitions produce a misunderstood interest that leads to a *one-sided* point of view and thereby to a misconception of the object. Only the well-understood interest of *humanity in general* can supply the correct point of view from which the duties and rights of human beings in this life and the ground for their expectation of a future life can be recognized

86 This selection of the 1790 edition (pp. 263–92) is an entirely new letter added where the *Merkur* letters ended.
87 As involving *posited* facts.

in their true shape – that is, in their genuine form grounded in the original nature of humanity.

Until *practical* reason arrives at a *distinct* consciousness of its spontaneity with regard to morality (purely and in the strictest sense), [265] the genuine and complete interest of humanity will necessarily be misunderstood, and the satisfaction of *self-interested* drives will be looked upon as the only – or at least the ultimate – object of that interest. Reason that misconstrues its calling and its worth takes itself to be a mere handmaiden of the drive for pleasure and believes that it has attained its highest status in this capacity when it has risen above the concerns of instinct to be their *supervisor*. Through its philosophizing representatives, reason does itself a great injustice today, and perhaps more than ever before, by ascribing actions of unselfish wisdom to self-interested prudence. Moreover, it does itself an injustice by explaining its interest in the common good – an interest that comes from the inner drive of its nature and from the abundance of its spontaneous power – in terms of the secured and increased advantage that individual members will be able to draw from the advantage of the whole society once the immense problem of a perfect political constitution and of universal and perpetual peace is solved.

Through the *particular needs* of the individual and unconnected states within which humanity gradually developed into a civil society, certain *positive* duties and rights of *citizens* were determined for the first time. These duties and rights were different in different states, and they contained only very weak traces of morality not only at the time of the emergence of individual states but also at the time of their highest cultivation. Whenever a state owes its self-preservation merely to the right of the stronger – or what amounts to the same thing, is capable of achieving it only through its encroachment on the inalienable rights of both its own members and those of other states – it turns its citizens into true barbarians. For it forces them, for its own benefit, to misconstrue everything that they as *human beings* owe to themselves, to their fellow citizens, and to foreigners. [266] If the enhancement of *physical* power ultimately becomes the political motivation of such a state, and if this power falls to the demagogic, aristocratic, or monarchic despots – as sooner or later is bound to happen – then the need for a civil society ceases to be the ground for determining positive laws. The caprice of arbitrarily acting rulers takes over in its place, former possessors of legislative power become mere instruments of the executive power, and citizens become slaves. It goes without saying that neither a moral disposition nor insights presupposing a use of the power of thinking that is *free*, yet guided by a moral disposition, can emerge in such states. Finally, if after a prolonged struggle from within and without, after many revolutions, and as a result of experiences that come to be just as costly for the oppressors as for the oppressed, political rulers gradually learn to understand their own interests better; if they begin to see that they can securely achieve their interests only by promoting the interests of their subjects and by protecting the interests of foreign states – only then and to that extent can a *moral disposition* develop, a disposition that remains bound as long as humanity is forced to battle for its mere existence either with the elements or with itself.

To the extent that the demands (self-interested drives) of humanity are restricted by the *spontaneity of reason*, the duties and rights of human beings as human beings in the strictest sense – that is, as *world citizens* – are determined by the *universal needs* of humanity that are grounded in human nature. With the complete development [267] and universal recognition of these duties and rights, all opposition, and thus all dispute between the interests of the states and their individual members, as well as between the individual states themselves, will fall away on its own. Neither differences of class nor differences in forms of government, in so far as they depend on external circumstances, can be abolished, and thus a variety of particular interests must always remain. But this very variety in particular and individual interests is bound to become the condition of an ever-progressing happiness and ennoblement of humanity to the same extent that it is subjected to a universal and highest rule of right. It goes without saying that the recognition of duties and rights of humanity by whole states – or rather, by the lawgiving power in those states – can be achieved only very gradually and slowly. But this recognition remains absolutely inconceivable until philosophizing reason, through its representatives – individual independent thinkers – has come to an agreement with itself about the principles of those duties and rights.

In human culture, *state citizenship* had to precede *world citizenship*, and the crude instinct of the senses had to be gradually refined by schooling in political education and restrained by the force of positive laws before it could make room for the spontaneity of reason and learn to obey its guidance. As a result, *political motives* (regardless of the fact that they themselves could be put in motion only by an instinct modified by moral predispositions) had to operate for a long time in place of *moral motives*, which, in so far as they are motives, can persist only in fully developed dispositions, in a capacity that has been elevated to an active power. *Civic* culture had to [268] prepare for genuine *moral* culture by way of *positive* laws and religions, and only with moral culture could cognition of the *pure* moral law and of the religion of *reason* gradually arise. – Just as this pure religion owes the ground for cognition of its basic truths to the theory of morality (which rests firmly on the fully developed form of reason) while it undergirds the moral disposition by the most powerful of motivations, so too positive laws and religions have guaranteed one another's existence and dissemination. The first forms of government were, on the whole, more or less *theocratic*, the oldest political laws were the *revealed* will of the deities, and the oldest positive religions were forms of *national divine worship*. Under the very same external circumstances in which variety sprung up in the needs of individual civil societies – circumstances in which different states' interests were subsequently generated – positive laws and religions were also multiplied and set in opposition to one another. And for a long time the national gods agreed as little amongst themselves as did their nations.

Once civil constitutions found a secure foothold, once subjects became accustomed to the force of positive laws and authorities came into possession of the means of force, the representatives of the deities began to rule in their own name, and theocracies gradually dissolved into monarchies, aristocracies, and democracies. Within the political regime, the gods gradually lost their *local character*. The *Hebrews*, who during the time of their genuine theocracy provided numerous proofs of their regard for their invisible king as only the God of their fathers, recognized him to be the ruler of all of nature after they had projected his royal dignity onto a ruler from their midst. Other nations, which [269] as a result of their basic constitution were not as exclusively isolated, took up foreign national gods along with the products of foreign arts the more a better-understood self-interest brought them closer to one another. And when Rome had combined almost all of the known nations at the time into a single body politic, the former tutelary gods of individual hordes of barbarians became the common protectors of the *orbis terrarum*.[88]

[88] World.

Just as protection by a national god was confined to his people alone, and his laws bound only the citizens of his state – laws that served no purpose beyond a merely political one – so too his influence on the weal and woe of his believers lasted only as long as the present life. The Hebrews hoped for and feared nothing but earthly goods and ills from their Jehovah; and in the entire code of his lawgiving, which has remained completely intact to our day, one finds nothing firmly established save temporal rewards and punishments. But the concepts of the deity became more refined the more the gods were relieved from the immediate management of worldly affairs. From this time on, whatever remained unrewarded or unpunished by their representatives in the present life, they rewarded or punished as evil in a future life, and whatever religion had lost in political motivation because of the end of theocracies, it gained in moral motivation. Laws now obtained a new sanction, which hastened the observance of those laws by means of a more general and subtle motive. This was a *more general* motive, for now no crime remained unpunished; and with the fear of an unavoidable and unbribable future tribunal, the hope of impunity was crushed – a hope that earlier was able to be grounded on examples of criminals who, by [270] deception or by open force, had escaped requital by earthly judges and were even overwhelmed by the gods with temporal prosperity. This was a *more subtle* motive, for, in mastering *present* impulses by means of the idea of a *future life*, the human spirit now expressed a higher degree of its spontaneity than when it had to leave their suppression to nothing but other impulses that were likewise present.

Which *laws* should religion have sanctioned in the peculiar period when *political laws* were gradually driven out of the whole cultivated world as a result of the despotism of the Roman emperors, when the *moral law* remained unknown outside a small circle of philosophers, and when its meaning was most heavily disputed among those schools (the *Stoic* and *Epicurean*) which were most preoccupied with it? With the decline of the positive laws that had been acting in place of moral laws, a universal corruption of morals[89] set in that in quick succession brought about the fall of the Roman Empire. Religion, which had lost along with the civil constitution its previous and most powerful ground of respect and the most important object of its influence, was now abandoned to the

[89] *Sitten*. Cf. below, n. 90.

fantasy of poets, to the self-interested speculations of altar servants, and to the nonbelief of pseudo-sages.

But precisely as a result of this fact, the form that religion had taken until this point, which was supposed to make way for a better one, became ripe for ruin. With *polytheism* the period of humanity's *political culture* ended, and with *Christianity* its period of *moral culture* commenced.

Christ was the first to advance *religion* in its distinctive and natural form by separating it wholly from *politics* and tying it directly [271] to *morality*. The new law to which Christianity gave its sanction does not obligate any one particular people but rather humanity as a whole. It is not imposed by force from the outside but rather contained in the rational will of everyone; it in no way has as its aim the outer prosperity of either whole states or their citizens but rather the *ennobling* of humanity; and it assures ennobled, individual human beings in this life nothing but contentment of the heart and the expectation of a better future life as a reward for their unselfish righteousness. As consequences of the ennoblement of its members, moreover, it assures civil societies continuing improvement of their forms, and it assures humanity in general a continuing decline of the woe that is inseparable from its nature. The author of this law can be neither a national god nor a political lawgiver, but must be the universal and only *father* of *all humanity*. The realm in which he determines the *ultimate* fates of *individual* human beings according to the measure of their observance of this law is not of this world precisely because the ennoblement of individuals, and not the improvement of their outer condition, is its only aim; and even the never fully completed decline of the woe that oppresses humanity in general is a direct *consequence* of this law. Thus, Christ tied religion to pure morality to the extent that he traced it back to its two genuine basic truths: namely, first, to the conviction in the existence of a cause of the world – a cause that is separate from it and *morally disposed* – and, second, to the conviction in a future life in which the ultimate fate of human beings is determined according to the *measure* of their *morality*.

Because Christ established the meaning of these basic truths neither by means of a philosophical system nor by means of incomprehensible [272] dogmas of blind faith, because he neither could nor wanted to build his religion upon metaphysics or hyperphysics, he indeed had to let the *purity of his teaching* depend on the *purity of the moral disposition*, which he expressed in his words and actions in a wholly unsurpassable way and which he sought to instill in his followers. And through this disposition in fact, which is directly tied to the true meaning of those basic truths, the understanding is saved from errors when thinking these truths no less than it is supported by its powerful influence on the heart when directing the will. Genuine *Christian orthodoxy* is conceivable to me only as a consequence of the purity of a heart that, because it unceasingly holds before the spirit the *one thing needed*, saves this spirit (even without any Critique of Reason or Theory of the Faculty of Representation) from all the strayings of speculation. It is enough for this heart – which alone, according to the teaching of *Jesus*, is allowed to *intuit God* – to know the will of the deity in the moral law, a will by which one recognizes the heavenly father without worrying about his *substance*. The more the moral disposition of a Christian develops, enlivens, and expands through *actions* characteristic of it, the more illuminating the one aspect of the deity becomes that is accessible to human reason, the *disposition of God*. And although it is on account of this very disposition that the Christian feels himself compelled to expect a better life beyond the grave, his own noble sense makes it impossible for him to waste his time – a time that is becoming too short for him to fulfill his duties in the present life – with speculations about the nature of the future life. For the man who is concerned not with rewards in the realm of immortality but solely with [273] *becoming worthy* of that realm, it should not be difficult to remain at ease about the incomprehensibility of these rewards.

In the period of *political* culture, *civic virtue* was suffocated by the despotism of the authorities, and civil constitutions degenerated because those who were supposed to be merely instruments of the laws imposed their arbitrary will in place of the laws. Similarly, in the period of *moral* culture, *Christian virtue* was suffocated by the despotism of the priests. And Christianity degenerated at the same rate that its teachers replaced the simple basic truths that were determined solely by the moral disposition with hapless, speculative elaborations of these basic truths, which were then forced upon the laity as expressions of the Holy Spirit, as mysteries of the kingdom of God, as *articles of faith*.

How quickly the purity of the moral disposition disappeared among Christians is known from church history, which unfortunately is attested in most detail by the writings and actions of the saints, heroes, and fathers of Christianity. This degeneration could have been prevented only by a miracle anyway, one which the wisdom of God did not favor partly for reasons that lie close enough even for human shortsightedness but are not relevant here. As the morality of the Christians gradually changed, so did their simple, modest, and pure manner of representing the deity and a future life. They misconstrued the moral law just as much as they deviated from it through their behavior. And because the law that they adopted in its place could be of interest only in terms of rewards and punishments of a future life, because they did not believe in a future life for the sake of the law but adopted the law for the [274] sake of a future life, a need arose for having a ground for conviction in that life, distinct from the moral disposition, and for seeking insights into its nature from inside and outside the domain of reason. They misconstrued the deity just as much as they misconstrued the will of the heavenly father. And because they could no longer infer from the disposition of God – which they otherwise encountered in their hearts – to what must be *thought* concerning the *incomprehensible* nature of God, a need arose to draw the features of the concept of the deity from metaphysical and hyperphysical sources.

The determination of the new form under which the basic truths of religion were to be thought now fell in a natural way to the discretion of the *teachers* of Christianity and, in accordance with its hierarchical constitution, to the discretion of the *bishops*, who at the *councils* practiced an aristocratic command over the faith of the subordinate clergy and laity. These bishops tied the manner of representation of the entire Christian world to certain formulas, and they advanced these formulas in the name of the Holy Spirit with the power of *infallibility* – a power which had partly become their own – and put them through against the objections of reason by means of spiritual anathema and secular arms.

In so far as it depended on the manner of representation of the few who prescribed formulas of faith – and because this manner was still not bound to any firmly fixed *church symbol* – the meaning that the basic truths of religion were supposed to hold for the entire Christian world depended on the *philosophy* of the age, which consisted in a combination of metaphysics and hyperphysics that is known by the name *Neoplatonism*. It is thus readily understandable how it came to pass that today even the lowest [275] social classes among all the Christian nations still carry on their tongues formulas that one rediscovers, not without consternation, among the handed-down remnants of the misunderstood speculations of *Plato* and *Pythagoras*. It is also readily understandable how a belief in these formulas – that is, a taking-to-be-true of a meaning that these formulas are supposed to have for the divine understanding alone – is still now and again taken as the first of all Christian virtues and as a condition of the *new covenant*, a condition that leaves no other choice but that between heaven and hell.

It is in this way that, in the unfortunate period during which ethics and the arts and sciences experienced a general decline, the degenerate and distorted *Platonic idea of immaterial intelligences* became the *foundation* for the orthodox manner of representation of the two basic truths of religion – that is, the manner of representation established by the ecclesiastical tribunal of faith. These two basic truths of religion had to relinquish their status to an ever-increasing number of *dogmas* in which they were merely presupposed and through which their rational meaning was more and more supplanted. Out of this religion, which was adulterated in its basic truths, and which now could no longer sanction reason's doctrine of morals,[90] there arose in opposition to *philosophical morality* a distinctly *theological morality*. This theological morality is most accurately described, perhaps, by the term *monkish* because it gave birth to monasticism in Christianity and has maintained itself up to the present day in its complete strictness, at least in theory, in the monasteries. This is true regardless of the fact that it also persists in more or less noticeable traces outside the monasteries, in the so-called *spiritual doctrine of morals* of all Christian religious denominations.

The moral law, which is necessarily misconstrued by philosophy whenever it is derived [276] from somewhere other than the *nature of reason*, was derived by the *Neoplatonists* from their enthusiastic speculations about the *nature of the soul* and the *nature of the deity*.

Because they held the *substance of the soul* – in all of its properties and constitution – to be the opposite of the *substance of bodies*, the flesh to be the prison of the soul, and a human being to be a spirit that finds itself in an unnatural state, they not only distinguished but also separated, in the strictest sense, the two essential components of the human faculty of desire and declared the demands of spiritual nature to be absolutely incompatible with the demands of physical nature. To be sure, the

[90] *Sittenlehre*. The term is used again at the end of this paragraph and also below, pp. 277 and 280. See above, the Third Letter from the *Merkur*, n. 59.

church fathers who had converted from paganism traded this ground of explanation of the *contradiction in human nature* for another explanation that their converters had found in the sacred books of their nation. But even the Jewish church fathers had drawn the *philosophy* that they applied in their exegesis from the same source as their pagan proselytes. The doctrine of the contradiction between the flesh and the soul could not possibly have been taken from the *Mosaic narration of the fall of the first human being*, for this narration contains no trace of that contradiction. Nonetheless, the story of the fall could have been considered quite suitable at that time for filling in the striking gap that was created by the Neoplatonists in the Platonic theory of the contradiction between spirit and matter. They created this gap not by assuming matter to be everlasting, as Plato did, or by explaining its evil character[91] in terms of the concept of its nature, but by deriving the origin of matter from the deity itself and thereby making it impossible for them to give the question concerning the *origin of evil*[92] any answer that did not [277] itself provoke this question again. The philosophizing Judeo-Christians believed that they had found such an answer: "Material (physical) nature, in so far as it arose from the deity, cannot possibly be evil. Its evil character must therefore be the consequence of a deed that cannot be ascribed to the deity. The fall of the first human being is such a deed, and its distressing consequence is the corruption of human nature, which consists in the contradiction between body and spirit. The curse that sin brought into the world concerns not only human beings but the whole of physical nature, which was created solely for the sake of human beings, and which is now deformed by physical ills to discipline them."

The contradiction between the flesh and the soul very soon became the principle of the Christian doctrine of morals. It is at all events the key to the thoroughgoing opposition between being human and being Christian, between worldly and spiritual interests, and between the present and the future life, which makes up the common content of all the exegeses and homilies of those times. Because drives, which have their ground in the sense organs, were considered to be evil in origin, there was no other duty for this life than a never-ending struggle that did

91 *Bösartigkeit.*

92 *Übel*; usually Reinhold uses *Böse* for this term. In this context, the issue of physical ills (see the end of the paragraph) as well as of moral evil may be meant to be relevant. Cf. Friedrich Nietzsche (1844–1900), *Genealogy of Morals* (Leipzig, 1887).

not, for instance, have the *guiding* of those drives as its goal, but rather their *suppression* and eradication. The sublime *Gospel* teachings of self-denial, mortification of the flesh, contempt for the world, etc. were taken in a crude literal sense and as a result were degraded to a mere commentary on the mystical doctrine of disembodiment.

Religion, which in ancient times helped to cultivate human beings into citizens, was now at the point of destroying its own work by imposing duties on them that [278] were incompatible with the needs of civil society. To be sure, religion had to ease the strictness of its demands if it did not want to destroy itself in the process of eradicating the human race; and the mystagogues were very soon forced to distinguish indispensable duties from the precepts of spiritual perfection – called *evangelical counsels* – which could not at all survive with the continuing existence of political states. Moreover, they were forced to *tolerate* the propagation of the species, the possession of property, and the use of a free will (in worldly affairs) by those who with God's allowance felt themselves too weak to begin the life of a disembodied spirit here below. But once monasticism became the ideal of perfection for Christianity, the *piety* of the *common* Christian that took the place of *morality* could consist only in the closest possible approximation to the holiness of the monk. The layperson led a *Christian* way of life by imitating the monk wherever he could and by *doing penance* for everything else.

The fact that a doctrine originally grounded on misbegotten speculations of metaphysics could find such general acceptance and could become so persuasive even outside the monasteries – despite all the unnatural constraint that it imposes on the most natural inclinations – will be less surprising to you, my friend, if you consider how much those speculations were supported in the present case by the *most common manner of representation*. The power of the imagination of the common man needs only very little aid if it is to perceive an opposed nature between the soul and the flesh in the *distinction* between the representing *I* and the represented sense organs that arises in the *self-consciousness* of every human being. [279] Even a very uncultivated understanding, once it has become familiar with that distinction, finds in its crude concepts enough premises for it to be easily led into grasping that the sex drive and all striving for enjoyment in which the instruments of the senses are employed have their ground in the flesh, that the soul, as distinct from the flesh, must be free from these drives, and that the enticement to evil lies in these drives and thus in the flesh, etc.

Practical reason announces its prohibitions *prior* to its commands, avoidance of evil necessarily precedes good works, and human beings learn to appreciate what the misuse of their sensible drives consists in long before they learn their rational use. As a result, during the standstill that the degeneration of Christianity caused in the moral culture that it had brought about, the human spirit was not only stuck at its discernment of that which was prohibited, evil, and misused; this spirit (misled by a religion that was adulterated in its basic truths) also extended its *prohibition* to commands unfamiliar to it, and it considered all use of sensible drives to be misuse and the good it had misconstrued to be evil. Too strong to let itself be guided by instinct and too weak to guide instinct, it made an attempt to suppress instinct, and in order to avoid vice, it fled all opportunity for virtue.

Because the philosophical idea of the deity, along with the idea of the soul, was drawn by the church fathers from one and the same source, the basic truth of God's existence and the basic truth of a future life had the very same fate and, consequently, also the very same influence on the degeneration of Christian morality into monkish morality.

Already with *Plato* the concept of the deity was determined by its opposition to *matter*, which he [280] took to be *original formlessness*, just as he took the deity to be the *original source of all forms*, which were to have been present since eternity in the understanding of God as the archetypes of finite things. Since, according to this manner of representation, finite substances could be *good* only in so far as they participated in the forms of the divine understanding and had to be *evil* in so far as they participated in the formlessness of matter, even the morality of human beings consisted in their distance from matter and their proximity to the deity. But because Plato recognized the forms of bodies as copies of divine ideas, he in no way rejected all enjoyment that presupposes the use of the instruments of sense; he rejected only that kind which has its basis in the evil character of matter, in disorderly drives, and which makes it impossible for the spirit to perceive the copies of divine ideas in matter and to arrive through this matter at the consciousness of the archetypes that are present in spiritual nature. For this reason, Plato recommended at every opportunity the enjoyment of the *beauties* of nature and art as a means to virtue, an enjoyment that was subsequently decried by monkish morality as unholy and dangerous. And on account of the healthiness of his soul, the correctness of his taste, and the noble, cultivated spirit of his era, his doctrine of morals, however enthusiastic it was in its basic concepts, was protected against the degeneration for which it contained the seed, and which was subsequently driven to an extreme by the Neoplatonists and monks.

To be sure, the inconsistent doctrine of the Neoplatonists deviated from the doctrine of Plato in so far as it derived matter itself from the deity. Yet not only had it conferred an *evil character* upon matter, but it had also projected this character onto all *finite beings* or onto the whole of *nature* in so far as [281] it assumed that even spiritual *nature*, to the extent that it is nature – that is, a *finite substance* – must degenerate when it is left to itself and not protected from degeneration by a special influence of the deity (*grace*). The character of the deity, which Christ revealed through a pure moral disposition, was defined by the philosophy of the church fathers in terms of an opposition to *nature*. As pure *incorporeal intelligence*, the deity could be pleased with human beings only in so far as they acted in that capacity as pure intelligences and consequently counteracted all those drives which had their ground in the organic body. And, as *supernatural intelligence*, the deity could sanction only those *spiritual* actions of the human soul which were implemented and performed *not from natural* motives but solely for the sake of the deity and under its direct influence. For this reason the Christian mystagogues declared to be *unholy* not only every satisfaction of sensible drives but even the act of thinking, whenever this act was not directed by the supernatural illumination of the Holy Spirit. Because this illumination with respect to the basic truths of religion was imparted only to the bishops representing the church, even thinking about the deity, to the extent that it deviated from the formulas of faith, was declared to be an unpardonable sin against the Holy Spirit. In contrast, the satisfaction of sensible drives, to the extent that it is indispensable for the existence of believers as *conditio sine qua non*,[93] could be reckoned to the indulgence of God's mercy.

Even in this idea of mystical metaphysics, uncultivated common sense meets up on one and the same path with stray philosophizing reason, and this fact makes very intelligible to us the speedy and universal [282] dissemination of this metaphysics in the Christian world as well as the

[93] A necessary condition.

important role that it played, and in part still plays, in folk religion. Here I find myself at the point where metaphysics and hyperphysics join hands. For regardless of the fact that hyperphysics, which is developed by philosophical minds, contains the materials for a system that deserves the name *philosophical* as much as any other previous system, it still belongs – to the extent that it is built on *supernatural facts* – to a common understanding that judges according to the testimony of the senses, an understanding that philosophizing reason, rightly or wrongly, is used to calling upon when desperate.

If nations that have not yet emerged from the state of barbarism, or have sunk back into it, have come by whatever path to believe in a *God that is separate from nature*, they will set this God in direct *opposition* to nature just as they set the soul in direct opposition to the flesh. But at the same time they will also *confuse* God with nature to the extent that they remain unfamiliar with nature. At the dawning of reason, the transition from any natural effect at hand to a supernatural cause can occur without a noticeable leap. For the ignorant worshiper of God, *nature* is the *little known* and *God* is the *infinitely unknown*, and wherever he fails to encounter the visible hand of the one, he feels compelled to accept the invisible hand of the other. The links of the chain in which every single event hangs are in most cases hidden from every human eye; only the last link, which holds them all fast to *Jupiter*'s throne, is large and visible enough to be universally observed.

[283] This was especially true of the *terrifying phenomena of nature* in the earlier youth of the human race. The *more unusual* such a phenomenon was, the less frequently the crude and inexperienced child of nature found something in the sequence of his previous experiences that he could specify as the *cause* of it. The *more horrifying* it was, the more troubled he was about its cause and the more inclined he was to seek this cause outside the sequence of his experiences (outside nature). The *more immense* its magnitude, and the more immeasurable it was for his benumbed power of representation, the more obvious the unknown supernatural cause became to him. However different from one another events of this kind may have been when they were merely *unusual*, *horrifying*, and *immense*, they always led him back to one and the same unknown supernatural being, which impressed itself deeper upon his fantasy at every similar opportunity. With the ever-growing urge to become better acquainted with a being that was so important to him,

nothing was more natural to him than believing that he could guess the properties and disposition of the deity from what he took it *to effect* and thus also *to will*.

Because God always effected and willed the *unusual* while nature effected and willed the *usual*, the idea gradually developed of an opposition between God's way of acting and willing and nature's way. They *acted against* one another, and, wherever a will had to be assumed in nature, an *evil* spirit was posited that *willed* the opposite of the deity.

Because God always willed and did the *terrifying*, while nature willed and did the *agreeable*, this opposition became all the more conspicuous. With their reverence [284] for the author of the terrifying, there was bound to arise amongst the more pious – or *more timorous*,[94] which in those times amounted to the same thing – a kind of indifference toward the efficient cause of the agreeable, which often passed over into contempt as a result of their long standing anxieties. To this the bad consequences were added of the misuse that was only too common in the enjoyment of the agreeable. What misled the imprudent into actions that made them unhappy was the *agreeable*; what held them back from such actions was the terrifying. The indeterminate concepts of the agreeable, the evil, and the natural on the one hand, and the terrifying, the good, and the divine on the other, ran together into two obscure principal ideas. It appeared settled that God pressed for *renunciation* just as nature pressed for *enjoyment*. Pain became holy, and joy unholy; generation became a service of nature, destruction a service of God.[95] It was believed that through floods, earthquakes, etc., and especially through flashes of lightning, the holy and beneficent will of God had been experienced; and one hastened forth with *burnt offerings* of fruits, animals, and human beings, preferring voluntarily to bring something in order not to be forced to give up everything. Nature, which is stronger than all prejudices, had nonetheless remained in possession of those enjoyments on which the survival of the individual as well as the species depends, and through such enjoyments human beings became conscious from time to time of having served nature. As a result, they trembled in anticipation of bad consequences and sought to rid themselves of their burdensome fear

[94] *Furchtsameren*, a term similar in German to *Furcht* (fear), *fürchterlich* (horrifying), *Ehrfurcht* (reverence or awe).

[95] *Gottesdienst*, the standard term for a church service.

by appeasing the deity from time to time through voluntary renunciation, through pain and destruction.

Finally, the fact that events *of great magnitude* were always traced back to God while smaller ones were traced back to nature inevitably drove the opposition between God and nature to an extreme. By allowing God himself directly to effect whatever appeared to surpass the [285] familiar powers of nature, one ultimately allowed God to will little more than what actually surpassed the powers of nature. Human beings did not have sufficient natural powers to satisfy God's demands on them. They had to be outfitted from above with a supernatural faculty, with what in the theological schools was subsequently called *grace*, whenever they were to take up something that was neither evil nor indifferent – that is, something that was to stand neither in contradiction nor in opposition to the will of God. Nature, to which one entrusted only small things, sank ever lower in the eyes of the pious when over time real and imagined needs arose that one did not know how to satisfy by natural means. At each of these occasions, one became used to calling upon the deity, passing over nature, and robbing oneself of all means in order to reach one's goal all the more certainly. The solution of difficult problems for the understanding was expected from *mysteries*, from the thoughts of God; and the execution of difficult undertakings was expected from *miracles*, from the actions of God.

The criterion used to measure the magnitude of an effect was the force of its sensory impression and the visible display of its powers. Hence it could not fail to happen often in those times that events very insignificant in and of themselves were credited to God's account while very important events were credited to nature's account. The presence of God was recognized not only in the majestic voice of thunder but also in the gout-ridden contortions of *Pythia*.[96] In contrast, even in much later times, the virtues of a *Socrates* were declared to be glaring vices because one had ascribed them to the natural powers of this man and not to any theological grace.

[286] Whatever was to please the author of the terrifying phenomena of nature had to cost violent efforts. Whatever happened with lightness and ease was either indifferent or evil. Thus, the hardships in sacrifice, renunciation, and self-torment shared a special sanction with the holiness

[96] The priestess of Apollo, who made oracular utterances at Delphi.

of these practices and caused one to regard effortless enjoyment as all the more unholy. If one enjoyed oneself at sacrificial feasts more liberally and with a freer conscience than before, this happened because one believed that one had purchased the permission or at least the indulgence of the deity by means of previous fastings and burnt offerings.

The more the experiences of the human race accumulated – and along with them its *familiarity with nature* – the more the unusual, terrifying, and strikingly immense phenomena diminished, and as a result the presumption of an opposition between God and nature found less and less sustenance. But this was true only of physical nature. The imagined sensory opposition between it and the deity finally disappeared almost entirely in brighter times, and supernatural powers were set in motion only on extraordinary occasions to elevate or replace nature's insufficient powers, not to work against her. The *moral opposition* between *God* and *human beings*, in contrast, not only remained but obtained new confirmation with every insoluble problem regarding the countless *collisions between sensibility and reason*. The sensible drive was called the "*human* will" or "the *natural* will left to itself"; moral reason, which expressed itself only in terms of commands, was called the "*will of God*."

This opposition was ultimately extended beyond the *will* [287] to *thinking reason* as well. The wisdom of reason, which in many cases naturally protected the demands of the sensible drive against misunderstood religiosity, became *foolishness* before God. The more often reason appeared in advancing culture, in doubts and objections against articles of faith and against the dominant manner of representation of the deity, the more the priests and pious laity hardened their opinion about the perversity and unholiness of natural reason. It had suffered just as much from original sin as the will had. Both were incurable by natural means. *Reason* could be helped only by *mysteries* and the *will* only by *miracles*, and their recalcitrance to the incomprehensible thoughts and unfathomable will of God could be bound by nothing but *blind faith* and *blind obedience*.

The gradual transition from the domination of mere instinct to self-control through reason seems to me to be the ultimate result of the *history of humanity*. When the point humanity set out from is compared to the point it is necessarily approaching, it becomes manifest that there was an age in which the spiritual powers of human beings were too weak, and that an age must be coming in which they will be too strong, to put up with the yoke of blind faith and obedience. Never have human beings been closer to the deity than in these times, when, according to the judgment of the guild of the pious, they are supposedly farthest from it.

In the period of mere instinct and the complete inactivity of reason, when young humanity lay as a suckling at the breast of nature and dreamed neither of [288] metaphysical ideas nor of hyperphysical articles of faith, the author of nature *revealed* its will to it through the voice of its uncultivated but also uncorrupted heart. Humanity fulfilled the law of this author through the satisfaction of its innocent drives, was guided by him in every one of its steps, and was perfectly of one mind with him without *being capable of distinguishing* him *from nature* – the organ through which alone this author could be visible to humanity. During this purest and most immediate communion that can occur between God and mortals *without the mediation of reason*, humanity experienced just as much of him as he allowed it to experience.

Soon enough the increase in population blocked the path of human instinct with obstacles, which could be overcome only gradually by means of a power that until then had resided as a mere undeveloped faculty in human beings, a power which was to attain victorious strength and effective freedom solely through a sustained and difficult struggle with those obstacles. This spontaneous faculty is called *reason*. Its unavoidable use *during the state of its weakness* – a use prompted by external circumstances – must have caused disorder in the sense for nature belonging to human beings, a disorder by which their former harmony with the deity had long been destroyed. The *first* step of reason was accompanied by a *fall*; it was a distancing from nature and from the deity that guided through nature.

Centuries of varied and mostly sad experiences passed before the *freed* pupil of nature learned to will no less correctly by *free choice* what in a *state of innocence* he had willed as a result of unavoidable drives – that is, before as a *citizen* of society he discovered through reason [289] the natural, innocent, and lawful things that had been characteristic of him through *instinct* as a merely natural human being in his narrow family circle. In a word, many centuries passed before he raised himself to a harmony between instinct and reason.

In the meantime, once humanity emerged as an imprudent, boisterous youth – a middle creature between man and child – it had on the one hand renounced its former obedience to instinct, and on the other had to learn from its mistakes before it could become its own leader through reason. From the combined, obscure feelings of both its power and impotence in controlling its faculty and obeying its need – of its dependence and freedom – a misconception gradually arose that ultimately came to dominate universally, a misconception that was all the more deceptive the more it actually borrowed from the truth. Human beings believed that they had to obey certain beings – yet, to be sure, only beings higher than they themselves were. They had to obey *incomprehensible* beings that *revealed* their properties by a means other than reason, and *supernatural* beings that *revealed* their wills by a means other than nature. The weakness of reason, taken together with the disorder of instinct, constituted a disposition which did not allow human beings to perceive that the properties they attributed to the deity were contradictory, and that the actions that could be commanded by those properties were inconsistent. This disposition is what we nowadays call *blind faith*.

Unsolicited *guardians* of human beings soon came forward who were keen enough to realize that a political building that is supposed to be covered with the lead roof of *blind obedience* can rest firmly on no other ground but *blind faith*. They appeared as [290] confidants and authorized agents of the aforementioned higher beings, and in this capacity confiscated from their inferiors their property, freedom, life, and – because reason started becoming dangerous to them – their reason as well. When a *Minos*, *Numa*, or *Lycurgus*[97] put into the mouths of the gods nothing other than what their correct insights into the art of governing and their love for their people had offered them, they became exceptions to the rule according to which the supposed deity was as abominable as the oppressor whom it had invested with *unrestricted power* as its political representative and with *infallibility* as the interpreter of its will.

At no time and place did the *most perfect being* become more foreign to human beings than whenever and wherever messengers and interpreters of higher beings swarmed about – where everything was settled in the name of the gods and where everything happened supernaturally. The author of nature was never less known than when human beings believed that they had several determinate concepts of him from experience, for these concepts seemed to make it a universally settled matter that he revealed his power only through *miracles* and his wisdom only through

[97] Founding rulers of ancient states: Minos, legendary king of Crete; Numa Pompilius (715–673 BC), second king of Rome; Lycurgus (ninth century BC), lawgiver of Sparta.

mysteries, and that one could lay claim to his goodness only through a blind faith in incomprehensible deeds and unintelligible propositions. One was afraid of degrading him to the level of a human being by thinking of his power, wisdom, and goodness in terms of ideas that belong to *human* reason. These attributes were ascribed to him, but they were also carefully separated from everything comprehensible and subjected in turn to an arbitrary will that was as blind as the *chance* and *fate* of pseudo-philosophy. On the other hand, however, one did not hesitate to proclaim him a *despot* who regarded the open attitude of reason as [291] a profanation of his majesty, who could be offended and then reconciled only through blood, who restricted his favor to arbitrarily chosen favorites, etc. This ruinous concept has displaced the beneficent and indispensable *ideal of highest perfection* long enough, an ideal that is evident only to pure hearts and will be attained only through pure reason. It has long enough estranged human beings from God and their happiness to the same degree that the preservers of mysteries and the distributors of miraculous gifts have been busy bringing them closer to the deity. And only recently – and by far not everywhere – was one able to say aloud, without danger of being regarded an atheist, that fortunately for human beings *no object corresponds* to that concept.

Nothing is more understandable than how this manner of representation managed to maintain its status among human beings for so long. When concepts developed and needs multiplied with the advances of civil societies, the earthly *representatives of the gods*[98] no longer felt capable of surveying at a glance their immense and ever-growing possessions. They divided themselves into two classes, one of which took up watch over the *physical* powers of human beings and the other watch over their *moral* powers. *Blind faith* guaranteed both of their possessions. It was thus very natural that with all their might – that is, with nothing less than the sum of all the physical and moral powers of human beings – they in turn guaranteed the possessions of blind faith. Whatever the one was not capable of with filled coffers and mounted on horseback, the other was capable of at the pulpits of churches and schools. But together they achieved their aims. *Pharaoh* organized *indigence* across the land, and his *priests ignorance*, and the people pressed from all sides [292] *to obey* them *blindly* for *bread* and *to believe* them *blindly* for *instruction*.

[98] Translating *Vizegötter* as "representatives of the gods."

I turn my glance from this terrible state of humanity, which, thank God, is for the most part over with now, and take respite in the uplifting prospect of the period that is in the making for humanity with the hard-won *self-cognition of reason*. The red dawn of innocence is breaking forth again, and the epoch is approaching when human beings will proceed on their own power along the path on which they had previously been guided by the hand of nature on the leading strings of instinct. The point in time is approaching when *as men* they rediscover through reason and feeling that happiness, ennobled and multiplied, which as children they had scarcely sampled through feeling alone. Infinite power, wisdom, and goodness, which had steered their tender hearts through a combined effect, is now emerging from the chaos of confused musings as the pure ideal of highest perfection and is becoming the highest rule guiding their reason as well as the foremost motive in their hearts. It is becoming the goal with which their *thinking* begins and to which their *willing* leads them back, the *ground* that they presuppose when seeking order, coherence, and final ends in the study of nature, and the *object* toward which they strive when bringing about order, coherence, and the well-being of humanity through their actions. *This is how the power of developed reason alone will restore the harmony of human beings with the deity, a harmony that seemed to be destroyed forever on account of the weakness of undeveloped reason.* O my friend, what bliss lies in the thought of both wanting and being able to contribute something, however small, that will draw this epoch more swiftly upon us!

Index

Cambridge Texts in the History of Philosophy

Titles published in the series thus far

Aristotle *Nicomachean Ethics* (edited by Roger Crisp)

Arnauld and Nicole *Logic or the Art of Thinking* (edited by Jill Vance Buroker)

Augustine *On the Trinity* (edited by Gareth Matthews)

Bacon *The New Organon* (edited by Lisa Jardine and Michael Silverthorne)

Boyle *A Free Enquiry into the Vulgarly Received Notion of Nature* (edited by Edward B. Davis and Michael Hunter)

Bruno *Cause, Principle and Unity* and *Essays on Magic* (edited by Richard Blackwell and Robert de Lucca with an introduction by Alfonso Ingegno)

Cavendish *Observations upon Experimental Philosphy* (edited by Eileen O'Neill)

Cicero *On Moral Ends* (edited by Julia Annas, translated by Raphael Woolf)

Clarke *A Demonstration of the Being and Attributes of God and Other Writings* (edited by Ezio Vailati)

Classic and Romantic German Aesthetics (edited by Jay Bernstein)

Condillac *Essay on the Origin of Human Knowledge* (edited by Hans Aarsleff)

Conway *The Principles of the Most Ancient and Modern Philosophy* (edited by Allison P. Coudert and Taylor Corse)

Cudworth *A Treatise Concerning Eternal and Immutable Morality* with *A Treatise of Freewill* (edited by Sarah Hutton)

Descartes *Meditations on First Philosophy*, with selections from the *Objections and Replies* (edited by John Cottingham)

Descartes *The World and Other Writings* (edited by Stephen Gaukroger)

Fichte *Foundations of Natural Right* (edited by Frederick Neuhouser, translated by Michael Baur)

Fichte *The System of Ethics* (edited by Daniel Breazeale and Günter Zöller)

Hobbes and Bramhall on Liberty and Necessity (edited by Vere Chappell)

Humboldt *On Language* (edited by Michael Losonsky, translated by Peter Heath)

Kant *Critique of Practical Reason* (edited by Mary Gregor with an introduction by Andrews Reath)

Kant *Groundwork of the Metaphysics of Morals* (edited by Mary Gregor with an introduction by Christine M. Korsgaard)

Kant *Metaphysical Foundations of Natural Science* (edited by Michael Friedman)

Kant *The Metaphysics of Morals* (edited by Mary Gregor with an introduction by Roger Sullivan)

Kant *Prolegomena to any Future Metaphysics* (edited by Gary Hatfield)

Kant *Religion within the Boundaries of Mere Reason and Other Writings* (edited by Allen Wood and George di Giovanni with an introduction by Robert Merrihew Adams)

La Mettrie *Machine Man and Other Writings* (edited by Ann Thomson)

Leibniz *New Essays on Human Understanding* (edited by Peter Remnant and Jonathan Bennett)

Lessing *Philosophical and Theological Writings* (edited by H. B. Nisbet)

Malebranche *Dialogues on Metaphysics and on Religion* (edited by Nicholas Jolley and David Scott)

Malebranche *The Search after Truth* (edited by Thomas M. Lennon and Paul J. Olscamp)

Medieval Islamic Philosophical Writings (edited by Muhammad Ali Khalidi)

Melanchthon *Orations on Philosophy and Education* (edited by Sachiko Kusukawa, translated by Christine Salazar)

Mendelssohn *Philosophical Writings* (edited by Daniel O. Dahlstrom)

Newton *Philosophical Writings* (edited by Andrew Janiak)

Nietzsche *The Anti-Christ, Ecce Homo, Twilight of the Idols, and Other Writings* (edited by Aaron Ridley, translated by Judith Norman)

Nietzsche *Beyond Good and Evil* (edited by Rolf-Peter Horstmann and Judith Norman)

Nietzsche *The Birth of Tragedy and Other Writings* (edited by Raymond Geuss and Ronald Speirs)

Nietzsche *Daybreak* (edited by Maudemarie Clark and Brian Leiter, translated by R. J. Hollingdale)

Nietzsche *The Gay Science* (edited by Bernard Williams, translated by Josefine Nauckhoff)

Nietzsche *Human, All Too Human* (translated by R. J. Hollingdale with an introduction by Richard Schacht)

Nietzsche *Untimely Meditations* (edited by Daniel Breazeale, translated by R. J. Hollingdale)

Nietzsche *Writings from the Late Notebooks* (edited by Rüdiger Bittner, translated by Kate Sturge)

Novalis *Fichte Studies* (edited by Jane Kneller)

Reinhold *Letters on the Kantian Philosophy* (edited by Karl Ameriks, translated by James Hebbeler)

Schleiermacher *Hermeneutics and Criticism* (edited by Andrew Bowie)

Schleiermacher *Lectures on Philosophical Ethics* (edited by Robert Louden, translated by Louise Adey Huish)

Schleiermacher *On Religion: Speeches to its Cultured Despisers* (edited by Richard Crouter)

Schopenhauer *Prize Essay on the Freedom of the Will* (edited by Günter Zöller)

Sextus Empiricus *Outlines of Scepticism* (edited by Julia Annas and Jonathan Barnes)

Shaftesbury *Characteristics of Men, Manners, Opinions, Times* (edited by Lawrence Klein)

Adam Smith *The Theory of Moral Sentiments* (edited by Knud Haakonssen)

Voltaire *Treatise on Tolerance and Other Writings* (edited by Simon Harvey)

Printed in Great Britain
by Amazon

50418710R00163